Y0-BQH-306

For Reference

Not to be taken from this room

Student Records Management

Recent Titles in
The Greenwood Educators' Reference Collection

Planning in School Administration: A Handbook
Ward Sybouts

School Law for the 1990s: A Handbook
Robert C. O'Reilly and Edward T. Green

Handbook of Academic Advising
Virginia N. Gordon

Handbook for the College and University Career Center
Edwin L. Herr, Jack R. Rayman, and Jeffrey W. Garis

Handbook of Cooperative Learning Methods
Shlomo Sharin, editor

Handbook of College Teaching: Theory and Applications
Keith W. Prichard and R. McLaran Sawyer, editors

The Training and Development of School Principals: A Handbook
Ward Sybouts and Frederick C. Wendel

Multiculturalism in the College Curriculum: A Handbook of
Strategies and Resources for Faculty
Marilyn Lutzker

Where in the World to Learn: A Guide to Library and Information
Science for International Education Advisers
Edward A. Riedinger

Planning and Managing Death Issues in the Schools: A Handbook
Robert L. Deaton and William A. Berkan

Handbook for the College Admissions Profession
Claire C. Swann, senior editor; Stanley E. Henderson, editor

STUDENT RECORDS MANAGEMENT

A Handbook

Edited by
M. Therese Ruzicka
and
Beth Lee Weckmueller

Published in Association with the
American Association of Collegiate Registrars
and Admissions Officers, Washington, D.C.

The Greenwood Educators' Reference Collection

GREENWOOD PRESS
Westport, Connecticut • London

Library of Congress Cataloging-in-Publication Data

Student records management : a handbook / edited by M. Therese Ruzicka
and Beth Lee Weckmueller.
    p.   cm.—(The Greenwood educators' reference collection,
ISSN 1056–2192)
    "Published in association with the American Association of
Collegiate Registrars and Admissions Officers, Washington, D.C."
    Includes bibliographical references and index.
    ISBN 0–313–29114–4 (alk. paper)
    1. College student records—United States.   I. Ruzicka, M. Therese.
II. Weckmueller, Beth Lee.   III. American Association of
Collegiate Registrars and Admissions Officers.   IV. Series.
LB2845.7.S88   1997
651.5'042—DC21   97–14467

British Library Cataloguing in Publication Data is available.

Copyright © 1997 by American Association of Collegiate Registrars and
Admissions Officers

Library of Congress Catalog Card Number: 97–14467
ISBN: 0–313–29114–4
ISSN: 1056–2192

First published in 1997

Greenwood Press, 88 Post Road West, Westport, CT 06881
An imprint of Greenwood Publishing Group, Inc.

Printed in the United States of America

The paper used in this book complies with the
Permanent Paper Standard issued by the National
Information Standards Organization (Z39.48–1984).

10   9   8   7   6   5   4   3   2   1

Copyright Acknowledgment

The authors and publisher are grateful for permission to reproduce portions of the
following copyrighted material.

From J. Berman and J. Goldman, *A Federal Right of Information Privacy: The Need
for Reform* (4). Washington, DC: Benton Foundation. Reprinted with permission from
Databanks in a Free Society: Computers, Record Keeping, and Privacy. Copyright
1972 by the National Academy of Sciences. Courtesy of the National Academy Press,
Washington, DC.

Contents

Introduction

Roman S. Gawkoski

Another book on management!? Why another one, when our library already holds shelves of them?

The answer is simple. The present volume is a production of the American Association of Collegiate Registrars and Admissions Officers (AACRAO). It is designed specifically for our professions. The subject matter of each chapter, the descriptions, the suggestions, and even the general principles are focused on the distinctive needs of our administrative areas.

But don't you realize that such a book is really superfluous, because you're not really going to be around for that much longer?

Many who read this will be too young to remember the predictions that the unit record computing equipment would not only eliminate manual manipulation of data (it did!) but in doing so would also decrease institutional staff size and budget (it did not!). As computing advanced, there were more predictions, such as the totally paperless office. There are very few of those around. These days one hears comments to the effect that the explosion in technology is so great that within a very short time such officers of higher education as the director of admissions, the registrar, and the director of student financial aid will be eliminated.

Possibly. But probably not. At least, I would suggest that it is not necessary for anyone in these professions to actively seek a new line of work.

Institutional development, evolution, does not proceed from the complex to the simple. It is the other way around. A rector, a beadle, and some lecturers in philosophy, theology, and rhetoric might have drawn students to the first medieval universities, but over time subject matter demanded by the students and offered by the institutions has expanded to include medicine, mathematics, physical science, languages, and on and on to the contents of the present-day catalog.

The student is not trained, for example, in some generalized physical science but rather in a specific category, such as chemistry, and indeed specializes in one of the specific subcategories of chemistry.

It cannot be denied that the work of the three professionals cited earlier will be changing in methodology over the course of time. But this is nothing new. One example: early registrars transcribed by hand the course work and grades of their students when the need for a transcript arose—thence the name of the document. With the advent of typewriters, the work of transcribing courses and grades was still manual but much faster. Then came Thermofax, and production really speeded up because handwork was virtually eliminated—but there was an annoyance, as Thermofax would not reproduce entries made in ink. When photocopying came on the scene, those problems were solved, but new ones emerged. Because we were now making Thermofax/photocopies of the entire hard copy record, everything on that record, including all manner of disciplinary actions, was being broadcast. The advent of computer-assisted transcript generation permitted the registrar to return to the original concept, and only basic and essential data were reproduced. Now the latest development, SPEEDE/ExPRESS, is permitting the transmittal of transcripts entirely electronically with no paper.

So over the years transcripts were produced more efficiently and more accurately. Did the size of the staff decrease? Because the number of students and the consequent demand for transcripts were dramatically increasing at the same time, the staff size did not decrease. It at least stayed the same and quite likely increased.

But even more important, who handled the human side of transcripts? When the student requested special service, who arranged it? Who answered the student's specific concern? Who explained university policy? Who arranged a duplicate transcript without charge when some problem arose at the receiving end? Who debated institutional policy on covering up private information before a transcript was run? Who, long before the Family Educational Rights and Privacy Act (FERPA), refused to let faculty examine student records to help them in assigning grades? Well, it certainly wasn't a typewriter, a photocopy machine, a personal computer, or a mainframe. No, indeed. It was a human: the registrar.

The Office of Admissions and the Office of Student Financial Aid also benefit from this human touch. Students and their parents—perhaps particularly the parents—may well be initially satisfied with a voice response telephone system that will provide general information, but when it comes to their particular question, then they will demand an attentive human whom they can question in detail to their satisfaction. Nothing mechanical will do.

We can all adduce examples of changes that have affected campuses over the years: the GI Bill and veterans' benefits, the riotous 1960s and their effects on curriculum and grading practices, the merging of institutions into multiple campuses, the Family Educational Rights and Privacy Act of 1974, the Student Right-to-Know Act, federal aid to education, the shrinking pool of traditional applicants and the increasing pool of nontraditional students—all of these needed to be explained to the university community, and the myriad details involved in each had to be kept in order. Can you guess to whom many, if not most, of these responsibilities fell? Right, to the stalwart academic watchdogs of the university.

The era of the information superhighway is upon us. Even more rapid advances in technology may be expected in the next decade, but human nature is not going to change. Prospective students will still need information about the institution. While the methods of providing that information may become more sophisticated, what information is to be provided and how it is to be disseminated and how that prospective student will be made to feel welcome as an individual will be within the accountability of the admissions office and the financial aid office. Once officially enrolled, the student will rely, either directly or indirectly, on the registrar for assistance in following those institutional prescriptions, policies, and procedures that will lead to successful completion of degree requirements. Direct reliance will, of course, be in areas such as registration that are under the specific control of the registrar. Indirect reliance will come about because the registrar is the custodian and interpreter of institutional policies through areas, such as advising, that are under the direct control of the deans.

In the long view, it is evident that the problems facing us daily are perennial, although always appearing in new and updated guise. It is our function to keep ourselves constantly aware of operational principles even as we struggle to define the question in particular and the constantly changing circumstances in general. How best can we ethically come to closure of the question in any organization that almost daily, it seems, advances technological efficiency? What means will enable us to provide information freely and yet maintain the control, security, and confidentiality we owe to our constituents? Students are impatiently waiting for printed grade reports. Institutions eagerly await receipt of transcripts for transfer students. How will we manage to improve our delivery systems? The needs of students (especially those with special needs) must be served in a system that seems to become increasingly more impersonal. We must avoid the "I'm just a number" syndrome. Credentialing is fast becoming a national obsession, so how will we respond to the demands for various certifications? Do we panic when change becomes inevitable, or are we anticipating and planning for change? What if disaster strikes? Are we to operate on some kind of uncertainty principle, or is there another road?

All in all, then, the best advice that can be given to you is this: learn all that you can about good management from the manual you now hold in your hand. Keep on learning, because you, as a resource your institution cannot possibly do without, are going to be around for a very long time.

1

Ethical Practices in Academe

C. James Quann
and David M. Birnbaum

Although ample newsprint is given to the "scandal of the day," not enough attention is focused on ethical considerations in higher education and academic affairs. A noted authority on higher education outlined the problem succinctly, stating "I still marvel at the large literature by academics on ethics in general and on medical and legal and business ethics in particular as compared with the slight literature on academic ethics" (Kerr, 1994).

Most higher education professional organizations publish statements on ethics and commend them to their academic colleagues, but the statements are usually general or boilerplate in nature. For instance, prestigious associations like the American Association of University Professors (AAUP), the National Education Association (NEA), and the American Association of Collegiate Registrars and Admissions Officers (AACRAO) regularly publish such codes of ethics. AACRAO's code lists thirteen commandments, each readily understandable and eloquent in its own way. The thirteen contain expressive and reverent words such as "a belief in," "adherence to," and "a sensitive appreciation of" but are so general that they seem to be simply ethical background music instead of authoritative advice that could be applied to the dilemmas and hard decisions that administrators must make every day. Where, then, do we turn for advice?

In *Guiding Standards and Principles*, H.J. Canon (1989) differentiates between formal ethical codes as described earlier and ethical principles, noting that codes tend to be doctrinaire, while principles offer a helpful degree of flexibility and permit consistency without rigidity. As a guide for decision making, Canon cites a set of principles offered by Kitchener (1985) that will provide useful guidelines for the case studies that follow: (1) do no harm, (2) benefit others, (3) be just, (4) be faithful, and (5) respect autonomy.

According to Kitchener, in "doing no harm," we honor the obligation to avoid actions that may inflict either physical or psychological injury. The act of "benefiting others" is self-explanatory and at the core of our reason for being student services professionals. "Being just" means giving appropriate attention to assuring equal treatment to all those for whom we have responsibility. "To be faithful" means keeping promises, telling the truth, being loyal, and maintaining respect and civility in human discourse. "Respecting autonomy" means acknowledging the right of individuals to decide how they live their own lives as long as their actions do not interfere with the rights and welfare of others.

The next section of this chapter deals with actual case studies that exemplify the types of dilemmas that admissions, financial aid, and records professionals face on a daily basis. Each case is followed by commentary that highlights the issues and proposed solutions that involve ethically based decisions. One or more of Kitchener's principles may be applied to each decision.

Minority Scholarship Eligibility. An outstanding prospective student indicates on his application for admission that he is Native American. The student is later awarded a minority scholarship from your institution. Ethnicity for the scholarship is based on self-reported information on the admission application. In the spring the student's high school counselor calls to inquire about the basis for the scholarship award and states that the awardee is not a minority student. When questioned, the student states that he sincerely believes he is part Native American. You are the director of financial aid and scholarship programs. Do you withdraw the award?

In the judgment of the authors, the scholarship offer should not be withdrawn. The institution is responsible for establishing and verifying scholarship criteria, such as grade point average (GPA) and ethnicity. If the scholarship selection committee relies on self-reported information rather than official transcripts or other documents, it needs to be accountable for the implications of its actions. The student involved could be contacted and questioned regarding the misinformation. This will help the director and the Scholarship Committee focus on these kinds of issues in the future. The Scholarship Committee might also reevaluate its requirements and procedures, but it should think twice before establishing special criteria for a single ethnic group such as Native Americans, because it would be unethical, and perhaps illegal, to make Native Americans meet special requirements not imposed on other ethnic groups.

Late Self-Confession. A student attended your law school for one year five years ago, then dropped out for three years, and later enrolled in another school of law, earning a JD degree. He recently wrote to you confessing that he had falsified his original application by not indicating his prior arrest and conviction records. His purpose for writing to you now was "to set the record straight." Apparently he sent a similar letter to the degree-granting school, and that registrar has now written to you asking for a copy of his original application to your institution. Can you provide this information?

This ethical dilemma presents at least two issues. What is the correct ethical response as far as the former student is concerned? What ethical posture should the registrar take with the colleague from the School of Law? FERPA allows several instances where one institution can forward confidential education records to another without the student's permission. However, this scenario doesn't appear to fit any of these circumstances.

Ethically, one of the first things the registrar should do is to make certain that the letter was actually written by the former student. This could be determined by first reviewing the former student's academic file and then by contacting the student to ask the types of questions only the former student could answer. When the former student has been properly identified, the registrar could explain the request from the other school, saying, in effect, "I am not at liberty to honor their request without your permission." If the former student is sincere about wanting to "set the record straight," he will grant permission. If he does, the registrar should request it in writing and then check the signature. If the former student says no to the request, that too sends a message to the degree-granting institution. Either way, the first registrar should respond to the second registrar in writing, noting that FERPA prevents compliance with the request, unless the student's permission has been granted.

> *Admissions Fraud.* As your staff processes a transfer record, it is discovered that a student reported attending only two previous colleges, but an entry on one of the transfer records indicates he attended a third. You call him in, and he admits attending the third school for one quarter with grades that would have made him inadmissible on transfer. The signature portion of your admissions application carries the normal statement about accuracy and concludes, "My signature below indicates I understand that admission to or enrollment in Central University may be denied if any information is found to be incomplete or inaccurate." On closer inspection, you discover the student failed to sign the application. It is obvious that the student omitted crucial information, but without his signature, can you cancel his admission and enrollment?

There are at least two issues here. First, the student did not meet the transfer admission GPA requirement. When confronted with the evidence, he readily admitted attending the third school, with grades that, if factored in, would have dropped his GPA to below the admissible level. There should be no dispute about that since the third record speaks for itself. Since he was not eligible based on published transfer criteria, the admissions officer is justified in canceling the student's admission or enrollment.

The second issue is honesty. Admissions personnel should always be able to count on applicants to submit honest and complete information, whether or not they sign the application form. The signature on the application is important primarily to know that the student filled out the form and completed the appropriate blanks or, as in this case, failed to indicate attendance at the third institution. If the admissions officer shows the student the application, and the student acknowledges filling it out, the fact that the student did not sign the form is of little consequence. Although it isn't necessary because of the GPA issue mentioned before, the admissions officer would also be justified in canceling the applicant's admission or enrollment because of the falsification (or omission) of the application, even though the form was not signed.

Ethically, it could do harm to other students if the admissions office didn't enforce the institution's admissions standards. If this student is allowed to continue, it may cast a shadow on other students who met minimum admission standards. By enforcing the policy, all of the other students benefit because institutional standards are being upheld.

A related issue is the importance of admissions literature clearly stating the need for complete and accurate information. It is helpful for the signature block on the application to list appropriate conditions such as: "I certify that I have considered each question carefully and that my statements are true and complete to the best of my knowledge. Further, I understand that admission to, or enrollment in, the university may be denied if any information is found to be incomplete or inaccurate."

> *Implied Contract.* In late July, your office receives the final transcript for a student who had been offered admission in March. Upon review, your staff notices codes on the record that were not recognized before. These codes indicate that much of the student's course work was "special education." Based on her high cumulative GPA, she had been offered admission, but, as you review her remedial work, you believe that she does not have the academic foundation to survive at your college. However, in the meantime, the student has paid her advance deposit, made a down payment on her food and housing contract, completed summer orientation, and registered for fall classes. Should you now rescind the offer of admission and refund her money?

Most institutions initially grant provisional admission with the understanding that final admission will be based on the receipt of final and complete transcript information. However, implicit in that understanding is that the final and complete transcript might contain new or different information that could justify a different admission decision. In this case, the final transcript did not contain anything new; it was simply that at this time the transcript was read correctly. Given that the error was the institution's, and the actions taken by the student relied on the admissions decision, revoking admission would be questionable legally. At the same time, the student is about to commit time and money to pursuing her degree. If she is doomed to academic failure, it would be unfair simply to do nothing but accept her fees and enroll her.

Perhaps the best resolution would be to meet with the student and explain the circumstances. If she wishes to withdraw at that point, she should be given a full refund of the money she has paid. If she wishes to enroll, she should be permitted to do so and given the same chance to succeed as any other student. You may wish to direct her to whatever tutoring or other academic support services the institution provides.

> *Federal Witness Protection Program.* A prospective student applies for admission to your institution, providing only limited information on his academic background. You deny admission based on lack of verifiable academic history and failure to meet minimum standards for admission. A few weeks later you receive a visit from a federal officer. After swearing you to secrecy, the government agent informs you that the prospective student is in the Federal Witness Protection Program, and the government is committed to giving the witness a new identity and supporting him in his degree endeavor. You are asked to admit him without high school or previous college records and to maintain absolute secrecy about him and the program. Do you admit?

This is a very complicated request. Before arriving at a decision, several issues need to be examined. Admitting this person of unknown identity without academic documentation means the admissions officer would be treating one prospective student differently than all others. One must ask, Is it just to do so? Also, would it be appropriate and ethically correct to admit without notifying other pertinent officials such as the dean of students and director of student health? If this unidentified person is wanted by a group such as an organized crime element, could his presence on campus endanger others? On the other hand, the more people who know of his circumstances, the greater the possibility that his federal witness status may become common knowledge.

Upon arriving at answers to these questions, the admissions officer would most likely conclude that the applicant could not be admitted under these circumstances. Moreover, the applicant should not even be considered without proper academic documentation of his previous education. Transcripts of all high school and college work must be submitted, but the admissions officer could allow the federal agent to obscure the name and identity of the student and the previous institutions, so long as the agent was willing to verify in writing that the records were true and unabridged copies of records of the subject candidate and that any transfer college or university was an accredited institution. The agent would also have to authenticate the state of residence, since the chances are rather great that the protected witness is from another state and therefore subject to out-of-state fees.

> *Admissions-Related Research.* Your institution has an integrated Student Information System, of which you are the cocustodian. Admission, registration, and academic record information is coalesced with cashier, billing, and financial aid data. A researcher with legitimate access to admissions and related data conducts research that seems to indicate in a statistically

significant way that Asian female students are the ethnic/gender group least likely to pay their bills and complete a term without withdrawing from classes. Can you allow this and related research findings to be published?

Provided the researcher is acting on behalf of the university and, under FERPA, "has a legitimate educational interest" allowing him to access confidential student information, he should be allowed to publish his findings provided:

• The procedures utilized and the report findings do not violate students' confidence;

• The students' names or other personal identifiers are not included in the study or in any way linked with the data;

• Case histories and records are sufficiently disguised to prevent identification.

In retrospect, before any such research is conducted involving student records for which I am custodian, I would require a very detailed proposal indicating the rationale for the research and the procedures to be followed. In other words, I would make an effort to be sure that the research was done responsibly and in a manner consistent with scientific principles. Consultation with faculty in an appropriate discipline might also be useful.

It might also be prudent to require the researcher to sign a statement accepting the conditions mentioned and agreeing to state that the research and findings were those of the researcher alone and did not represent the conclusions or analysis of the university.

> *Enrollment Deception.* A student's mother called on you in your office without an appointment. She confided that she was about to send her daughter the funds for tuition for the ninth consecutive quarter but was concerned that her daughter never shared her grades with her and was evasive about her college experience and progress toward a degree. As registrar, you explained the salient issues of the federal Family Educational Rights and Privacy Act and campus policies on confidentiality. The mother left the office stating that she was going to give her daughter tuition money for only one more quarter, unless her daughter provided some proof of progress. After the mother left, you checked the files and found that the daughter's enrollment had been academically barred, and she had not been enrolled for the past six quarters. Also, the daughter has never filed a "Do Not Release" request under FERPA. Should you contact the mother and blow the whistle?

One of our ethical principles is "to do no harm." Based on our response, is the potential harm to the student or her mother? Who benefits if we allow the lie to continue? What is the right or "just" thing to do? Can the registrar be "faithful" without telling the truth?

The daughter is a former student, and she has not been enrolled for the past two years. Many aspects of FERPA apply to former students enrolled since

1976. The daughter attended one full year before being barred due to her poor academic performance. When enrolled and since, the records indicate that she never asked to have directory or public information withheld. One of the elements of public information, approved by the institution and printed in proper student publications, is "dates of attendance." Thus, it would be proper, honest, and legal to provide basic enrollment information to the mother, but only after the registrar determines that the mother is in fact who she says she is and in response to a request for such information from the mother. Following proper identification, the mother might be told that the institution can share certain information with her at her request. If she asks, she would then be told that the institution's records indicate that the student in question was enrolled from fall quarter 1990 through spring quarter 1991, and there is no indication of any enrollment since that time.

The registrar should not reveal the student's poor academic standing or that her enrollment has been barred; that is not public information. As with other cases of this kind, it would also be helpful to suggest to the mother that she obtain other necessary information directly from her daughter.

The preceding deception was an actual case. In retrospect, it might have been better had the registrar sought proper identification from the mother on the spot, left the room to check on the daughter's record, and then provided the appropriate information to the mother at that time, if she requested it. This approach would have also allowed the opportunity to discuss in more detail with the mother why the institution does not send grades and other sensitive information to the parents.

> *Nondiscrimination.* A student has been admitted and enrolled and has paid full tuition and fees at your public university. Midway through the first quarter and well beyond the deadline for full refund, the student states that she cannot continue in the university because classes are offered and facilities/activities provided that recognize, if not support, gay and lesbian orientations. Upon further questioning, she reveals that her religion strongly condemns homosexuality. Your institution does not discriminate on the basis of handicap, race, color, ancestry, religion, national origin, age, sexual orientation, or sex in admission to, or participation in, its programs, activities, or services. Do you withdraw the student and refund her tuition and fees?

As we consider a response, we must remember our ethical guideposts—to do no harm, considering the harm to other students as well as the petitioner; to benefit others, considering the other students as well as the institution's educational mission; to be faithful respecting contracts; and to respect the dignity of others. This is a public institution, with a well-published refund deadline of a complete refund the first week, 50 percent refund for the next three weeks, and no refund after the fourth week of instruction. This student's appeal was made halfway through the term, beyond the deadline for any refund, except, of course, for the unused portion of the room and board contract.

The institutional statement on diversity and nondiscrimination appears in all publications, and the catalog clearly mentions programs and student organizations dealing with gay, lesbian, and bisexual issues. Also, we must assume that the educational community is dedicated to the pursuit of truth and knowledge and committed to diversity. Gay, lesbian, and bisexual issues clearly coalesce with the missions of education and diversity. So, with that background, the student could be invited to the office to discuss the matter. Although it would be inappropriate to try to convince the student to change her mind, one could point out that she is well past the final deadline for refund of tuition and fees; that the institution is dedicated to nondiscrimination; and that the institution cannot, in good conscience, refund her fees, as they are already committed and essentially spent. As a corollary to her request, I would mention that our Zoology Department teaches a course on evolution, but we don't allow students who disagree with the evolution theory to withdraw and receive a full refund of fees, unless they do so according to the published refund deadlines.

It would also be prudent to help the student become aware of the number of businesses, agencies, and organizations she will continue to come in contact with that will likely support a variety of political, religious, and lifestyle choices, many of which may be in direct opposition to her own. It might also be helpful to suggest that she consider finishing the term so as to get the benefit of the money already spent and volunteer to help her select another college or university that would be more in keeping with her philosophy.

> *Former Student Requests a Name Change on All Official Records.* The registrar's office receives a registered letter from a former student requesting an official name change. The student was last enrolled ten years ago. Included with the letter are a certified copy of a court order changing the former student's name and a request that the name be changed on all university records and a new diploma be issued. Must you make the changes?

Current laws in the various states must be observed with respect to name changes. The ethical solution in this case lies within AACRAO guidelines and published institutional policy. The latest *AACRAO Academic Record and Transcript Guide* states: "The student's full name includes family name and all given names. Institutions have no obligation to record name changes for students not currently enrolled. Name changes for currently enrolled students should be recorded only when there is evidence of a legal basis for change." The AACRAO statement does not specify the grounds for change or documents that could constitute a "legal basis" for change, although most records officers would agree that a certified court order, marriage certificate, or decree of dissolution will suffice.

The AACRAO statement does, however, differentiate between current and former students, and, although it is not spelled out, it recognizes the difference between the two groups and implies that separate policies are in order. If the institution has a clear statement of policy on name changes, then the registrar or records officer need only follow that policy. If there is no such statement, the AACRAO guidelines should be followed in this case, and a prudent records officer should then draft a policy for consideration by the appropriate institutional committee(s). The policy could differentiate between current and former students, allowing changes in the first category (with proper documentation) and no changes in the second. A rationale for such a policy follows.

Many records are collected and maintained on file for each student. After the student's admission and enrollment, the registrar's office uses these documents to create an official academic record that is maintained on file for ready access during the student's tenure at the institution. Upon graduation, the files are closed, and important source documents are archived on microfilm or optical disk and kept on file in perpetuity. A change of name after the student leaves the institution disrupts the continuity of records and complicates record-keeping policies. Since the registrar may not alter the various records received from other institutions and agencies, a serious problem of record accuracy and continuity occurs if some, but not all, records are changed. Moreover, because of various archiving practices and types of equipment used, it is often extremely difficult, if not impossible, to change records of former students. Hence, the reason for dual policies. (For more complete information on name-change issues, see "Changing the Nom de Plume; A Name-Change Protocol," *College and University* [Winter 1994].)

> *Release of Social Security Number.* Your state Higher Education Coordinating Committee (HECC) annually requests formatted tapes with enrollment-related information. To be in compliance with the Federal Educational Privacy Act of 1974, you normally assign a sequential number to each student and withhold the Social Security numbers. Now the HECC is demanding release of the Social Security numbers so the agency can match enrollments with individually specific information. HECC has limited, but resource-specific, authority over state two- and four-year institutions. Do you release the Social Security numbers?

Our fear, in a case like this, is that if we release the Social Security identifiers for a specific purpose, the agency may later use the numbers for another purpose, and the second purpose may be totally unacceptable (e.g., matching the Social Security number with parental income or identifying students who have received state-funded, need-based financial aid in excess of $20,000). The federal Family Educational Rights and Privacy Act (FERPA) makes it clear, in Section 438.6.B, that confidential student information can be released to "authorized representatives of the Comptroller General of the United States, the Secretary of Education, an administrative head of an education agency as defined in Section 408 of the Act, or state educational authorities." Thus, FERPA is permissive on this point, but individual state educational authorities are not specified (that is up to the state). If the Higher Education Coordinating Committee is so designated, then as records officer, you are free to provide the Social Security numbers as requested. If it is not so designated, then it would be prudent to continue assigning the sequential numbers and withholding the Social Security information.

Another approach would be, at the time you ask students for their Social Security numbers, to advise them of uses that will be made of the numbers, including sharing information with the HECC or similar agencies. By giving their Social Security numbers after receiving such advice, the students would be consenting to sharing the information. It should also be noted that supplying the university with one's Social Security number must be a voluntary act, and a student has the right to refuse and to demand an alternative student number.

> *Age Discrimination.* A former student and graduate is older than most and is worried that she may lose out on a good job because her date of birth (DOB) is recorded on her college transcript. She asks that the DOB be removed, citing the possibility of age discrimination in the hiring process. The former student points out that listing the DOB is also potentially harmful for extremely young graduates as well. Do you comply with the request?

This case raises an issue that deserves attention. Records officers have generally recorded birth dates on transcripts for purposes of identification and security. This may have been necessary in precomputing days, but most modern databases now allow the storage of tracking data that need not be printed when producing a computerized transcript. Thus, to store the DOB in the system but not reproduce it on transcripts respects the autonomy of the individual, avoids doing harm, and is the "just" thing to do. If the institution's student information system does not allow the suppression of the DOB, then the records officer should consider listing only the day and month of birth, not the year. In this way, the limited dates will help identify the student without giving out the year of birth and, hence, the graduate's age. This procedure was outlined by Mary Gunn (1990) in a recent article.

> *Clerical Error.* Prior to the beginning of her final semester, a student received her degree audit report from the registrar, listing all remaining degree requirements. She completed all of the listed requirements during the spring term (a total of thirteen credits), but a staff member in the graduation section discovered a three-credit error when conducting the final graduation audit. As registrar, you are obligated to ensure that all students meet all requirements, including the minimum 120 semester credit hours, but because of the error, the student completed only 117. Do you require the student to complete the additional three credits?

The solution to this vignette brings into focus at least three of the ethical principles stated earlier: to be faithful (to our promises), to be just, and to do no harm. Certainly, the student must bear some of the responsibility for the omission, but the graduation section made the error and misinformed the student. The student's adviser or major department might have caught the error as well, but that didn't happen. Also, had the student known, she could have easily carried seventeen credits and graduated with her class. Thus, because there was considerable institutional error, it seems the officials should do everything within their power to assist the student without diminishing the academic standards of the institution. As registrar, you might consider the following to resolve the problem (no order intended): (1) if it can be done, with the support and approval of the academic department, file an appeal, on the student's behalf, to the appropriate person or committee asking for consideration of a three-credit waiver; (2) if the student was a transfer, review all transfer records to determine if there are remaining credits that might be considered transferable; (3) review the student's record and recommend an appropriate course challenge or credit-by-examination procedure for a three-credit course; (4) waive summer session fees and allow the student to complete an acceptable three-credit course in summer.

> *Confidentiality of Medical Records.* A woman student is the victim of an attempted rape. She was able to fight off her assailant and run to safety, but before she escaped, she was severely beaten. She reported to the campus police that she bit the assailant in the neck and shoulder as hard as she could and drew a fair amount of blood. She thinks the injury was serious enough that the assailant will seek medical treatment. Three days later a police officer goes to the medical records office of the Student Health Center and asks for the names of anyone treated for a neck or shoulder injury. The police have no suspect, and the reported injuries are their strongest clue. The Medical Center director calls you, the registrar, and asks if the records can be released. Do you release?

FERPA makes it very clear that "medical records," although highly confidential, are not student records if they are created, maintained, or used only in connection with treatment, and this is certainly the case here. Surely, we would all like to help the campus police catch the would-be rapist. But maintaining the confidential nature of student health files is also of utmost importance, and if we do not respect confidentiality in this or similar instances, then we will not be able to expect students to share confidential, health-related information with the medical staff. If that happens, the quality of health care will deteriorate, and some students may even find themselves in life-threatening situations because their medical files are incomplete and therefore of limited use.

Surely the campus police have other methods that will help identify the criminal in this case. A widely circulated artist's sketch is only one that comes to mind. Alternatively, the police can seek a search warrant or a subpoena from the courts to allow them access to the student medical records. Thus, the recommendation should be that the medical records not be released for this purpose.

> *Serious Disciplinary Problem—To Record or Not Record?* A student is found guilty of rape and is suspended for two years. He is required to obtain counseling and provide a psychiatric release before he can petition to reenroll. Before the two years have expired, you learn that he has applied to another university and is likely to be admitted. The transfer institution has no knowledge of his prior conduct since, as a student disciplinary record, it is not maintained as part of the student's official academic record (transcript). This is a most grievous crime, and you don't want it to be repeated on another campus. Do you advise the transfer institution of the student's disciplinary history?

This is a case in which the ethical and morally right solution is in direct conflict with a cautious legal approach to the dilemma. The student's disciplinary record is a student record, protected from disclosure without the consent of the student. While the student has consented to disclosure of his transcript, the transcript does not contain any reference to the serious disciplinary problem. Thus, the "legal" approach to the problem is to forward only the transcript to the transfer institution and to avoid any reference to the disciplinary problem. But what is the ethical decision that will "do no harm"? What decision will benefit others? What is just and faithful? In a grievous case such as rape, the aforementioned solution is very distressing for all concerned, especially the original victim and potential future victims. An alternative would be to characterize the issue as one that the transfer university should address. If a university receives a transfer application, shouldn't the admissions officer ask the student applicant whether there had been any disciplinary problems at the first school and then request permission for the parent institution to release any disciplinary records? If the student declines to sign the release, this could be a deciding factor in whether or not to accept the student as a transfer. This approach also solves the legal issue. However, as professionals in the admissions business, we know that it would be overly burdensome for an institution to ask for waivers on disciplinary records from all of its transfer applicants.

Another possibility, although it is similar to "closing the barn door," would be for the university to begin recording serious disciplinary actions on student transcripts. There could be a notation when a student has been suspended or dismissed, for example, which would indicate to another university that there had been a serious disciplinary problem. This is fair warning, and then it is up to the prospective transfer institution's admissions officer to ask the student for a waiver to allow the disciplinary records to be sent. This approach allows the admissions office to limit its inquiries about discipline to those cases in which the school has been alerted by the transcript notation.

If an institution wishes to begin noting serious disciplinary sanctions on a transcript (a policy recently adopted by all nine campuses of the University of California), it is important to give all students notice in advance of the new policy implementation. Students will then be aware that a notation on the transcript is one of the consequences of serious misconduct, and the policy would have the effect of preventing one institution from exporting serious behavior problems to another college or university. Students would also be on notice that when they ask to have their transcripts sent to another institution, they are also consenting to having the reference to any serious disciplinary problems sent as well.

Another approach that would accomplish the same thing without recording the disciplinary action would be for the dean of students or judicial officer to "freeze the record" by adding an internal code to the rapist's file to indicate: "This file or a transcript therefrom may not be released without the permission of the dean of students." Then following a request for release, the standard operating procedure would be for the dean or judicial officer to notify the offender that "under the circumstances, I cannot release your record unless you consent to share your disciplinary history with the other institution." Legally, however, the student's records could not be frozen in this way unless the "freeze" was made part of the official disciplinary action or sanction imposed on the offending student.

> *Revocation of an Academic Degree.* A graduate student completed all of his course work, passed his written and oral examinations, and completed an acceptable dissertation. He was awarded a doctoral degree by your institution and returned to his teaching position in another state. Two years later your institution obtains irrefutable evidence that the doctoral student plagiarized a major portion of his dissertation. Should you revoke the degree?

Courts in the United States increasingly have held that colleges and universities with the power to grant a degree also have the power to revoke a degree for good cause. Action in this specific case may hinge on whether or not the institution has a policy in place for revoking degrees. Assuming that the institution has irrefutable evidence, the "just" thing to do is to revoke the degree. To do otherwise causes potential harm to other degree recipients and to the integrity of the institution.

While requiring that educational institutions provide procedural safeguards such as notification and a hearing (due process), in *Crook v. Baker* (1986), the court concluded that under Michigan state law, a university has the power to revoke a degree without a court proceeding. In this case, the master's degree of a graduate who university officials and faculty determined had fabricated data in support of his thesis was revoked. Similarly, in *Waliga v. Board of Trustees* (1986), an Ohio court stated that the power to grant a degree implies the power to revoke it for good cause, such as fraud, deceit, or error.

The preceding cases are simply examples of the types of academic dishonesty that administrators must occasionally face. Readers of this case study should determine whether or not their institutions have a published policy covering revocation of a degree. If they do not, it is recommended that they work with counsel and the appropriate faculty committee to establish such a policy. It is recommended that any such policy limit revocation of degrees to circumstances in which it is learned that the student did not, in fact, meet the requirements for the degree. Revoking a degree in other circumstances, such as punishment for vandalism or other misconduct, is not appropriate.

> *Privacy Rights after Death.* A former student and successful politician re-
> cently died after years of public service. He was well known throughout
> the state as a champion of several controversial issues. During his public
> life, even "directory" or public information was not releasable without his
> written permission. Following his death, personnel representing various
> news media request public and confidential information from his records.
> Do you comply?

Information practices vary by state, so the records officer should seek the advice of legal counsel before disclosing heretofore confidential information that could embarrass the family of the deceased. The court case of *Lugosi v. Universal Pictures* (1979) considered this type of situation in 1979. Although the Lugosi case did not address the issue directly, counsel concluded that the right of privacy is personal and does not survive after death. Thus, if the college were to release records covered by the privacy law after the death of the person, there would be no living plaintiff to file an invasion of privacy action. Hence, the college would not be exposed to any liability for such a disclosure.

The preceeding statement may resolve the legal issue but not the ethical question. Obviously, the deceased cannot object, but the interest in maintaining confidentiality now rests with the institution and third parties, such as the family or heirs. If confidential information is released, are we being just, are we doing harm, are we being faithful? Would disclosure bring discredit to the family?

The institution also has the interest of protecting those who contributed to the former student's academic record: professors, advisers, the dean of students, and others. Simply put, it behooves the records officer to examine the facts of each individual case of this type. Based on the laws in each state and after weighing the variety of competing interests, the records officer must determine whether or not the records should be released. If the decision is made to continue to withhold confidential information, the requesters can still turn to the court and subpoena the information under any applicable public records act laws, thereby relieving the institution of responsibility. Alternatively, the institution might contact any known family members and notify them of the request for information. If the applicable law appears to require disclosure, the institution could advise the family that disclosure will occur unless the family obtains an order to the contrary from the court. This places the burden of a court action on those with an interest in confidentiality.

Sexual Harassment. As registrar, you have hired a group of work-study students to work for you during the academic year. After the first day of training on procedures and confidentiality, which all student employees must attend, you are approached by a female student employee who tells you that during the previous spring, she filed "sexual harassment charges" against one of the male student employees. She states that she is still frightened by this individual and does not feel that she can work in the same office with him. She also states that the male student has honored the voluntary resolution instituted by the campus sexual harassment officer and has not contacted her since the resolution was implemented. She further states that the male student "must go," or she will resign and seek redress. Do you discharge the male employee?

Once again we must remember our ethical guideposts: to "do no harm" (in this case to the victim); to be just; to respect the dignity and autonomy of others; to honor contracts. Sexual harassment is a serious problem, and students are protected from sexual harassment by Title IX legislation, state law, and campus policy.

Resolution of disciplinary problems is usually handled in one of two ways: through voluntary resolution or through action of a campus judicial board. In this case voluntary resolution was the agreed-upon method selected by the male student.

As registrar, my first action would be to visit with the dean of students or the campus judicial officer and determine what happened last spring and what action was taken. The chances are very good that the voluntary resolution signed by the aggressor included sanctions, and the chances are also good that one of the sanctions was that the male student keep away from the victim in class, socially, and on the job. If the male student cannot hold the job without being in close proximity to the victim, then the male student should be advised to seek employment elsewhere.

You may want to make some effort to determine whether it is possible for the male student to work in an area that will not put him in close proximity to the victim, assuming that he is acting in good faith and does not wish to violate the terms of his disciplinary sanctions. A more difficult situation exists if the male student is already working when the victim applies for a job. It does not seem reasonable to require the male student to resign, since it is the victim in this case who is choosing to place herself in proximity to the male student. If it is not possible for them to work without being in close proximity, she may need to choose whether she wishes to take that job under those circumstances or to look for another position. If she chooses to look elsewhere, every effort should be made to facilitate her finding an alternative position.

FURTHER READING

For interesting reading on ethical matters and ethical decision making, see *Ethics and Higher Education*, edited by William W. May (1990). In *Applied Ethics in Student Services* (1985), Canon and Brown provide a basic primer on ethical problems in daily practice and on ethical principles and ethical decisions in student affairs. Good background information on professional ethics and the ethical codes of the American Association of University Professors (AAUP), the National Education Association (NEA), the American Association of School Administrators (AASA), and related topics can be found in *Professional Ethics in Education* by John M. Rich (1984).

Fair Practices in Higher Education, a report of the Carnegie Council on Policy Studies in Higher Education (1979), offers good advice on institutional rights and student responsibilities and student rights and institutional responsibilities. *Managing Admissions, Records and the Law*, a 1994 publication by Kent M. Weeks, provides information on recent court decisions that pertain to recruitment and admissions, students with disabilities, disclosure and retention of students' records, the college catalog, and other topics of interest.

The American Association of Collegiate Registrars and Admissions Officers (AACRAO) publishes the "AACRAO Code of Ethics" in the annual *AACRAO Member Guide* (1991). AACRAO also publishes a "Statement of Principles of Good Practice with Reference to College Admissions," "Standards and Responsibilities in International Educational Interchange," and the "Joint Statement: Transfer and Award of Academic Credit," all of which set forth ethical standards for the profession. These AACRAO codes are printed in *Admissions, Academic Records, and Registrar Services* (1987).

Finally, for those who would like to review ethical issues presented in a lighthearted way, *Ethics and Other Liabilities* by Harry Stein (1982) is must reading.

REFERENCES

American Association of Collegiate Registrars and Admissions Officers (AACRAO). 1996. *AACRAO Academic Record and Transcript Guide*. Washington, DC: AACRAO.
———. 1991. *AACRAO Member Guide 1992–93*. Washington, DC: AACRAO.
———. 1987. *Admissions, Academic Records, and Registrar Services*. Washington, DC: AACRAO.
Canon, Harry J. 1989. Guiding standards and principles. In *Student Services: A Handbook for the Profession*, by Ursula Delworth and Gary R. Hanson et al. San Francisco: Jossey-Bass.
Canon, Harry J., and Brown, Robert D. 1985. Applied ethics in student services. In *New Directions for Student Services*. San Francisco: Jossey-Bass.
Carnegie Council on Policy Studies in Higher Education. 1979. *Fair Practices in Higher Education*. San Francisco: Carnegie Council on Policy Studies in Higher Education.

Crook v. Baker, 57 *American Law Reports 4th*, Section 3, "View That a College or University Has Power to Revoke Degree," 1986.

Gunn, Mary. 1990. The date of birth and the student transcript. *College and University* 65(4).

Kerr, Clark. 1994. Knowledge ethics and the new academic culture. *Change, the Magazine of Higher Learning* (January/February).

Kitchener, Karen S. 1985. Ethical principles and ethical decisions in student affairs. In *Applied Ethics in Student Services*, ed. Harry J. Canon and Robert D. Brown. San Francisco: Jossey-Bass.

Lugosi v. Universal Pictures, 25 Cal 3d 813, 1979, 425.

May, William W. 1990. *Ethics and Higher Education*. New York: Macmillan.

Quann, C. James. 1994. Changing the nom de plume: A name-change protocol. *College and University*.

Quann, C. James, et al. 1987. *Admissions, Academic Records, and Registrar Services*. San Francisco: Jossey-Bass.

Rich, John M. 1984. *Professional Ethics in Education*. Springfield, IL: Charles C. Thomas.

Stein, Harry. 1982. *Ethics and Other Liabilities*. New York: St. Martin's Press.

Waliga v. Board of Trustees, 57 *American Law Reports 4th*, Section 3, "View That a College or University Has Power to Revoke Degree," 1986, 1246–47.

Weeks, Kent M. 1994. *Managing Admissions, Records and the Law*. Nashville, TN: College Legal Information.

2

When Major Change Becomes Inevitable

Roman S. Gawkoski
and Anthony D. Tortorella

Routine can be so comfortable. How secure we can feel with a procedure that works, where the glitches seem far and few between, where administrators, support staff, faculty, and students know what to expect, and only the occasional newcomer needs instruction.

Yet—caution! No one can seriously deny that change is a fact of life—these days at an accelerating pace, it seems—and that it plays a major role in our daily professional lives. Granted, it is often the type of change we can accommodate with an undiminished sense of equanimity, albeit not necessarily without some soto voce grumbling (e.g., That darned department is changing its course numbers *again!*). But eventually there does come the day when we are faced with implementing a new procedure that is major.

Perhaps the idea for this innovation sprang from within your own office. Possibly there was criticism of current procedure from students and/or faculty. Or, maybe after years of your pleading for money to initiate a project, the Business and Finance Office suddenly came up with the cash, and your boss now says the equivalent of ''Have it ready to run yesterday.'' Whatever the background, you now have a major procedural change to implement.

STRESS

Springboarding a new procedure of major proportions certainly can be stress-ful over and above the normal (and therefore productive) anxiety associated with any venture into the unknown. However, much—perhaps most—stress in this situation can be ameliorated, if not eliminated, by following some general planning guidelines that come from both experience and common sense.

Numerous case studies might be adduced to illustrate these guidelines. A change in grading system is one example. Another is a move from manual preparation of transcripts to a computer-assisted procedure. A third might be the introduction of a computerized degree audit system. But the example par excellence, the one with which everyone in the institution can identify, is the switch from an arena registration to a fully automated, decentralized, Touch-Tone voice response registration system.

For the remainder of this chapter, we use the change in registration format as the model for developing our general principles for attacking change intelligently. The story of "Composite University" (CU) that we will be relating is based on the experiences of several institutions that successfully, if not totally painlessly, brought up the new registration procedure.

BACKGROUND ON THE EXISTING SYSTEM

CU is a large, midwestern, independently supported institution with an enrollment of approximately 12,000 undergraduate students, 5,500 graduate students, and 1,500 professional students in dentistry, law, and pharmacy. Students meet with an adviser after midsemester for "preregistration" for the following semester. Using a preliminary version of the *Timetable*, students merely indicate the courses (but not sections) they are interested in taking. The colleges tally these course requests and submit them to the departments, which then determine their specific section needs for each course offered and add this information for the final version of the *Timetable of Classes*. Actual registration occurs at the opening of the semester, at which time students are given an opportunity to meet with their adviser just prior to their actual registration appointment. The Office of the Registrar has made several modifications in the mode of registration and over the last 20 years has managed to consolidate all registrations in the gymnasium. After experimenting with various methods of distributing registration assignments, the registrar has settled upon random assignment of students with proportional representation by college and class within each fifteen-minute assignment period as optimal. It actually has worked so well that over a period of years, lines in the gym have virtually disappeared. Graduate assistants supervised by faculty distribute computer course cards. Advisers from several colleges are also on duty in the gym throughout registration to handle on-the-floor problems that may arise. The whole registration procedure works so well that it can be accomplished in the space of three days. Classes begin on the fourth day, with class lists having been run overnight and ready for the first class. Late registration takes place on Monday, Tuesday, and Wednesday of the following week. "Smooth" is the consensus. It is also very cost-effective!

BUT ...

The registrar and staff are well aware that time has been taking its toll on the current registration system. Despite efforts by the Registrar's Office to hide the system's wrinkles, the old system is showing its age, particularly in the fact that the equipment and technology supporting the system are rapidly becoming obsolete. In addition, registrar and staff have been attending American Association of Collegiate Registrars and Admissions Officers (AACRAO) meetings, and for several years word has been out about a brilliant registration system that eliminates the need for a gymnasium and punched cards. The office staff feel it is time to make a move toward this improvement, and the registrar has floated toward the deans and administration the idea for a Touch-Tone voice response registration system. Stone wall! Money is dear, and the present system is working so well. The registrar and staff commiserate—they have done themselves in by having done too good a job with the existing system.

[October, Year 1] Then comes the dreaded news. The Computer Center director reports that not only is punched-card equipment no longer being produced, but old equipment for cannibalization of parts, should our present equipment break down, is now virtually impossible to find. With luck, the present equipment may produce for another year, at most two.

At this news, the registrar experiences several emotions. Initial dismay, however, is rapidly transformed into elation by the realization that this is a repeat opportunity to promote the long-desired registration update—except now the arguments in favor of a new system will be buttressed by the realities identified by the Computer Center.

[November, Year 1] The first step taken is to marshal these dismal facts to lay out for the Board of Deans and Directors and to seek its approval to proceed with the gathering of data for the updating of registration. The board recognizes the need to move forward without delay and unanimously authorizes the registrar to take whatever investigatory steps are necessary to present the board with its recommendation.

[November–December, Year 1] Wasting no time, the Office of the Registrar initiates a series of intensive meetings seeking the advice of the entire university community: deans, directors of both academic and nonacademic units, selected department chairs, faculty, and representatives from the Student Senate. Participants in these meetings are asked to identify those characteristics of the current system that are good and that therefore should be retained in a new system but also those characteristics that should be eliminated. (One interesting, albeit unexpected, outcome of these discussions is the unusual number of participants who remarked that they are learning for the first time how complex are the elements involved in registration.)

[January, Year 2] Knowledge and materials provided by vendors at AACRAO meetings prove invaluable as a foundation for initial meetings with Computer Center staff. Also sought are the experience and advice of registrars of other universities that have recently undergone changes in their registration systems. Telephone calls to several of these institutions yield additional ideas, and visits by staffs of both the Office of the Registrar and the Computer Center

to nearby universities both in-state and out-of-state provide invaluable discussions with both registrarial and technical staff.

Five possible modifications are identified: arena registration using bar-coded cards (in place of punched cards), three variations on computer-assisted registration, and Touch-Tone voice response. Vendors are invited to make presentations, cost estimates are prepared, tentative implementation schedules are laid out, and the pros and cons of each modification are vigorously debated. Particular attention is paid to how they satisfy the "retained" and "eliminated" characteristics that had previously been identified within the current registration system.

The result of these preliminary investigations is a presentation by the registrar's staff to the Board of Deans and Directors concerning the possibilities and the joint recommendation by the Office of the Registrar and the Computer Center that, in their judgment, the most effective registration system that ought to be adopted by Composite U is a Touch-Tone voice response registration system. The registrar arranges with an institution already on Touch-Tone to use its registration system, hooks up a speaker phone, and arranges a live show-and-tell demonstration of a Touch-Tone voice response registration. The board is convinced by the arguments and the demonstration presented by the registrar, votes unanimous support for Touch-Tone voice response, and forwards its recommendation to the Office of Academic Affairs, which, *mirabile dictu*, also takes immediate action not only to approve the registrar's recommendation but to obtain the necessary funding.

[January–February, Year 2] The next step taken by the registrar is a series of intensive meetings with administrators, department heads, faculty, and students. They are asked to respond to the summary of those features of the current system earlier identified as desirable and retainable in the new system. After each discussion, each representative is also asked to send the registrar in writing a wish list of features that the new system should have. The registrar's staff then summarizes all the points. Interestingly, a second major issue has emerged: the faculty insist upon replacing the historic midsemester preregistration with "a real registration," and they want it introduced simultaneously with the new registration system. Yes, they think this is so important that they are willing to make all the necessary accommodations concerning decisions about what classes they intend to offer—including the much earlier preparation of the *Timetable of Classes*. The administration asks that all colleges of the university and all students be brought onto the new system simultaneously rather than piecemeal. Thus were dashed the registrar's hopes of gradualism in introducing change.

[February and continuing, Year 2] An ad hoc Committee on Remodeling Registration is also immediately appointed—representatives of the deans, administrators, Computer Center, the Student Senate, and Office of the Registrar, with the registrar as chair. The registrar will also prepare the minutes of the meetings, especially the agreements that have been reached. This committee will meet weekly for six months and biweekly thereafter. The Office of the Registrar

begins by presenting a broad summary of requests—*and their implications for the various production calendars.* Following discussion, sometimes heated, the registrar's staff set to work again to prepare production calendars demonstrating the interacting effects of the committee's decisions for the following meeting. Committee members are often startled by the "domino effect" that has been produced by the "small change" they had insisted upon. Can this one item really have affected so many others? More discussion. Much changing of mind. Revision. It is obvious that the registrar's staff are fully cognizant of the university-wide effects of even small changes but that the reactions of the other committee members are generally limited to their own constituency. The Office of the Registrar, then, must diplomatically and prudently move these diverse interests not only to see the broader picture but also to accommodate their particular interests to that broader picture.

[March, Year 2] The committee makes one very important recommendation: next fall's registration will be the last gymnasium registration, and the first Touch-Tone voice response early registration will occur next March; it will be the advanced registration for the first semester of the next academic year. Special arrangements have been made for the early registration of freshmen in July following the initial early registration—a first for CU. The Board of Deans and Directors, the academic vice president, and the president approve. This now becomes the fixed point about which those previously volatile production calendars are finalized.

[April and continuing, Year 2] Communication is an important tool. Accordingly, the registrar inaugurates a newsletter that reports on the latest developments in CU's new registration system. The newsletter begins by announcing to the university community the fact of a new registration system and then regularly reporting on developments. It also dubs the new system "TOTO" for Touch-Tone (and hopes the student newspaper won't remember that Toto was a dog, should difficulties arise with the system).

[April and continuing, Year 2] The staffs of the Office of the Registrar and the Computer Center have jointly reached the decision concerning the vendor from whom the registration system should be purchased. The computer hardware and software have now arrived and are being installed and tested. A system is not simply put into place, period. It must be carefully customized to reflect the peculiar needs of the institution. The number of details appears overwhelming. Coordinating these details requires an enormous amount of the Office of the Registrar staff's time and energy. Just one example is the writing of the voice response script (which must be carefully done so that precious storage space is conserved) and then the recording of the voice so that disparate words and phrases flow together as smoothly as possible into sentences.

[April and continuing, Year 2] The Computer Center staff is also working feverishly not only to make the modifications needed in the registration program—for example, a very sophisticated wait and wait/drop procedure is being developed—but also to write all the new programs required, such as the program

for direct entry of timetable information by each department and the program that will permit departments to monitor registration activity in their courses. The registrar breathes a sigh of relief because these new programs are going to place full control and accountability for course enrollment size exactly where they belong—in the department.

[May, Year 2] Deans and students alike agree that the random proportional representative assignment of registration appointments used in the past should be continued with the new system. The Business Office has identified the cutoff dates for billing and notification of student schedule to be followed by (reluctant!) cancellation of the registration if payment is not received by the deadline.

The year is going by swiftly, but the registrar's diplomatic guidance is paying off. Disagreements, misunderstandings, and revisions are becoming fewer and farther between. All the pieces of this intricate puzzle are dropping into place.

[June–August, Year 2] The summer before the last two gym registrations is difficult indeed because the Office of the Registrar is now juggling two types of registrations, closing out the old while simultaneously bringing up the new. It is also engaged in the production of a registration video to present to students in addition to the entire university community. Training seminars in the numerous timetable building and registration control programs built for TOTO have been developed for college offices, academic departments, and support staff and are scheduled throughout this period.

[September–December, Year 2] With the opening of fall semester, there ensues an intensive advertising/education campaign of meeting with student and faculty groups to show the video and to answer questions. Most prove stimulating and exciting. A mock-up of a portion of a *Timetable of Classes* with call numbers is prepared, and a random sample of students (a select group of marketing students and some of the best engineering computer students) is asked to study the effectiveness of the system. The engineers, noted for creative shenanigans at gymnasium registration, are asked to try to "break" the system. Mercifully, the pilot study is quite successful and is not "broken," and the feedback from participating students proves valuable in further refining procedures. One of the outcomes of the pilot study is the decision to keep Touch-Tone voice response registration on-line eighteen hours per day, seven days a week, over a three-week period for early registration and then to keep it open during the same hours for add/drop activity throughout the days up to and including the first week of classes.

[January, Year 3] The spring semester commences with a gala farewell to the last old-style gym registration (balloons, T-shirts, buttons, soft drinks, brownies, and other goodies) and the first days of classes.

[January–February, Year 3] The production calendar for the *Timetable of Classes* for the first advanced registration calls for the submission of class information for the following fall semester within a few days of the opening of classes for the spring semester—a calendar change emphasized repeatedly from the very first meetings with faculty and department heads. But almost immediately there is a rumbling from some of the departments that they have never

before had to submit class data so early. (Yes, these are the same people who earlier had sworn they would accommodate any calendar change that would provide for that urgently needed early "real" registration!) We are glad we kept the minutes and repeatedly called attention in our newsletter to all the implications of an advanced registration. Once again diplomacy is called for, and the situation is resolved, albeit not without some gnashing of teeth. Somehow the class information is produced, and the first *Timetable of Classes* for Touch-Tone voice-response registration is published. It is a masterpiece of updating from the old document. No sooner is the *Timetable* printed than the departments are making changes. The desktop publisher is kept busy churning out addenda listing the changes for the departments and the advisers and student bulletin boards.

The registrar reassures a nervous administration that, yes, there are several variations on a backup plan in readiness should the new system prove a failure. No, we do not expect difficulties necessitating the implementation of a backup plan, but we are ready if one should be needed.

[March, Year 3] Midsemester passes; advising passes; and the first TOTO begins. From the registrar's point of view it is quite successful but not wildly so—the registrar perceives some flaws—but students really like it, and even the student newspaper has kind words for it. Prepared for the worst, the Office of the Registrar had installed several TOTO Helplines and had assigned full staffing. To their delight, the phone calls are far fewer than expected.

TOTO is a success! Mostly congratulations come in—but, yes, there are the inevitable few negatives as well. Most administrators are enthusiastic. Most faculty appreciate being freed from gymnasium duty. Most departments appreciate the total control they have in monitoring and controlling the enrollment numbers in their courses—but, not unexpectedly, some are dismayed by the accountability they now have.

[April, Year 3] This final formal phase of the implementation of TOTO and advanced registration partakes of the character of a television "sweeps" week as questionnaires soliciting evaluation of the new procedures are sent to a large, random, representative sample of students. When the results come in, well over 98 percent give it an A grade.

[April and continuing, Year 3] The ad hoc committee continues to meet bimonthly over the next eighteen months to solve the few problems that continue and is then discharged. Neither the registrar's staff nor the Computer Center staff, however, relax. They continue to implement more enhancements that provide a wider and more sophisticated range of options to the students and easier monitoring capability and control to the departments.

THE PRINCIPLES OF MASTERING CHANGE

This story of the way in which Composite University effected a major change in its registration system, interesting in itself, has been designed to illustrate a number of general principles for dealing with major change.

1. *Research your idea thoroughly.* Professionals in our fields are noted for their willingness to exchange information. They will invariably be happy to share their files with you—an invaluable source of data! Visit several schools that have implemented the system or the procedure. One-on-one question-and-answer is an excellent opportunity for obtaining information, particularly if it is coupled with a demonstration of the system/procedure itself. Absent the opportunity for a personal visit, use the telephone. Conferences and seminars can be great training sessions. Don't limit yourself to the spoken word, but also check out *College and University*, other publications, conference proceedings, and so on. Make use of computer network listservers.

2. *Be secure in your belief that your idea constitutes a realizable goal and that it is practical for your institution.* Remember that change always involves some risk, and be ready to take action, even though there is risk involved. Using a statistical analogy, progress would never occur if a zero level of significance were set.

3. *Persevere.* Don't give up the fight should your idea be turned down when you first present it. Press your points diplomatically. Recall such homely maxims as "A soft answer turns away wrath" and "Make haste slowly." Once your project is approved and funded, don't be surprised when the inevitable opposition surfaces. Even if it originates in downright ignorance of facts, take heart.

4. *Seek input from the university community broadly, but remember that you are the expert.* You will know most positively the how, when, and where the project fits into the university-wide scheme of things. As a practical matter, much of the "counsel" you will receive will, in fact, be a quite legitimate vocalization of parochial doubts and fears. In a major project, it is impossible that every dean's, every faculty member's, every student's ideas and needs can be accommodated. Compromise where possible so as to foster a mentality of collegiality concerning the development of the project. But stand firm—diplomatically, logically—on principles where compromise is unwise.

5. *Document all agreements reached.* You and members of your staff will be on project committees. Try to chair the committee. Usually nobody wants to serve as secretary, so take on that job, too. As the project moves toward completion, details will constantly be changing, and calendar dates will be shifting. As chair/secretary, you will be able to set the strategy of the agenda so as to lead discussions into the most productive directions to effect a smooth transition. You will be certain that the documentation of agreements is completely and accurately reflected in the minutes.

6. *Keep others informed.* Don't depend on your committee members to spread the word. The campus grapevine is notoriously counterproductive. Use stories in the student newspaper, distribute a project newsletter to departments and administrators, offer to participate in departmental faculty meetings, address student groups, use e-mail, prepare a video presentation. Keep the channels of communication open.

7. *Provide training for everyone who will be involved with new programs and procedures.* Staff of deans' and departmental offices need the benefit of thorough training. Training your own professional and support staff will reap dual benefits: they will immediately pick up on potential problems that can be corrected before implementation, and, because of their input, they will assume a proprietary interest in the system they are beginning to implement.

8. *Thoroughly test the new project.* Many quirks and glitches can be identified and removed from the program well in advance. At the same time, also work out a backup plan, ready to put into place, should unexpected problems arise during the implementation phase.

9. *Evaluate.* If the first run-through of your new project is successful, don't be afraid to publicly claim credit but be sure to share it with all those who contributed to the success. If there were problems, acknowledge them without lame excuses. Analyze the difficulty and seek counsel, if appropriate, to eliminate it. Don't become discouraged.

10. *Enhance.* No new major system is perfect at implementation. Continue to work out enhancements that will make it ever more efficient, ever more productive, over time.

3

Data Control, Security, and Confidentiality in an Electronic Environment

Kay Magadance

INTRODUCTION

Institutions of higher education have developed sophisticated management information systems to support their academic mission and to help them manage their institutional data. Faculty, students, deans, academic and administrative department heads, administrators, and even the public have a need to interact with these management information systems. Higher education has an obligation to make access available to these systems. At the same time, it must control that access, protect the integrity of the system, and maintain confidentiality. The report of the *AACRAO Task Force on the 90s* shows that in the "open" responses, 93 indicated the key issues in higher education in the 1990s are technology, communications, data processing, data systems, and so on, with the most frequently mentioned subset (26) being records integrity related to security of computer systems (AACRAO, 1988). In the academic computing environment the philosophy is toward open access to information. However, in administrative computing, "access restriction to particular information is implicit; often mandated by law or policy" (Hawkins, 1989, p. 148).

DATA OWNERSHIP/RESPONSIBILITY

Administrative management information systems have many components and serve multiple purposes. By nature, these systems serve both operational and strategic planning purposes. The integration of these systems, the need for broad access, and the proliferation of hardware and software require that in addition to the development of the systems themselves, an institution needs a plan to manage these systems. This plan must complement the institution's mission and goals and should include (1) designation of responsibility for the data, (2) a written policy on information management, and (3) a process for controlling access to information (NACUBO, 1981).

If it has not already been done, your institution needs to identify one or more offices or functional areas with responsibility for its information. A literature review of information management systems in higher education reveals there is very little written on the subject of administrative data ownership and responsibility in higher education. Literature on information management systems in government, business, and industry indicates there are differing approaches and outcomes to determining who owns the data. These approaches appear to fall into two primary categories. One is that ownership rests with the office identified as responsible for the data storage, or, more specifically, the data-processing center. The second is that ownership resides with the "managers" of the information. According to this second approach, for example, the business officer would be the manager considered responsible for all data in the accounts payable system. Regardless of the approach your institution chooses, it is responsible for controlling and managing its information systems.

Most colleges and universities place responsibility for data ownership and electronic access to data with the managers of the information, the same offices that have responsibility for the administrative function and the paper version of the information. In student information systems, generally the registrar has primary responsibility for managing student and curricular data. This includes responsibility to maintain the integrity of the academic records and to safeguard them in accordance with institution, system, state, and federal regulations. When making this determination, your institution should consider which office has responsibility for the administrative function; has the best understanding of the meaning and status of the data; and is the most knowledgeable about its use, the regulations that apply to it, and its interrelationship with other databases or information management systems. Authorizing access, educating users, determining standards of security, and ensuring compliance with local, state, and federal guidelines relating to the data will be most effective if ownership and the responsibility for authorizing access to the information reside with the office that has the greatest interest in both using and protecting the data.

Today's information technology explosion, the necessity for computerized operational systems, the expansion of data systems and databases, and the need to manage those data and make them accessible in a meaningful form require coherent institutional policy on information management. Highland (1993, p. 636) states that this explosion of the past several years makes it necessary to radically change our concepts, principles, and implementation of information security. Such a policy needs to include assignment of responsibility for implementation of database management, designation of the office(s) or functional area(s) responsible for data, minimum acceptable standards of security, reference to legal guidelines affecting the information, and procedures for dealing with instances of security violation. The policy must be approved and supported at all administrative levels. It must be flexible enough to allow for hardware, software, and function changes but rigid enough to ensure that security and confidentiality will not be compromised.

A written policy on information management that includes data responsibility should also include a definition of the type and scope of institutional data to which the policy relates and the consequences of violating or abusing access privileges. It is assumed that colleges and universities complied with the Family Educational Rights and Privacy Act (FERPA) when it was passed in 1974 and established policy on access to records covered under FERPA. Since that time, elaborate databases have been developed to store and manage data protected by FERPA and other laws and regulations. Today these policies need to be reviewed and updated. Operational information systems need to be reviewed, and policy on appropriate levels of access established or reestablished. The review should be followed by documentation that lists and describes both the "education" records covered under FERPA and other categories of records and the office responsible for controlling their access and retention.

At the University of Wisconsin (UW)–Eau Claire, an ad hoc committee appointed by the chief academic officer was charged with reviewing access to student information and developing guidelines for this access. The committee members categorized information into broad groupings such as directory information, admission data, personnel data, non-class advising data, class data, academic progress data, and so on. They likewise categorized requesters into groups based on functional need, educational interest, need for advising, student support services, and so on. They used a grid approach to indicate the level of access ("yes," "no," or "limited") each requester group needed for access to each category of information. An example of the outcome of this policy is the access provided to faculty who advise students. At UW–Eau Claire all faculty are responsible for student advising. The guidelines, supported by the grid, indicate that faculty need access to academic progress data for their advisees and for students whose major program is in the faculty member's academic discipline. The grid is now part of the institution's policy on student records and is used to guide the data owners in granting appropriate access to users of the various database systems.

In addition to identifying responsibility for data ownership, a well-conceived campus data management policy should identify responsibility for data security and should designate an information technology security manager. The data managers, Computer Center personnel, and the security manager should jointly establish minimum acceptable security standards.

"Today all executives are being held to new and higher standards of accountability, both because society is growing increasingly litigious, and because, in a ferociously competitive marketplace, jobs are on the line, companies and their reputations are at risk, and our wealth of future technological advantage is threatened" (Weiss, 1993, p. 5). A formal process for authorizing access to information should be established. This process should clearly identify the parties responsible for authorizing access, should specify the criteria for determining access, and should delineate the authorization procedures used to obtain access. Both the personnel involved and the security system itself need to recognize and enforce the institutional policy through this process. Formalizing these responsibilities will "protect the integrity, availability, confidentiality and privacy of information resources" (Weiss, 1993, p. 5).

Approval and sign-off by the manager(s) of the data must be incorporated into the process for granting access. However, in order to have appropriate checks and balances, the process should be separated between the manager responsible for the data and the security manager. Developing procedures along these principles puts the data manager in charge of authorizing and controlling the access, while the security manager is in charge of enforcing and maintaining the security system. Both areas share responsibility for educating the users.

In summary, higher education has recognized that information is a valuable asset and should be made available to a broad audience. The institution must define data ownership, develop a written policy on information management that recognizes data ownership and supports the philosophy of distributed access, and establish procedures that provide a secure basis for implementing this broad-based access.

SECURITY

As indicated earlier, the responsibility for security should be shared between the managers of the data and the data-processing personnel. One proposed solution for implementing security incorporates distributed responsibility for input into the requirements of the system and centralized implementation (Fagan, 1993). Menkus (1991, p. 293) states: "A critical element in successful information security too often is overlooked by most organizations. That is the construction and maintenance of effective control in those information systems whose protection is at issue." Determining the security requirements is a shared responsibility. It involves identifying the important elements of security and developing a system that incorporates these elements at all levels, from the database to the end user attempting to access the data. Hawkins (1989, p. 148) warns, "Failure to provide adequate access controls may be costly to the campus through either loss of funding or damage awards."

The security system should support the institution's objectives and should not be so rigid as to inhibit these objectives or cause personnel to attempt to circumvent the controls. Pottas and von Solms (1991) point out that the critical issue in access control software today is flexibility. Elements to be considered in designing an appropriate security system need not be limited to those in the following discussion. However, the major aspects of security should include standards for hardware and software security, audit records and procedures, authorization procedures, training, system cross-checks, and backup protection and disaster recovery. Most of us are familiar with hardware and software security. However, we need to deal with the other elements as well.

SYSTEM STANDARDS

The security system should include minimum standards to protect against physical access to the hardware, interception of data in transit, unauthorized electronic access, inappropriate use of applications or systems software, and data corruption (Vaughn, Saiedian, and Unger, 1993).

"Physical security is certainly the best-understood protection measure and the most readily accepted. It encompasses such solutions as guards, walls, locks, key entry systems, uninterrupted power supplies, backup or archival files, fire protection systems, disaster recovery procedures, etc." (Vaughn et al., 1993, p. 81).

Related to physical security is the need to protect data transmission. The interconnection of systems implies the transmission of data across various communication media (Vaughn et al., 1993). The electronic transmission of data needs to be protected against inappropriate interception, intervention, or manipulation. There are encryption methods available throughout the industry. An institution needs to make its own decision about the type and level of encryption to employ and how to protect its data during transmission. It is also important that network links, access on and off the systems, and points vulnerable to interception be tested to ensure that the data are protected. To illustrate this, consider a situation in which access coming through a remote port, which has security to disconnect a user after a set period of inactivity, disconnects the user before he or she is disconnected from the computer system itself. The system connection coming through the port thus remains available to the next user, with all of the prior user's privileges. In this case, both the port and the mainframe have security; however, their link leaves the security system open to unauthorized access.

SOFTWARE SECURITY

The security system should be capable of recognizing and protecting against unauthorized or inappropriate access to the database by both the people and the software programs that process against the database. Providing software security involves hardware, software, and users and is often achieved through the use of verification techniques. These verification techniques must be at the core of the security system and must be considered part of the system's trusted computing base. They should be built into the operating system and run in a protection level higher than the supervisory software (Vaughn et al., 1993). These verification techniques are used to authenticate users and terminals, to detect unauthorized access attempts, to prohibit unauthorized data manipulation, and to support multilevel security that trusts the system to segregate the users and data (Vaughn et al., 1993).

AUDIT PROCEDURES

The audit approach should be determined in the early stages of systems development and implemented to track or trail activity to the data. An audit record can serve several functions. The following two are directly related to data control, security, and confidentiality. The first is to provide verification to the responsible party that appropriate action was taken. The second is to provide a system that allows for reconstruction of events if inappropriate action was taken. "They [audit trails] should provide the ability to reconstruct accurately essential elements of a system's history, in order to detect misuse of privileges" (Sandhu and Jajodia, 1991, p. 416).

Further, audit trail activity should not be limited to the operational databases. It should be extended to audit changes in security. Authority to invoke audit trails for changes to the system or changes to the authorization process needs to be distributed and audited in such a way that prevents the monitor of the security system from changing this audit process, thus allowing undetected privileges.

ACCESS AUTHORIZATION PROCEDURES

The process of authorizing access is almost as important as the security system itself in controlling data access. Access procedures should mirror the institution's access policy and, as indicated earlier, include a separation of responsibilities between the owner of the data and the provider of the security system. The owner authorizes access to the information and identifies the minimum/maximum level of privileges being authorized. The security system should recognize and enforce the data ownership and allow authorizers to grant access only to the data they own.

The authorization process should include a system for an individual or office to request access to information. The first level is to authorize electronic access for the individual. This can be done on a need-to-know or need-to-do basis and should be based on a formal request from the supervisor to the security manager (Olson and Abrams, 1990). The next level in granting access is to determine the kind of information and the type of access an individual should be granted. Again, the need-to-know versus need-to-do test must be administered. The owner of the information requested is the authorizer for both the kind of information and the user's type of access. The determination for the kind of information should be directly related to the function that this individual performs and should be tested against the institution's policy. The type of access, view only or view and modify, can be determined using the same logic. Again, the security system should be in control and allow authorizers to grant access only to data that they own.

TRAINING ON SECURITY

In addition to receiving requests and granting appropriate access to the information, the information authorizer should have responsibility for training the user. Each authorizer of data should have in place a system for training about security, informing the user how to access the information, interpret it, and use it. The training process should also include discussion of the issues of confidentiality and security of the information. In addition to the training, the user should be informed of the consequences of security and confidentiality violations. Highland (1993, p. 637) points out that if our security systems are to be effective, we cannot overlook today's most important component—"wet-ware." Training users and obtaining their understanding of the need for, and support of, security are probably the biggest challenges to data control, security, and confidentiality.

SECURITY SYSTEM CROSS-CHECKS

The database management system and the security system should also interact to provide data integrity checks. The database contains the attributes of the data dictionary, including security. The software should interact with the database to prevent erroneous data from being entered in the system. The database also contains the ownership and privilege information. The security system should cross-check the owner information in the data dictionary against the authorization that has been granted. The security system should also recognize users who have been given access to the system, the type of access they were granted, and the type of information the user is attempting to access. Periodic reports showing the individuals authorized and their access should be distributed to the authorizers.

BACKUP PROTECTION AND DISASTER RECOVERY

The security system should provide for electronic backup on a regular basis. Regular, automated backup is a requirement for any computer system, whether it is mainframe or personal computer (PC)–based. Many computer systems have their own backup/recovery systems. In addition, procedures should outline a routine backup of the electronic databases, an off-site storage location, provision for a "hot" site should a disaster occur, and individual office backup plans in the event a main "host" is not available for daily operations. There is a significant amount of literature available on this subject.

LEVELS OF SECURITY

Defining security levels is the very technical aspect of translating your institution's policy on access to administrative information systems into your actual database management systems. The lowest level of security begins at the database where each data item contains the attributes of the policy. The database and the security system work together to deliver the security and control the access according to policy. This control continues from the data element level through the screens that are created to access data, the software that runs against the data, the devices or terminals that are used for remote access, and the individuals authorized to access the data. The following is a detailed description of how a database and security system can be used to support and enforce all levels of security. It is based on the system used at UW–Eau Claire. Computer systems, security systems, and database management systems vary from one institution to another. Appropriate staff at each institution will have to take into account their particular computing environment to determine how they might implement their particular levels of security. Further, to keep the discussion simple and more focused, only on-line access control will be addressed. However, the concepts that support this type of access can be applied to query access, data file transfers, program access, and so on. As stated earlier, levels of security begin at the data item level and continue through the screens and terminals used to access the database to the individuals using the system.

Data Item

Each data item in a database should have associated with it the office of responsibility; the privilege level to read, write, modify, append, execute, copy, and so on; and the type(s) of audit trail activity required. This is in addition to the other attributes of the data item. At UW–Eau Claire, a security account is associated with each user office. When systems are developed, and data items are added to the database, the office or functional area responsible for the data is identified. The security account of the responsible office is then coded on the data item. The security account for an office needing access to the data item, but not officially responsible for the data, can be authorized by the owner and coded on the data item also. When programs are written to access the data, when screens are created to display the data, or when queries are executed to report the data, the software then uses this security account in conjunction with the database to validate approved access. The security system validates approved access between the software and the data items. This limits an office or individual from retrieving data for which they have not been authorized. The data item is also coded with a level of privilege such as view, modify, and so on. When the data item is placed on a screen, reported in a query program, or used by system software, the security system recognizes the level of access that has been authorized. For example, the security system would not allow placing a data item on a screen that is being created under an account that does not have clearance for that data item. Likewise, placing a "programmatic update only" item on a screen with update privilege would also be denied.

Ownership and control also require monitoring and accountability. In addition to defining access for each data item, the database and the security system should be used to define the type of audit record that needs to be generated and who needs to receive that audit record. An audit record is a trail of changes to a data item and should contain at minimum the before/after image of the data, the identity of the user making the change, the location of the device from which the change was made, and the date and time of the change. As indicated earlier, this is an element of the software security used to help protect the integrity of a database. It can serve as a verification tool or a reconstruction source. Audit trails can also be set up to detect exceptions to security.

Defining access parameters at the data element level can provide additional opportunity for security and control. For example, the policy at UW–Eau Claire states that advisers are permitted access to academic data on their advisees. Coded on the database, specifically the academic program data item, is the account of the academic department authorized to access information about students enrolled in specific academic programs. Using these data, the transaction programs and the security system work together to limit faculty to accessing information pertaining only to their advisees or students in a program in their department or academic discipline.

Developing a security system that begins at the database level may seem very complex and appear to require additional work to maintain. However, when the security approach is determined in the early stages of systems development, the workload can be distributed over a manageable period of time. Adding new data items, changing existing data items, and so on become a routine part of managing the database.

Screen Security

The next level of security is to consider the relationship between the data items and their presentation on a screen. When screens that will be used to display or modify data are created, they should be associated with the responsible office. At UW–Eau Claire the security account code is recorded as one of the screen attributes. As each data item is coded on a screen (or report layout), the system validates the access authorization and privilege level back to the database. It validates that the account under which the screen is being created has authorization for each of the items placed on it. For example, placing the "name" field on a screen for update is possible only if the account under which the screen is created has both authorization and update privilege on the data item. At UW–Eau Claire each screen is associated with a transaction program, and both the screen and the transaction program, as approved by the data owner, are recorded on the security system by the security manager. This prevents someone from creating a screen for his or her own purpose, using it to access or change data, and then deleting the screen without leaving a trail or otherwise informing the data manager or security manager. Likewise, report formats are associated with query programs and checked against the database security.

Additional security can be added to the system by using the database in conjunction with the screen and the transaction program. The system can recognize the status of a record being requested and not allow access or provide alternate access. Another feature that can be built into the database, transaction programs, and the screens can restrict display of data based on certain information on the record. For example, the system could hide directory data for a student who has requested restriction to the release of those data.

Terminal

The security system should be made to recognize a terminal accessing the database and, in some cases, the transactions for which this terminal has been approved. In today's environment, where the distribution of access devices is moving away from hardwired terminals toward networked PCs and remote access, the need for security at this level is greatly magnified. There may be transactions that are of such a critical nature that only recognized terminals may have access to them. An example to help illustrate this concept is to consider responsibility for entering an academic action to a student's record. A very controlled approach is to have the security system recognize both the user and the terminal from which the transaction is being transmitted. When terminals are set up for access to data, and electronic connections are established, they should also be authorized for access to various transactions. For example, only terminals with direct connection to the database are typically authorized for a transaction such as changing a student's academic record. It may also be advisable to prevent the most protected data from access via remote, networked devices, since it is more secure to require a direct relationship between the transaction and the device from which it is coming. Less controlled security may be appropriate for general access. However, the security system should provide for recognition of the remote access, via network, modem, and so on. In a network environment, the server that processes the communication must have adequate security and protection to detect unauthorized or inappropriate access. In situations where dial-in capabilities exist, the system should include some kind of recognition and acknowledgment of approved access.

Individual Access

Individual access begins with approval as an authorized user. All individuals given access receive their access under a security account. The access procedures include identification of the person responsible for authorizing individuals under a specific security account. Thus, the registrar can authorize computer access only for those individuals in the organization who report to that office. (Note, however, that the registrar authorizes all data and screen access for data that are controlled by the registrar's office.) The security system should keep track of the person's user name or sign-on name, the password, the security account under which access is being given, and any time restrictions on the individual's access. In addition to a sign-on name, the individual must have a password. The password should be known by the individual only and should not be electronically retrievable by any individual or program. It should be so encrypted that, if forgotten, the individual's access must be reestablished. The security system should allow only a set number of failed attempts at access. When an individual is not able to enter the correct log-on name and password, the security system should disconnect the terminal after a specified number of tries. This will reduce the possibility of an unauthorized person's guessing passwords in order to use someone else's access. The security system should also provide for the length of time the individual's sign-on access is valid. When an individual connected to the system has not conducted a transaction within a specified period of time, the individual is automatically disconnected. When appropriate, setting an expiration date on the individual's access should also be used to control access. Employees separating from the organization, temporary staff, or staff who perform functions only on a cyclical basis can have access denied upon their separation from the organization or after their seasonal need for access has ended.

In addition to an individual's receiving access to the system, the set of functions or screens for which permission has been given should be recorded in the security system. The security system should recognize the level of access that has been granted, that is, access to view or modify. For example, an individual may have access to a screen that has both viewable and updatable data items. The individual's access to the screen would specify if it was for update or view only.

Under a sophisticated system, control can be extended to specific data items on a screen. Since the security system contains the individual's user account, the system is made to check against the database to determine if the account has been approved to view or modify the data. Thus, an individual may have update access to a screen, but if functional responsibility for maintaining certain data items on that screen has not been authorized for the account, the access defaults to a view only.

These levels of security will provide an institution with a security system that is controlled by transaction, rather than blanket, permission (Sandhu and Jajodia, 3.4, para. 2). Each data item has an owner, each screen has an authorizer, each terminal has security, and each individual has a specified set of privileges.

DOCUMENTATION

Data ownership and the determination of data responsibility for information in an electronic environment are a critical issue for every institution in higher education. Requests for access to information and the "open" records concept have put pressure on institutions to make decisions about their information management systems, the need to make these systems available, and the need to provide manageable security to accompany these systems.

The National Association of College and University Business Officers (NACUBO) (1977) recommendation states that while local, state, and federal laws have an impact on the institution's development of a system to manage access to its data, the institution is still left with a considerable amount of discretion concerning the openness or confidentiality of its records.

Regardless of where ownership and responsibility are placed, the institution is responsible for making available its information and at the same time securing it from unauthorized access release. As part of this responsibility, the institution needs to put forward its policy on electronic information access and ownership. The information, whether stored physically or electronically, is both an asset and a liability for the institution and, as such, needs a well-written policy on access and control. The policy needs to be officially recorded as an institution policy and communicated to its constituents.

REFERENCES

American Association of Collegiate Registrars and Admissions Officers (AACRAO). 1988. *Emerging Issues, Expectations, and Tasks for the 90s. Report of the Task Force of the 90s.* Washington, DC: AACRAO.

Fagan, P. 1993. Organizational issues in IT security. *Computers and Security* 12: 710–715.

Haugen, S.D., Korn, W.M., and LaBarre, J.L. 1996. Procedures for improving security of local area networks. *Mid-American Journal of Business* (March).

Hawkins, B.L. 1989. *Organizing and Managing Information Resources on Campus.* Reading, MA: Addison-Wesley.

Highland, H.J. 1993. A view of information security tomorrow. *Computers and Security* 12: 634–639.

Hussain, D., and Hussain, K.M. 1985. *Information Processing Systems for Management.* Homewood, IL: Richard D. Irwin.

Menkus, B. 1991. "Control" is fundamental to successful information security. *Computers and Security* 10: 293–297.

National Association of College and University Business Officers (NACUBO). 1981. Management information systems. *College and University Business Administration* 6(3): 1–10.

———. 1977. A personnel database. *College and University Business Administration* 2(9): 1–8.

Olson, I.M., and Abrams, M.D. 1990. Computer access control policy choices. *Computers and Security* 9: 699–714.

Pottas, D., and von Solms, S.H. 1991. A computerized management reporting aid for a mainframe security system. *Computers and Security* 10: 653–660.

Sandhu, R., and Jajodia, S. 1991. Integrity principles and mechanisms in database management systems. *Computers and Security* 10: 413–427.

Vaughn, R.B., Saiedian, H., and Unger, E.A. 1993. A survey of security issues in office computation and the application of secure computing models to office systems. *Computers and Security* 12: 79–97.

Weiss, K.P. 1993. Data integrity and security: Who's in charge here anyway? *Information Management and Computer Security* 1(4): 4–9.

4

The Family Educational Rights and Privacy Act of 1974

Bobbye G. Fry

In Greek mythology, the course of each man's destiny in life was set by three sisters known as the Fates, daughters of the god Zeus. Clotho spun the thread of life, Lachesis measured its length, and Atropos cut it. Those whom the Fates smiled upon were given a long and bright thread; those whom the Fates did not favor learned to their anguish that no effort on their part could reverse the "implacable decree" of the Three Sisters. A friendly god might be able to help an individual "cheat the Fates" temporarily, as by diverting the attention of a god who was watching a battle to see that the apportioned judgment took place. But the Greeks accepted the idea that each individual's progress in life unfolded as the Fates had determined it.

In modern society, of course, we live by different myths. But as Americans entered the post–World War II era, it seemed as though the role of the Three Fates might be reappearing in modern dress. The life thread of each person was now spun in the formal records that gatekeeper organizations began to keep about him or her at birth. This person was measured at each step of his or her growth according to the information woven into these proliferating files. When critical decisions affecting his or her adult life were made by managers of the government agencies, commercial enterprises, and private institutions that controlled the destiny of individuals in industrial civilization, the individual's personal record was perhaps the most important single resource used to make those judgments. The Three Sisters with shuttle and shears had been replaced by the record-weaving looms of large organizations.

Then, in the 1960s, another symbolic image began to take shape. The record-keeping looms were automated. With the advent of electronic data processing and the rapid adoptions of the technology by large organizations, information about individuals moved from the filing cabinet to the computer. For the supporters of a high-tech society, the power of computer systems was welcome, since it promised to enable organizational evaluators to obtain the timely and complete information with which to make truly informed decisions about individuals (Westin and Baker, 1972, p. 3).

INTRODUCTION

The Family Educational Rights and Privacy Act (FERPA) of 1974 was created to ensure accuracy and protection of the information we give to others and entrust to them to keep private from those who do not have access to the information. When we recorded and maintained information on hard-copy documents, protection of the information was relatively simple. However, the technological explosion of the 1980s and 1990s has dramatically changed the manner in which we collect, disseminate, and store information. For this reason, FERPA is even more significant today than it was when first introduced on the floor of Congress in 1974.

HISTORICAL BACKGROUND

Since the early 1800s, Congress has been involved in the matter of protecting an individual's right to privacy. With the collection of information from tax and census reports, federal financial assistance programs, and civil service employment, American citizens provide countless data elements for use, and possible misuse, by our federal government. The birth of the information age only adds to our concerns for the security of the information we are required by our own government to provide.

According to a report funded by the Benton Foundation:

Congress has struggled with the problems posed by increasing information collection and use, and the development of new information technologies that transform the way institutions handle information. In the 1960s and early 1970s, Congress held a series of hearings on computers, privacy, and the protection of personal information. Throughout most of the 1960s, Congress considered a proposal to create a centralized national data center on all U.S. citizens containing information such as Social Security numbers, and income and census data. Backers of the proposal argued that the center was necessary to serve the needs of the "welfare state." After years of hearings, studies and debates, the national data center was overwhelmingly condemned as "Big Brother" government, and a threat to individual autonomy, dignity and liberty. (Berman and Goldman, 1989, p. 10)

Once thought to be the panacea to control information and privacy abuses, the Fourth Amendment proved ineffective when confronted with the technologies of the information age. The Fourth Amendment was written to prevent unauthorized search and seizure of personal property (namely, the home) and could not address current data exchange applications, information piracy, or fraudulent documentation issues. "In the 1700s, personal information was difficult to collect, and files were handwritten, rarely reproduced, and easily lost. However, despite major changes in the way individuals handle their papers, the Court has been reluctant to extend the reach of the Fourth Amendment to protect records from intrusion once they are held by someone else" (Berman and Goldman, 1989, p. 4).

Americans' attention to their own privacy was alarmingly awakened during the 1970s, thanks to the abuses of governmental entities that were exposed through the Watergate hearings. "The 'Watergate era' focused public attention on the illegitimate use of personal information that had been collected in federal files for legitimate purposes" (Trubow, 1989, p. 8). American citizens questioned the uses of the information they provided, gained a heightened awareness of data security, and called for regulations to govern their own privacy.

By 1973, the Watergate scandal contributed to what had become a national crisis of faith in government institutions and a heightened sensitivity to the unfettered ability of the government to intrude into the personal affairs of its citizens. In this environment, the public became increasingly concerned about the unhampered collection and use of personal records by the government: "Accelerated data sharing of such personally identifiable information among increasing numbers of federal agencies through sophisticated automated systems, coupled with the recent disclosures of serious abuses of governmental authority represented by the collection of personal dossiers, illegal wiretapping, surveillance of innocent citizens, misuse of tax data, and similar types of abuses, have helped to create a growing distrust or even fear of their government in the minds of millions of Americans." (Berman and Goldman, 1989, p. 12)

The controversy and resulting uproar over Watergate gave birth to the Privacy Act of 1974, which "[gave] notice to the public of federal information systems that store personal data, give a data subject the right to review and challenge the accuracy of files about him or her, and restrict the exchange or disclosure of personal information" (Trubow, 1989, p. 8). In May of the same year, FERPA was passed to protect educational records from unauthorized third-party disclosure. This Act proved to substantively affect institutions, students, and parents, and yet it received little debate when presented for congressional approval.

FERPA was a significant legislative breakthrough in the area of student rights. Yet, this important amendment was enacted with little of the study normally attached to a major bill. In May of 1974 an amendment for the "Protection of the Rights and Privacy of Parents and Students" was introduced on the floor of the Senate by Senator James Buckley (R-NY) as an amendment to an omnibus education bill. No public or committee hearings were held, and there was substantive debate on only a few of the Amendment's provisions. A fellow New Yorker, Representative Jack F. Kemp, had introduced a short amendment to the House version of the education bill in March of that same year. Mr.

Kemp's bill was designed to protect parental rights regarding their children's classroom experiences. The Buckley and the Kemp amendments were adopted by their respective bodies. In conference, the Senate proposal was incorporated with only one substantive addition made from the House bill: a provision allowing parental review of instructional material. The Educational Amendments of 1974, of which FERPA was a part, were signed into law by President Ford. (Hyman, 1982, p. 567)

Many of us espouse the necessity of compliance with FERPA, and some may even hide behind the regulations to avoid confrontation. Indeed, "when discussing student records, we frequently invoke the Family Educational Rights and Privacy Act of 1974 (the Buckley Amendment) to support our position, whatever that position may be. The Federal Act outlines what educational institutions must do, may do, and must not do regarding maintenance of and access to student records and parent financial data" (Alexander, 1988, p. 47). Few administrators, though, are thoroughly versed in all of the intricacies of the law, or at least to a level of confidence that one may cite the entire law without hesitancy.

APPLICATION OF FERPA REGULATIONS

How, then, does an institution maintain the information it needs to conduct its business, protect the information it collects, and provide a beneficial service to the student, state, and nation? The regulations of FERPA, in short, are:

1. Educational institutions must adopt a policy that stipulates adherence to the FERPA regulations. This policy must be in writing and made available to parents and students upon request.
2. Educational institutions must allow the students to examine the contents of their educational records.
3. Educational institutions must allow requests for amendment of the student's education record and respond accordingly and within a reasonable amount of time.
4. Educational institutions may not release personally identifiable information about a student without the written consent of the student.
5. Educational institutions must maintain a record of authorized disclosure of personally identifiable information from a student's record. Likewise, educational institutions must maintain a record of every request made by individuals without authorization to the information. Requests for information made by institutional employees with authorized access need not be recorded.

While these regulations seem rather straightforward and concise, their application often raises more questions than answers. An examination of each regulation, with an exploration into the intent of the regulation, may provide clarity with regard to current application. For the sake of consistency, an eligible student is defined as a student attending a postsecondary institution who is beyond the age of eighteen years. Citations are from the 1988 Rules and Regulations version of the 1974 Act unless otherwise noted by a more recent rule or regulatory change.

Institutional FERPA Policy

Regulation. Educational institutions must adopt a policy that stipulates adherence to the FERPA regulations. This policy must be published annually and made available to parents and students upon request (1988 Rules and Regulations, Sections 99.6 and 99.7).

Intent. It is the intent of the federal government that all citizens should know their rights under FERPA. Toward this aim, educational institutions must annually report how they comply with the Act. More specifically, this regulation requires that institutions examine privacy issues and develop a policy to be enforced by the entire institution—not just those offices that routinely maintain student files. The policy must state the following:

1. how students are informed of their rights;
2. how students may inspect and amend their records;
3. how access may be denied;
4. what fees may be assessed for copies of records;
5. what types of records are maintained and by what offices;
6. who employed by the institution has access to the records and by what method that access is determined;
7. the definition of directory information as designated by the institution; and
8. that the institution maintains a record of all disclosure requests, both authorized and unauthorized.

Application. A statement printed in the institutional catalog is sufficient for the publication of the policy provided it contains all of the information as required by law. If the institution deems the policy statement excessive in length, administrators may publish the policy in a separate document and make it available upon the request of the student or the parent. Many institutions include the policy statement as part of the university catalog and student handbook and send copies of the policy document to parents. The policy statement should also become part of the faculty and staff employee handbooks. Administrators trained in FERPA regulations should regularly monitor compliance and conduct seminars to keep policy compliance foremost in every employee's mind. Failure to comply with FERPA regulations may cost the institution federal, even state and local, funding. Ideally, an institutional representative should be identified, in the absence of institutional legal counsel, who regularly trains new employees and student employees and who reports to administrative officers on compliance issues (an example of institutional policy, from California State University, Fullerton, is provided at the end of this chapter).

The Right to Inspect and Review Educational Records

Regulation. Educational institutions must allow students to examine the contents of their education records (1988 Rules and Regulations, Sections 99.3, 99.5, 99.10, and 99.11).

Intent. Under the provisions of FERPA, eligible students have the right to inspect most, but not all, records that an educational institution maintains on the student. Educational records are defined as "those records which (1) are directly related to a student; and (2) are maintained by an educational agency or institution or by a party acting for the agency or institution" (*Department of Health, Education, and Welfare* [HEW], 1988, p. 11944). Records that are not considered educational records are those that may infringe upon the privacy rights of the parents (such as financial statements), letters provided under assurances of confidentiality (such as letters of recommendation for admission, employment, or honor), law enforcement records, records to which the student initially waived his or her right to inspect, placement files, and records that include confidential information about other students. The Act further stipulates that, upon the request of the student, the record will be supplied for review within a "reasonable period of time, but in no case more than 45 days after the request has been made" (HEW, 1988, p. 11944). Copies of the educational record will be provided to the student or eligible parent in those cases where "failure to do so would effectively prevent the parent or student from exercising the right to inspect and review the records" (HEW, 1991, pp. 256–257). Institutions may charge a fee for copies as long as the fee is not prohibitive to the extent that access would be denied.

Application. This regulation frustrates administrators, parents, and students more than all of the others. Who has the right to view the records, and what right does the parent have? Until a student reaches the age of eighteen years, the parents have the right of access to the records. Upon reaching the age of eighteen years, the student becomes the "eligible student," and the right of access transfers from the parent to the student. However, "a parent of a postsecondary student may have access only if the student is dependent on the parent as defined by the Internal Revenue Code [and] has a legitimate basis for seeking information" (Weeks, 1993, p. 96). Institutions should state clearly—and apply consistently—their policy on parental dependence. "In practice, some colleges assume the student is dependent unless the student notifies the institution otherwise. Other colleges assume the student is independent unless the parents demonstrate otherwise" (Weeks, 1993, p. 96). The statement of dependency should be strictly enforced, regularly monitored, and made available to offices that routinely maintain and release information about students. If the registrar's office does not have access to student and parental financial records, a system should be developed whereby the registrar's office staff may be informed of the dependency status. The institutional policy may be more restrictive than FERPA, and parental access may be denied based on this institutional policy. However, this should be clearly delineated in the FERPA policy statement.

Records that do not meet the definition of "educational records" should not be kept in the student's educational file. While these records (e.g., law enforcement records, medical records, and notes recorded by faculty or university officials for university business) may pertain to the student and are exempt under FERPA, they are not "educational" in content. According to the definition of educational records as developed by the U.S. Department of Education, these records are considered educational in content if law enforcement officials could not have access to them, and law enforcement records are maintained separately from them.

Institutions must provide access to, but are not required to provide copies of, the student's record, except under the condition previously cited. Often students will request copies of the file and may be familiar enough with FERPA regulations to cite this portion of the regulation, confusing the provision of access with the provision of copy. Allowing a student to inspect and manually take notes pertaining to the file's content complies with the FERPA regulation. However, administrators must use their own judgment to determine when to allow copies of the file, when to charge a fee for copying services, and what fee should be assessed (an example of institutional policy, from California State University, Fullerton, is provided at the end of this chapter).

Requests for Amendment of Educational Records

Regulation. Educational institutions must allow requests for amendment of the student's educational record and respond accordingly and within a reasonable amount of time. Hearing requests from the student must be allowed to permit the student to contest the contents of his or her educational record (1988 Rules and Regulations, Sections 99.20, 99.21, and 99.22).

Intent. The student has the right, upon inspection of his or her record, to request amendment of the record should it be "inaccurate or misleading or violates the privacy or other rights of the student" (HEW, 1988, p. 11946).

Application. While the student has the right to request amendment of his or her educational record, the institution is not required to amend the record based on the information received from the student. The institution is required, however, to evaluate the amendment request and respond to the student within 45 days. A record of the communication must be maintained by the institution. Should the institution's response be in the negative, the institution must also notify the student of his or her right to a hearing. Should the student not agree with the institutional official's decision, the student may request a hearing, and the institution must comply with the hearing request. The requirements for a hearing include the following: (1) a request by the eligible student or parent with dependency rights; (2) responding notification within a reasonable amount of time of a hearing by the institution, which includes the day, date, time, and location of the hearing; (3) a hearing official (this official may not necessarily be involved with the record under investigation); (4) evidence presented by the eligible student or parent pertinent to the hearing under legal counsel (at the student's expense) or with the assistance of corroborating witnesses; (5) a decision by the institution within a reasonable amount of time based on the information presented at the hearing; and (6) documentation of the hearing and evidence presentation and the resultant action taken by the institution (HEW, 1991, pp. 257–258). If the hearing does not result in an amendment of the record, the institution must notify the student of his or her right to ''place a statement in the record commenting on the contested information in the record or stating why he or she disagrees with the decision of the agency or institution, or both'' (HEW, 1988, p. 257). The institution must then maintain the statement for the life of the record and must release the statement along with the contested portion of the record (an example of institutional policy, from California State University, Fullerton, is provided at the end of this chapter).

Release of Personally Identifiable Information

Regulation. Educational institutions may not release personally identifiable information about a student without the written consent of the student, except in those instances provided by law (1988 Rules and Regulations, Sections 99.30, 99.31, 99.33, 99.34, 99.35, 99.36 and 99.37).

Intent. Obviously, the intent is to protect the confidentiality of the student's record and to deny access to third parties that may attempt to invade the student's privacy for legitimate or even illegitimate reasons.

Application. This portion of the law delineates the application of FERPA much more succinctly than any other portion. The student must make his or her request in writing if the record is to be sent to, or viewed by, any person other than the eligible student or parent (if the student is a dependent), provide the purpose of the request, and identify who may have access to his or her records at the time of each request. All requests for access to personally identifiable information must be signed and dated.

Information that is considered ''directory'' and does not contain personally identifiable information may be released without the consent of the student provided the institution provides annual notification of this fact to the eligible student (or parents of the dependent student). Eligible students and parents of dependent students must be informed about the institutional definition of what constitutes directory information and of their right to restrict the release of such information. Those who wish to withhold information from public disclosure must indicate so within the time frame established by the institution.

There are instances when personally identifiable information can be released without the consent of the student. While the consent to release information in these instances is not required, institutional administrators ''must be careful that the data they release does not exceed the scope granted by the regulations''

(Hyman, 1982, p. 598). In all instances of the release of information, the institutional administrator must advise the receiver that the information is protected by FERPA and thus should be protected from release to other parties. Further, the administrator must advise the receiver that once the information is of no further use, the information (if in hard-copy form) should be completely and appropriately destroyed. The instances when release of information without consent is permissible are:

1. Eligible students or parents of dependent students may request access to the student's educational record and need not provide written consent.

2. Records may be released to employees of the educational institution who have been previously identified as persons with legitimate use of student records or to other educational institutions where the student seeks application for admission.

3. The student's consent is not required to release information to "the Comptroller General of the United States, the Secretary, the Commissioner, the Director of the National Institute of Education, the Assistant Secretary for Education, or State educational authorities" (HEW, 1988, p. 11947).

4. Information may also be released to agencies or institutions awarding financial aid provided the purpose of the information is for the determination of eligibility, financial aid award amount determination, conditions of awarding aid, and enforcement of terms that are based on the student's attendance at an education institution (HEW, 1991, p. 258).

5. Information may be released to organizations or institutions conducting educational studies for assessment purposes on behalf of the institution or educational agencies provided the organization ensures the protection of privacy of the information.

6. Information may be released to regional accrediting agencies in the performance of their functions.

7. Information may be released in compliance with a "lawfully issued subpoena; *provided* [*sic*] that the educational agency or institution makes a reasonable effort to notify the parent of the student or the eligible student of the order or subpoena in advance of compliance therewith" (HEW, 1991, p. 258).

8. Information may be released to medical personnel in the event of an emergency that may affect either the student or other parties. Institutional administrators must consider the "seriousness of the threat to the health or safety of the student or other individuals; the need for the information to meet the emergency; whether the parties to whom the information is disclosed are in a position to deal with the emergency, and the extent to which time is of the essence in dealing with the emergency" (HEW, 1991, p. 258).

Many institutions have instituted elaborate systems of student identification to permit requests for transcripts by telephone and to ensure the protection of privacy for the student. However, many institutions rely solely on the written request from the student to enforce privacy policy. In part, the reason for this policy is that many institutions, perhaps most, require payment for the transcript and may not have an equitable system of processing the request without the payment. Further, the process of identifying the student over the telephone re-quires the institutional employee to ask a cadre of questions of the student to ascertain that the student calling is who he or she purports to be. Some student information systems (SIS) or student history transcript systems (SHTS) may not contain the information needed that only the student or parent might know. For example, should the mother's maiden name be an identification element, and that field is not part of the SIS or SHTS, and the folder containing the infor-mation has been destroyed as part of the records retention schedule, the insti-tutional employee, using this identification element, cannot ascertain the identity of the calling party as the student. Institutions that allow telephone requests for transcripts must ask information of the student that is easily accessible and permanently available.

With regard to the various sections applicable to this regulation, while FERPA allows for the release of information, institutions are free to develop and enforce institutional policies that are much more restrictive and prohibitive than FERPA. According to Hyman, "[T]he parent's ability to review the student's file has caused significant debate within the higher education community. Many insti-tutions deny parents' access as an institution policy while still adhering to the philosophy of FERPA and allowing the student full access" (1982, pp. 602–603). When developing the institutional policy for compliance with FERPA, administrators should also develop the institutional policy on parental access to the students' educational records (an example of institutional policy from Cal-ifornia State University, Fullerton, is provided at the end of this chapter).

Documentation Requirements for Release of Information

Regulation. Educational institutions must maintain a record of authorized dis-closure of personally identifiable information from a student's record. Likewise, educational institutions must maintain a record of every request made by indi-viduals without authorization to the information. Requests for information made by institutional employees with authorized access need not be recorded (1988 Rules and Regulations, Sections 99.32, 99.33, and 99.36).

Intent. As with any matter relative to receiving funds from the federal gov-ernment, institutions are required to document all activities pertaining to requests for access to student educational records. This, in part, ensures that the institu-tion has knowledge of FERPA regulations and is making an attempt to comply.

Application. Records must be kept for each request for access to personally identifiable information contained within an educational record for each student for the life of the educational record. This regulation applies to both authorized and unauthorized requests for information, whether or not information is pro-vided. The documentation must include the name of the party or parties re-questing the information and the purpose of the request. Requests for inspection or copies of records by the student, parent of a dependent student, or authorized institutional officer need not be recorded. Further, requests by "part[ies] with written consent from the parent or eligible student or part[ies] seeking directory information'' (HEW, 1988, p. 11948) need not be recorded. While the FERPA regulations do not state documentation requirements for the release of information in the event of a medical emergency, administrators should consider doing so for their protection and that of the institution should legal action occur as the result of the release of information.

COMPLIANCE ISSUES AND ENFORCEMENT PROCEDURES

(1988 Rules and Regulations, Sections 99.62, 99.63, 99.64, 99.65, 99.66, and 99.67)

Occasionally, institutions cannot comply or experience difficulties with compliance because of state or jurisdictional laws that are in opposition to FERPA. In these instances, the administrative officer must notify the Department of Education ''within 45 days, giving the text and citation of the conflicting law'' (HEW, 1988, p. 11949). The Family Compliance Office of the Department of Education will make the determination of compliance and will notify the institutional officer who will, in turn, provide the documentation to those representing the conflicting law.

In the event of a violation of the Act, the student, the parent of the dependent student, the institutional administrator, or any individual with knowledge of the incident or alleged violation must contact the Department of Education and provide evidence supporting the claim of violation. This complaint must be submitted ''within 180 days of the date of the alleged violation or of the date that the complainant knew or reasonably should have known of the alleged violation'' (HEW, 1993, p. 3189). The Family Compliance Office will investigate the allegations and document the following: (1) that a complaint against the institution or individual has been received, (2) the circumstances of the violation, and (3) the right of the institution or individual to respond in writing to the allegations (HEW, 1993, p. 3189). Once deliberations and investigations have concluded, the Family Compliance Office will notify all parties of its findings. Institutions found not in compliance will be informed of the procedures required to comply with FERPA regulations within a specified time period. Should the institution fail to comply within the probationary period, the Office will notify the institution of the termination of funds issued to the institution through federal aid programs.

FURTHER ISSUES RELATED TO FERPA

As with any regulation, there are problems associated with application of the regulation due to technological advancements, matters not covered specifically by the original regulation, or newly enacted regulations. Questions arise because of the lack of specificity and the hesitancy of the university administrator to make a judgment call that may ultimately place the institution in legal difficulties. What follows are but a few of the problems relative to compliance with FERPA.

1. *Who may have access to the educational records upon the death of a student?* According to the Family Policy Compliance Office of the U.S. Department of Education, upon the death of a student, the release of educational records is no longer restricted according to the regulations of FERPA. However, institutional policy may protect these records further in the absence of FERPA protection. Some institutional administrators require a copy of the death certificate and a copy of the letter of testamentary to release the records to those who seek information, as this verifies the death of the student and releases the institution from the FERPA restriction and/or institutional policy. It is essential that the institutional administrator ascertain that the student is indeed deceased before any or all records or information is released.

2. *How should you secure records in an electronic age?* When FERPA was written, "paper records were the traditional mode of record retention" (Hyman, 1982, p. 568) and not under scrutiny by those who evaluated security of computerized systems. The laws governing an individual's right to privacy "cannot, has not, and will not keep pace with the lightning-like speed of technological change" (Curran, 1989, p. 14). As Robert Curran points out, "the 200-year-old U.S. Constitution never mentions the word 'privacy,' and microcomputers weren't even a gleam in a Univac's eye" (1989, p. 14). As student records go on-line, and access is provided to faculty and other administrative units, registrars lose some of the control they previously held over the security of the records. Accessibility to student records by individuals not accustomed to the procedures of privacy protection raises questions of security and confidentiality. A catch-22 situation has developed because of the technological advances and the ease with which information can be retrieved. Institutional research directors, grants researchers, academic advisers, and assessment directors need the information found in student files and therefore need access to those files. Registrars have the responsibility to control access to the student files. However, to deny access to individuals with a legitimate need would increase the workload of the registrar's office personnel, as they would be constantly providing information for other university offices. Registrars consequently have become institutional watchdogs for the security of the student files distributed to the entire campus. "With electronic records, your level of responsibility is far higher than your level of control. An institutional approach to the security of records is absolutely essential" (DeLoughry, 1989, pp. A1, 32).

Many registrars conduct workshops with individuals requesting access in order to ensure that such individuals are advised of the FERPA regulations and apprised of institutional policies concerning use of student-related files. By doing so, registrars have developed security systems and policies for the campus that were once in only a few administrative offices. "Questions of *who* is allowed *what* access to *which* databases at *what* point in time cuts across all activities of an institution, including data about finances, students, and personnel, among others. The type and extent of problems engendered by the relatively simple question of data access are confounded by combining the desire for data with legal, data security and data validity concerns'' (McKinney et al., 1986, p. 6).

In addition to educating novice student record users about their legal responsibilities, registrars must address ethical responsibilities. Computer ethics may seem a strange topic when speaking of student files, but consider the availability of student files to administrative offices that routinely employ other students who also have access to the computer. Previous to the technological information age, files currently on-line and accessible to other administrative or faculty offices were accessible only to staff in the registrar's office. As access is provided to individuals beyond the registrar's control, protection of student record confidentiality and adherence to privacy laws come into question. Computer security and computer ethics must be considered hand in hand and are an integral responsibility and concern of the registrar. As Sally Webster indicates:

In the last few years, many of us have worked hard to protect the rights of individual users and to let faculty and student computer users know what is and is not acceptable. We have beefed up security systems; forced users to change passwords more often; put microcomputers on local area networks which prevent or discourage software theft; made more and better signs to hang on computer lab walls; required applicants for computer accounts to sign statements that they have read and understood the rules; put specific language about computer abuses into institutional organs, such as policy manuals for faculty and students; published handbooks detailing policies, laws, and consequences; and on occasion taken student offenders before judicial boards. In short, we have concentrated on finding and closing loopholes and in putting out the word about specific computing violations. And still we feel uneasy, as if we should do more and yet more, as if the computer terrorists, hackers, cavaliers, and blockheads will inevitably breach our defenses. (1989, p. 51)

While many erect defenses to protect their systems from the "computer terrorists" and "hackers," most are primarily concerned with the "cavaliers and blockheads" whose careless disregard of the law or institutional policy places the institution at risk. While some may view it as an inconvenience, policymakers deem it a necessity to ensure privacy protection. Toward this end, many student records administrators have developed elaborate contracts that the faculty member or other authorized institutional employee must read and sign prior to receiving a computer account that allows access to the student records. (See the appendix for examples reprinted with permission from Patricia Marsh Cavanaugh, University of Houston.) Some computer systems are designed to display a FERPA warning message on the screen when the approved and authorized employee accesses the protected files. While no one can absolutely guarantee a perfect system "because perfect is not an absolute and nothing is absolutely perfect" (R. Wingrove, personal conversation, 1993), student records administrators continue to communicate reminders and warnings and take every measure possible to inform all users about FERPA regulations.

The following illustrates the FERPA statement that is displayed on a computer screen upon access to the student files by faculty members at McMurry University in Abilene, Texas:

The Family Educational Rights and Privacy Act, a federal law, and McMurry University policy require that confidentiality of student information be upheld. Each McMurry University employee is expected to protect the confidentiality of student information.

McMurry University provides access to confidential student information that should only be accessed based upon a legitimate educational interest (need to know). Student information should be provided only to other McMurry University employees who have a legitimate educational interest. Information should not be given to non-McMurry University parties unless it is unrestricted "directory information," authorized in writing by the student, or in accordance with specific McMurry University policies. Student confidentiality must be insured should you leave your office or computer terminal unattended or should you employ student assistants.

For additional information regarding the confidentiality of student information and the release of information, consult the Faculty Handbook or contact the University Registrar. (Fry, 1994)

3. *How should institutions inform all employees about FERPA policies?* In addition to the creation of the access screen mentioned earlier, student records administrators should ensure that they are integral players in the enforcement of FERPA and the development of institutional policies related to FERPA. FERPA compliance administrators and student records administrators should regularly review legislation and conduct workshops to keep FERPA compliance issues at the forefront of administrative policy. Other suggestions include:

- Develop a newsletter that details FERPA regulations or devote a regular feature section to FERPA in the institutional newsletter or newspaper;
- Participate in all new employee orientations to inform employees about FERPA;
- Prepare a fact sheet of FERPA regulations and institutional policy to give to every employee;
- Ensure that the compliance policies relative to FERPA regulations and institutional policy are in the institutional handbook(s); and
- Develop a policy for judicial review of policy infractions. "This policy should include steps for removal of computer privileges and employee termination" (Harris, 1993, p. 24).

4. *How to keep current with FERPA regulations and changes. Which version is accurate? How do you receive updates?* The *Federal Register*, a publication of the U.S. Government Printing Office, provides updates relevant to FERPA compliance. These updates are identified in the section pertaining to changes within the Department of Education. Further, an annual index published in January as part of the *Federal Register* provides a compilation of all regulatory changes or proposals. The Department of Education may on occasion send a

letter that specifically delineates proposed changes to registrars or legal counsel to elicit their responses prior to effecting the change.

However, not all student records administrators regularly receive copies of the *Federal Register*. The institution should receive a copy either by subscription through the library or other administrative offices. Student records administrators should identify the recipient of the publication and request access to the monthly issues. Further, they should scan the annual index and examine all notices listed that are relevant to FERPA. Once changes or rulings are noted, student records administrators should circulate the changes to all employees and update the institutional policy manual and other vehicles by which FERPA regulations are distributed throughout the campus.

SUMMARY

University administrators must develop an institutional policy manual that delineates FERPA regulations and institutional policy relative to student records. While ''out of sight'' may be out of your control, it should never be out of mind. The protection of our students' privacy and the protection of their records are essential for the reputation of the student records administrator, the institution, and the broader state of education as a whole.

APPENDIX 4.1: FAMILY EDUCATIONAL RIGHTS AND PRIVACY ACT; FINAL REGULATIONS; MONDAY, APRIL 11, 1988

Dated February 19, 1988.

William J. Bennett,

Secretary of Education.

The Secretary revises Part 99 of Title 34 of the Code of Federal Regulations to read as follows:

PART 99—FAMILY EDUCATIONAL RIGHTS AND PRIVACY

Subpart A—General

Authority: Sec. 438. Pub. L. 90–247, Title IV, as amended, 88 Stat. 571–574 (20 U.S.C. 1232g), unless otherwise noted.

Subpart A—General

§ 99.1   To which educational agencies or institutions do these regulations apply?

(a) This part applies to an educational agency or institution to which funds have been made available under any program administered by the Secretary of Education that—

(1)(i) Was transferred to the Department under the Department of Education Organization Act (DEOA); and

(ii) Was administered by the Commissioner of Education on the day before the effective date of the DEOA; or

(2) Was enacted after the effective date of the DEOA, unless the law enacting the new Federal program has the effect of making section 438 of the General Education Provisions Act inapplicable.

(Authority: 20 U.S.C. 1230, 1232g, 3487, 3507)

(b) The following chart lists the funded programs to which Part 99 does not apply as of April 11, 1988:

Name of program	Authorizing statute	Implementing regulations
1. High School Equivalency Program and College Assistance Migrant Program..............	Section 418A of the Higher Education Act of 1965 as amended by the Education Amendments of 1980 (Pub. L. 96–374) 20 U.S.C. 1070d-2).	Part 206.
2. Programs administered by the Commissioner of the Rehabilitation Services Administration, and the Director of the National Institute on Disability and Rehabilitation Research.	The Rehabilitation Act of 1973, as amended. (29 U.S.C. 700, *et seq.*).	Parts 350–359, 361, 365, 366, 369–371, 373–375, 378, 379, 385–390, and 395.
3. Transition program for refugee children..................	Immigration and Nationality Act, as amended by the Refugee Act of 1980, Pub. L. 96–212 (8 U.S.C. 1522(d)).	Part 538.
4. College Housing..................	Title IV of the Housing Act of 1950, as amended (12 U.S.C. 1749, *et seq.*).	Part 614.
5. The following programs administered by the Assistant Secretary for Educational Research and Improvement: Educational Research Grant Program. Regional Educational Laboratories Research and Development Centers. All other research or statistical activities funded under Section 405 or 406 of the General Education Provisions Act.	Section 405 of the General Education Provisions Act (20 U.S.C. 1221e), and section 406 of the General Education Provisions Act (20 U.S.C. 1221–1).	Parts 700, 706–708.

Note: The Secretary, as appropriate, updates the information in this chart and informs the public.

(c) This part does not apply to an educational agency or institution solely because students attending that agency or institution receive non-monetary benefits under a program referenced in paragraph (a) of this section, if no funds under that program are made available to the agency or institution.

(d) The Secretary considers funds to be made available to an educational agency or institution of funds under one or more of the programs referenced in paragraph (a) of this section—

(1) Are provided to the agency or institution by grant, cooperative agreement, contract, subgrant, or subcontract; or

(2) Are provided to students attending the agency or institution and the funds may be paid to the agency or institution by those students for educational purposes, such as under the Pell Grant Program and the Guaranteed Student Loan Program (Titles IV–A–1 and IV–B, respectively, of the Higher Education Act of 1965, as amended).

(e) If an educational agency or institution receives funds under one or more of the programs covered by this section, the regulations in this part apply to the recipient as a whole, including each of its components (such as a department within a university).

(Authority: 20 U.S.C. 1232g)

§ 99.2 What is the purpose of these regulations?

The purpose of this part is to set out requirements for the protection of privacy of parents and students under section 438 of the General Education Provisions Act, as amended.

(Authority: 20 U.S.C. 1232g)

(Note: 34 CFR 300.560–300.576 contain requirements regarding confidentiality of information relating to handicapped children who receive benefits under the Education of the Handicapped Act.)

§ 99.3 What definitions apply to these regulations?

The following definitions apply to this part:

"Act" means the Family Educational Rights and Privacy Act of 1974, as amended, enacted as section 438 of the General Education Provisions Act.

(Authority: 20 U.S.C. 1232g)

"Attendance" includes, but is not limited to—

(a) Attendance in person or by correspondence; and

(b) The period during which a person is working under a work-study program.

(Authority: 20 U.S.C. 1232g)

"Directory information" means information contained in an education record of a student which would not generally be considered harmful or an invasion of privacy if disclosed. It includes, but is not limited to the student's name, address, telephone listing, date and place of birth, major field of study, participation in officially recognized activities and sports, weight and height of members of athletic teams, dates of attendance, degrees and awards received, and the most recent previous educational agency or institution attended.

(Authority: 20 U.S.C. 1232g(a)(5)(A))

"Disclosure" means to permit access to or the release, transfer, or other communication of education records, or

the personally indentifiable information contained in those records, to any party, by any means, including oral, written, or electronic means.

(Authority: 20 U.S.C. 1232g(b)(1))

"Educational agency or institution" means any public or private agency or institution to which this part applies under § 99.1(a).

(Authority: 20 U.S.C. 1232g(a)(3))

"Education records" (a) The term means those records that are—

(1) Directly related to a student; and

(2) Maintained by an educational agency or institution or by a party acting for the agency or institution.

(b) The term does not include—

(1) Records of instructional, supervisory, and administrative personnel and educational personnel ancillary to those persons that are kept in the sole possession of the maker of the record, and are not accessible or revealed to any other person except a temporary substitute for the maker of the record;

(2) Records of a law enforcement unit of an educational agency or institution, but only if education records maintained by the agency or institution are not disclosed to the unit, and the law enforcement records are—

(i) Maintained separately from education records;

(ii) Maintained solely for law enforcement purposes; and

(iii) Disclosed only to law enforcement officials of the same jurisdiction;

(3)(i) Records relating to an individual who is employed by an educational agency or institution, that—

(A) Are made and maintained in the normal course of business;

(B) Relate exclusively to the individual in that individual's capacity as an employee; and

(C) Are not available for use for any other purpose.

(ii) Records relating to an individual in attendance at the agency or institution who is employed as a result of his or her status as a student are education records and not excepted under paragraph (b)(3)(i) of this definition.

(4) Records on a student who is 18 years of age or older, or is attending an institution of postsecondary education, that are—

(i) Made or maintained by a physician, psychiatrist, psychologist, or other recognized professional or paraprofessional acting in his or her professional capacity or assisting in a paraprofessional capacity;

(ii) Made, maintained, or used only in connection with treatment of the student; and

(iii) Disclosed only to individuals providing the treatment. For the purpose of this definition, "treatment" does not include remedial educational activities or activities that are part of the program of instruction at the agency or institution; and

(5) Records that only contain information about an individual after he or she is no longer a student at that agency or institution.

(Authority: 20 U.S.C. 1232g(a)(4))

"Eligible student" means a student who has reached 18 years of age or is attending an institution of postsecondary education.

(Authority: 20 U.S.C. 1232g(d))

"Institution of postsecondary education" means an institution that provides education to students beyond the secondary school level; "secondary school level" means the educational level (not beyond grade 12) at which secondary education is provided as determined under State law.

(Authority: 20 U.S.C. 1232g(d))

"Parent" means a parent of a student and includes a natural parent, a guardian, or an individual acting as a parent in the absence of a parent or a guardian.

(Authority: 20 U.S.C. 1232g)

"Party" means an individual, agency, institution, or organization.

(Authority: 20 U.S.C. 1232g(b)(4)(A))

"Personally identifiable information" includes, but is not limited to—

(a) The student's name;

(b) The name of the student's parent or other family member;

(c) The address of the student or student's family;

(d) A personal identifier, such as the student's social security number or student number;

(e) A list of personal characteristics that would make the student's identity easily traceable; or

(f) Other information that would make the student's identity easily traceable.

(Authority: 20 U.S.C. 1232g)

"Record" means any information recorded in any way, including, but not limited to, handwriting, print, tape, film, microfilm, and microfiche.

(Authority: 20 U.S.C. 1232g)

"Secretary" means the Secretary of the U.S. Department of Education or an official or employee of the Department of Education acting for the Secretary under a delegation of authority.

(Authority: 20 U.S.C. 1232g)

"Student", except as otherwise specifically provided in this part, means any individual who is or has been in attendance at an educational agency or institution and regarding whom the agency or institution maintains education records.

(Authority: 20 U.S.C. 1232g(a)(6))

§ 99.4 What are the rights of parents?

An educational agency or institution shall give full rights under the Act to either parent, unless the agency or institution has been provided with evidence that there is a court order, State statute, or legally binding document relating to such matters as divorce, separation, or custody that specifically revokes these rights.

(Authority: 20 U.S.C. 1232g)

§ 99.5 What are the rights of eligible students?

(a) When a student becomes an eligible student, the rights accorded to, and consent required of, parents under this part transfer from the parents to the student.

(b) The Act and this part do not prevent educational agencies or institutions from giving students rights in addition to those given to parents.

(c) If an individual is or has been in attendance at one component of an educational agency or institution, that attendance does not give the individual rights as a student in other components of the agency or institution to which the individual has applied for admission, but has never been in attendance.

(Authority: 20 U.S.C. 1232g(d))

§ 99.6 What information must an educational agency's or institution's policy contain?

(a) Each educational agency or institution shall adopt a policy regarding how the agency or institution meets the requirements of the Act and of this part. The policy must include—

(1) How the agency or institution informs parents and students of their rights, in accord with § 99.7;

(2) How a parent or eligible student may inspect and review education records under § 99.10, including at least—

(i) The procedure the parent or eligible student must follow to inspect and review the records;

(ii) With an understanding that it may not deny access to education records, a description of the circumstances in which the agency or institution believes it has a legitimate cause to deny a request for a copy of those records;

(iii) A schedule of fees (if any) to be charged for copies; and

(iv) A list of the types and locations of education records maintained by the agency or institution, and the titles and addresses of the officials responsible for the records;

(3) A statement that personally identifiable information will not be released from an education record without the prior written consent of the parent or eligible student, except under one or more of the conditions described in § 99.31;

(4) A statement indicating whether the educational agency or institution has a policy of disclosing personally identifiable information under § 99.1(a)(1), and , if so, a specification of the criteria for determining which parties are school officials and what the agency or institution considers to be a legitimate educational interest;

(5) A statement that a record of disclosures will be maiintained as required by § 99.32, and that a parent or eligible student may inspect and review that record;

(6) A specification of the types of personally identifiable information the agency or institution has designated as directory information under § 99.37; and

(7) A statement that the agency or institution permits a parent or eligible student to request correction of the student's education records under § 99.20, to obtain a hearing under § 99.21(a), and to add a statement to the record under § 99.21(b)(2).

(b) The educational agency or institution shall state the policy in writing and make a copy of it available on request to a parent or eligible student.

(Authority: 20 U.S.C. 1232g(e) and (f))

(Approved by the Office of Management and Budget under control number 1880–0508)

§ 99.7 What must an educational agency or institution include in its manual notification?

(a) Each educational agency or institution shall annually notify parents of students currently in attendance, and eligible students currently in attendance, at the agency or institution of their rights under the Act and this part. The notice must include a statement that the parent or eligible student has a right to—

(1) Inspect and review the student's education records;

(2) Request the amendment of the student's education records to ensure that they are not inaccurate, misleading, or otherwise in violation of the student's privacy or other rights;

(3) Consent to disclosures of personally identifiable information

contained in the student's education records, except to the extent that the Act and the regulations in this part authorize disclosure without consent;

(4) File with the U.S. Department of Education a complaint under § 99.64 concerning alleged failures by the agency or institution to comply with the requirements of the act and this part; and

(5) Obtain a copy of the policy adopted under § 99.6.

(b) The notice provided under paragraph (a) of this section must also indicate the places where copies of the policy adopted under § 99.6 are located.

(c) An educational agency or institution may provide this notice by any means that are reasonably likely to inform the parents and eligible students of their rights.

(d) An agency or institution of elementary or secondary education shall effectively notify parents of students who have a primary or home language other than English.

(Authority: 20 U.S.C. 1232g(e))

(Approved by the Office of Management and Budget under control number 1880–0508)

Subpart B—What are the Rights of Inspection and Review of Education Records?

§ 99.10 What rights exist for a parent or eligible student to inspect and review education records?

(a) Except as limited under § 99.12, each educational agency or institution shall permit a parent or eligible student to inspect and review the education records of the student.

(b) The educational agency or institution shall comply with a request for access to records within a reasonable period of time, but in no case more than 45 days after it has received the request.

(c) The educational agency or institution shall respond to reasonable requests for explanations and interpretations of the records.

(d) The educational agency or institution shall give the parent or eligible student a copy of the records if failure to do so would effectively prevent the parent or student from exercising the right to inspect and review the records.

(e) The educational agency or institution shall not destroy any education records if there is an outstanding request to inspect and review the records under this section.

(f) While an education agency or institution is not required to give an eligible student access to treatment records under paragraph (b)(4) of the definition of "Education records" in § 99.3, the student may have those records reviewed by a physician or other appropriate professional of the student's choice.

(Authority: 20 U.S.C. 1232g(a)(1)(A))

§ 99.11 May an educational agency or institution charge a fee for copies of education records?

(a) Unless the imposition of a fee effectively prevents a parent or eligible student from exercising the right to inspect and review the student's education records, an educational agency or institution may charge a fee for a copy of an education record which is made for the parent or eligible student.

(b) An educational agency or institution may not charge a fee to search for or to retrieve the education records of a student.

(Authority: 20 U.S.C. 1232g(a)(1))

§ 99.12 What limitations exist on the right to inspect and review records?

(a) If the education records of a student contain information on more than one student, the parent or eligible student may inspect, review, or be informed of only the specific information about that student.

(b) A postsecondary institution does not have to permit a student to inspect and review education records that are—

(1) Financial records, including any information those records contain, of his or her parents;

(2) Confidential letters and confidential statements of recommendation placed in the education records of the student before January 1, 1975, as long as the statements are used only for the purposes for which they were specifically intended; and

(3) Confidential letters and confidential statements of recommendation placed in the student's education records after January 1, 1975, if—

(i) The student has waived his or her right to inspect and review those letters and statements; and

(ii) Those letters and statements are related to the student's—

(A) Admission to an educational institution;

(B) Application for employment; or

(C) Receipt of an honor or honorary recognition.

(c)(1) A waiver under paragraph (b)(3)(i) of this section is valid only if—

(i) The educational agency or institution does not require the waiver as a condition for admission to or receipt of a service or benefit from the agency or institution; and

(ii) The waiver is made in writing and signed by the student, regardless of age.

(2) If a student has waived his or her rights under paragraph (b)(3)(i) of this section, the educational institution shall—

(i) Give the student, on request, the names of the individuals who provided the letters and statements of recommendation; and

(ii) Use the letters and statements of recommendation only for the purpose for which they were intended.

(3)(i) A waiver under paragraph (b)(3)(i) of this section may be revoked with respect to any actions occurring after the revocation.

(ii) A revocation under paragraph (c)(3)(i) of this section must be in writing.

(Authority: 20 U.S.C. 1232g(a)(1) (A) and (B))

Subpart C—What are the Procedures for Amending Education Records?

§ 99.20 How can a parent or eligible student request amendment of the student's education records?

(a) If a parent or eligible student believes the education records relating to the student contain information that is inaccurate, misleading, or in violation of the student's rights of privacy or other rights, he or she may ask the educational agency or institution to amend the record.

(b) The education agency or institution shall decide whether to amend the record as requested within a reasonable time after the agency or institution receives the request.

(c) If the educational agency or institution decides not to amend the record as requested, it shall inform the parent or eligible student of its decision and of his or her right to a hearing under § 99.21.

(Authority: 20 U.S.C. 1232g(a)(2))

§ 99.21 Under what conditions does a parent or eligible student have the right to a hearing?

(a) An educational agency or institution shall give a parent or eligible student, on request, an opportunity for a hearing to challenge the content of the student's education records on the grounds that the information contained in the education records is inaccurate, misleading, or in violation of the privacy or other rights of the student.

(b)(1) If, as a result of the hearing, the educational agency or institution decides that the information is inaccurate, misleading, or otherwise in violation of the privacy or other rights of the student, it shall—

(i) Amend the record accordingly; and

(ii) Inform the parent or eligible student of the amendment in writing.

(2) If, as a result of the hearing, the educational agency or institution decides that the information in the education record is not inaccurate, misleading, or otherwise in violation of the privacy or other rights of the student, it shall inform the parent or eligible student of the right to place a statement in the record commenting on the contested information in the record or stating why he or she disagrees with the decision of the agency or institution, or both.

(c) If an educational agency or institution places a statement in the education records of a student under paragraph (b)(2) of this section, the agency or institution shall—

(1) Maintain the statement with the contested part of the record for as long as the record is maintained; and

(2) Disclose the statement whenever it discloses the portion of the record to which the statement relates.

(Authority: 20 U.S.C. 1232g(a)(2))

§ 99.22 What minimum requirements exist for the conduct of a hearing?

The hearing required by § 99.21 must meet, at a minimum, the following requirements:

(a) The educational agency or institution shall hold the hearing within a reasonable time after it has received the request for the hearing from the parent or eligible student.

(b) The educational agency or institution shall give the parent or eligible student notice of the date, time, and place, reasonably in advance of the hearing.

(c) The hearing may be conducted by any individual, including an official of the educational agency or institution, who does not have a direct interest in the outcome of the hearing.

(d) The educational agency or institution shall give the parent or eligible student a full and fair opportunity to present evidence relevant to the issues raised under § 99.21. The parent or eligible student may, at their own expense, be assisted or represented by one or more individuals of his or her own choice, including an attorney.

(e) The educational agency or institution shall make its decision in writing within a reasonable period of time after the hearing.

(f) The decision must be based solely on the evidence presented at the hearing, and must include a summary of the evidence and the reasons for the decision.

(Authority: 20 U.S.C. 1232g(a)(2))

Subpart D—May an Educational Agency or Institution Disclose Personally Identifiable Information From Education Records?

§ 99.30 Under what conditions must an educational agency or institution obtain prior consent to disclose information?

(a) Except as provided in § 99.31, an educational agency or institution shall obtain a signed and dated written consent of a parent or an eligible student before it discloses pesonally identifiable information from the student's education records.

(b) The written consent must—
(1) Specify the records that may be disclosed;
(2) State the purpose of the disclosure; and
(3) Identify the party or class of parties to whom the disclosure may be made.

(c) When a disclosure is made under paragraph (a) of this section—
(1) If a parent or eligible student so requests, the educational agency or institution shall provide him or her with a copy of the records disclosed; and
(2) If the parent of a student who is not an eligible student so requests, the agency or institution shall provided the student with a copy of the records disclosed.

(Authority: 20 U.S.C. 1232g (b)(1) and (b)(2)(A))

§ 99.31 Under what conditions is prior consent not required to disclose information?

(a) An educational agency or institution may disclose personally identifiable information from an education record of a student without the consent required by § 99.30 if the disclosure meets one or more of the following conditions:
(1) The disclosure is to other school officials, including teachers, within the agency or institution whom the agency or institution has determined to have legitimate educational interests.
(2) The disclosure is, subject to the requirements of § 99.34, to officials of another school, school system, or institution of postsecondary education where the student seeks or intends to enroll.
(3) The disclosure is, subject to the requirements of § 99.35, to authorize representatives of—
(i) The Comptroller General of the United States;
(ii) The Secretary; or
(iii) State and local educational authorities.
(4)(i) The disclosure is in connection with financial aid for which the student has applied or which the student has

received, if the information is necessary for such purposes as to—
(A) Determine eligibility for the aid;
(B) Determine the amount of the aid;
(C) Determine the conditions for the aid; or
(D) Enforce the terms and conditions of the aid.
(ii) As used in paragraph (a)(4)(i) of this section, "financial aid" means a payment of funds provided to an individual (or a payment in kind of tangible or intangible property to the individual) that is conditioned on the individual's attendance at an educational agency or institution.

(Authority: 20 U.S.C. 1232g(b)(1)(D))

(5)(i) The disclosure is to State and local officials or authorities, if a State statute adopted before November 19, 1974, specifically requires disclosures to those officials and authorities.
(ii) Paragraph (a)(5)(i) of this section does not prevent a State from further limiting the number or type of State or local officials to whom disclosures may be made under that paragraph.
(6)(i) The disclosure is to organizations conducting studies for, or on behalf of, educational agencies or institutions to—
(A) Develop, validate, or administer predictive tests;
(B) Administer student aid programs; or
(C) Improve instruction.
(ii) The agency or institution may disclose information under paragraph (a)(6)(i) of this section only if—
(A) The study is conducted in a manner that does not permit personal identification of parents and students by individuals other than representatives of the organization; and
(B) The information is destroyed when no longer needed for the purposes for which the study was conducted.
(iii) For the purposes of paragraph (a)(6) of this section, the term "organization" includes, but is not limited to, Federal, State, and local agencies, and independent organizations.
(7) The disclosure is to accrediting organizations to carry out their accrediting functions.
(8) The disclosure is to parents of a dependent student, as defined in section 152 of the Internal Revenue Code of 1954.
(9)(i) The disclosure is to comply with a judicial order or lawfully issued subpoena.
(ii) The educational agency or institution may disclose information under paragraph (a)(9)(i) of this section only if the agency or institution makes a reasonable effort to notify the parent or

eligible student of the order or subpoena in advance of compliance.
(10) The disclosure is in connection with a health or safety emergency, under the conditions described in § 99.36.
(11) The disclosure is information the educational agency or institution has designated as "directory information", under the conditions described in § 99.37.
(12) The disclosure is to the parent of a student who is not an eligible student or to the student.

(b) This section does not forbid or require an educational agency or institution to disclose personally identifiable information from the education records of a student to any parties under paragraphs (a) (1) through (11) of this section.

(Authority: 20 U.S.C. 1232g (a)(5)(A), (b)(1) and (b)(2)(B))

§ 99.32 What recordkeeping requirements exist concerning requests and disclosures?

(a)(1) An educational agency or institution shall maintain a record of each request for access to and each disclosure of personally identifiable information from the education records of each student.
(2) The agency or institution shall maintain the record with the education records of the student as long as the records are maintained.
(3) For each request or disclosure the record must include—
(i) The parties who have requested or received personally identifiable information from the education records; and
(ii) The legitimate interests the parties had in requesting or obtaining the information.

(b) If an educational agency or institution discloses personally identifiable information from an education record with the understanding authorized under § 99.33(b), the record of the disclosure required under this section must include—
(1) The names of the additional parties to which the receiving party may disclose the information on behalf of the educational agency or institution; and
(2) The legitimate interests under § 99.31 which each of the additional parties has in requesting or obtaining the information.

(c) The following parties may inspect the record relating to each student:
(1) The parent or eligible student.
(2) The school official or his or her assistants who are responsible for the custody of the records.
(3) Those parties authorized in § 99.31(a) (1) and (3) for the purposes of

auditing the recordkeeping procedures of the educational agency or institution.

(d) Paragarph (a) of this section does not apply if the request was from, or the disclosure was to—

(1) The parent or eligible student;

(2) A school official under § 99.31(a)(1);

(3) A party with written consent from the parent or eligible student; or

(4) A party seeking directory information.

(Authority: 20 U.S.C. 1232g(b)(4)(A))

(Approved by the Office of Management and Budget under control number 1880–0508)

§ 99.33 What limitations apply to the redisclosure of information?

(a)(1) An educational agency or institution may disclose personally identifiable information from an education record only on the condition that the party to whom the information is disclosed will not disclose the information to any other party without the prior consent of the parent or eligible student.

(2) The officers, employees, and agents of a party that receives information under paragraph (a)(1) of this section may use the information, but only for the purposes for which the disclosure was made.

(b) Paragraph (a) of this section does not prevent an educational agency or institution from disclosing personally identifiable information with the understanding that the party receiving the information may make further disclosures of the information on behalf of the educational agency or institution if—

(1) The disclosures meet the requirements of § 99.31; and

(2) The educational agency or institution has complied with the requirements of § 99.32(b).

(c) Paragraph (a) of this section does not apply to disclosures of directory information under § 99.31(a)(11) or to disclosures to a parent or student under § 99.31(a)(12).

(d) Except for disclosures under § 99.31(a) (11) and (12), an educational agency or institution shall inform a party to whom disclosure is made of the requirements of this section.

(Authority: 20 U.S.C. 1232g(b)(4)(B))

§ 99.34 What conditions apply to disclosure of information to other educational agencies or institutions?

(a) An educational agency or institution that discloses an education record under § 99.31(a)(2) shall—

(1) Make a reasonable attempt to notify the parent or eligible student at the last known address of the parent or eligible student, unless—

(i) The disclosure is initiated by the parent or eligible student; or

(ii) The policy of the agency or institution under § 99.6 includes a notice that the agency or institution forwards education records to other agencies or institutions that have requested the records and in which the student seeks or intends to enroll;

(2) Give the parent or eligible student, upon request, a copy of the record that was disclosed; and

(3) Give the parent or eligible student, upon request, an opportunity for a hearing under Subpart C.

(b) An educational agency or institution may disclose an education record of a student in attendance to another educational agency or institution if—

(1) The student is enrolled in or receives services from the other agency or institution; and

(2) The disclosure meets the requirements of paragraph (a) of this section.

(Authority: 20 U.S.C. 1232g(b)(1)(B))

§ 99.35 What conditions apply to disclosure of information for Federal or State program purposes?

(a) The officials listed in § 99.31(a)(3) may have access to education records in connection with an audit or evaluation of Federal or State supported education programs, or for the enforcement of or compliance with Federal legal requirements which relate to those programs.

(b) Information that is collected under paragraph (a) of this section must—

(1) Be protected in a manner that does not permit personal identification of individuals by anyone except the officials referred to in paragraph (a) of this section; and

(2) Be destroyed when no longer needed for the purposes listed in paragraph (a) of this section.

(c) Paragraph (b) of this section does not apply if—

(1) The parent or eligible student has given written consent for the disclosure under § 99.30; or

(2) The collection of personally identifiable information is specifically authorized by Federal law.

(Authority: 20 U.S.C. 1232g(b)(3))

§ 99.36 What conditions apply to disclosure of information in health and safety emergencies?

(a) An educational agency or institution may disclose personally identifiable information from an education record to appropriate parties in connection with an emergency if knowledge of the information is

necessary to protect the health of safety or the student or other individuals.

(b) Paragraph (a) of this section shall be strictly construed.

(Authority: 20 U.S.C. 1232g(b)(1)(I))

§ 99.37 What conditions apply to disclosing directory information?

(a) An educational agency or institution may disclose directory information if it has given public notice to parents of students in attendance and eligible students in attendance at the agency or institution of—

(1) The types of personally identifiable information that the agency or institution has designated as directory information;

(2) A parent's or eligible student's right to refuse to let the agency or institution designate any or all of those types of information about the student as directory information; and

(3) The period of time within which a parent or eligible student has to notify the agency or institution in writing that he or she does not want any or all of those types of information about the student designated as directory information.

(b) An educational agency or institution may disclose directory information about former students without meeting the conditions in paragraph (a) of this section.

(Authority: 20 U.S.C. 1232g(a)(5) (A) and (B))

Subpart E—What are the Enforcement Procedures?

§ 99.60 What functions has the Secretary delegated to the Office and to the Education Appeal Board?

(a) For the purposes of this subpart, "Office" means the Family Policy and Regulations Office, U.S. Department of Education.

(b) The Secretary designates the Office to—

(1) Investigate, process, and review complaints and violations under the Act and this part; and

(2) Provide technical assistance to ensure compliance with the Act and this part.

(c) The Secretary designates the Education Appeal Board to act as the Review Board required under the Act.

(Authority: 20 U.S.C. 1232g (f) and (g), 1234)

§ 99.61 What responsibility does an educational agency or institution have concerning conflict with State or local laws?

If an educational agency or institution determines that it cannot comply with the Act or this part due to a conflict with State or local law, it shall notify the

Office within 45 days, giving the text and citation of the conflicti..g law.

(Authority: 20 U.S.C. 1232g(f))

§ 99.62   What Information must an educational agency or institution submit to the Office?

The Office may require an educational agency or institution to submit reports containing information necessary to resolve complaints under the Act and the regulations in this part.

(Authority: 20 U.S.C. 1232g (f) and (g))

§ 99.63   Where are complaints filed?

A person may file a written complaint with the Office regarding an alleged violation under the Act and this part. The Office's address is: Family Policy and Regulations Office, U.S. Department of Education, Washington, DC 20202.

(Authority: 20 U.S.C. 1232g(g))

§ 99.64   What is the complaint procedure?

(a) A complaint filed under § 99.63 must contain specific allegations of fact giving reasonable cause to believe that a violation of the Act or this part has occurred.

(b) The Office investigates each timely complaint to determine whether the educational agency or institution has failed to comply with the provisions of the Act or this part.

(Authority: 20 U.S.C. 1232g(f))

§ 99.65   What is the content of the notice of complaint issued by the Office?

(a) If the Office receives a complaint, it notifies the complainant and the educational agency or institution against which the violation has been alleged, in writing, that the complaint has been received.

(b) The notice to the agency or institution under paragraph (a) of this section—

(1) Includes the substance of the alleged violation; and

(2) Informs the agency or institution that the Office will investigate the complaint and that the educational agency or institution may submit a written response to the complaint.

(Authority: 20 U.S.C. 1232g(g))

§ 99.66   What are the responsibilities of the Office in the enforcement process?

(a) The Office reviews the complaint and response and may permit the parties to submit further written or oral arguments or information.

(b) Following its investigation, the Office provides to the complainant and the educational agency or institution written notice of its findings and the basis for its findings.

(c) If the Office finds that the educational agency or institution has not

complied with the Act or this part, the notice under paragraph (b) of this section—

(1) Includes a statement of the specific steps that the agency or institution must take to comply; and

(2) Provides a reasonable period of time, given all of the circumstances of the case, during which the educational agency or institution may comply voluntarily.

(Authority: 20 U.S.C. 1232g(f))

§ 99.67   How does the Secretary enforce decisions?

(a) If the educational agency or institution does not comply during the period of time set under § 99.66(c), the Secretary may take an action authorized under 34 CFR Part 78, including—

(1) Issuing a notice of intent to terminate funds under 34 CFR 78.21;

(2) Issuing a notice to withhold funds under 34 CFR 78.21, 200.94(b) or 298.45(b), depending upon the applicable program under which the notice is issued; or

(3) Issuing a notice to cease and desist under 34 CFR 78.31, 200.94(c) or 298.45(c), depending upon the program under which the notice is issued.

(b) If, after an investigation under § 99.66, the Secretary finds that an educational agency or institution has complied voluntarily with the Act or this part, the Secretary provides the compl'anant and the agency or institution written notice of the decision and the basis for the decision.

(Note: 34 CFR Part 78 contains the regulations of the Education Appeal Board.)

(Authority: 20 U.S.C. 1232g(g))

Corrections

DEPARTMENT OF EDUCATION

34 CFR Part 99

Family Educational Rights and Privacy

Correction

In rule document 88-7764 beginning on page 11942 in the issue of Monday, April 11, 1988, make the following corrections:

§ 99.6   [Corrected]

1. On page 11945, in the second column, in § 99.6(a)(4), in the fifth line, "§ 99.1(a)(1)" should read "§ 99.31(a)(1)".

§ 99.7   [Corrected]

2. On the same page, in the second column, in the heading for § 99.7, "manual" should read "annual".

§ 99.20   [Corrected]

3. On page 11946, in the second column, in § 99.20(b), in the first line, "education" should read "educational".

§ 99.31   [Corrected]

4. On page 11947, in the first column, in § 99.31(a)(3), in the second line, "authorize" should read "authorized".

5. On the same page, in the second column, in § 99.31(a)(5)(ii), in the third line, "or State" should read "of State".

§ 99.36   [Corrected]

6. On page 11948, in the third column, in § 99.36(a), in the first and second lines, "of safety or" should read "or safety of".

§ 99.67   [Corrected]

7. On page 11949, in the second column, in § 99.67(b), in the sixth line, "complainant" was misspelled.

8. On page 11950, in the third column, in "*Section 99.3*", in the second paragraph, in the 11th line, "statue" should read "statute".

9. On page 11953, in the second column, in the sixth indented paragraph, in the first line, "Two" should read "The".

10. On page 11954, in the third column, in the fourth line, "disclosed" should read "disclose".

11. On page 11956, eleven lines from the bottom, "student" should read "statute".

12. On page 11957, in the second column, eleven lines from the bottom, after "the" insert "student as".

BILLING CODE 1505-01-D

APPENDIX 4.2: U.S. DEPARTMENT OF EDUCATION, FERPA FACT SHEET

UNITED STATES DEPARTMENT OF EDUCATION

OFFICE OF HUMAN RESOURCES AND ADMINISTRATION

FACT SHEET

FAMILY EDUCATIONAL RIGHTS AND PRIVACY ACT OF 1974

(FERPA)

FERPA is a Federal law designed to protect the privacy of a student's education records. The law applies to all schools which receive funds under an applicable program from the U.S. Department of Education.

FERPA gives certain rights to parents regarding their children's education records. These rights transfer to the student or former student who has reached the age of 18 or is attending any school beyond the high school level. Students and former students to whom the rights have transferred are called eligible students.

-- Parents or eligible students have the right to inspect and review all of the student's education records maintained by the school. Schools are not required to provide copies of materials in education records unless, for reasons such as great distance, it is impossible for parents or eligible students to inspect the records personally. The school may charge a fee for copies.

-- Parents and eligible students have the right to request that a school correct records believed to be inaccurate or misleading. If the school decides not to amend the record, the parent or eligible student then has the right to a formal hearing. After the hearing, if the school still decides not to amend the record, the parent or eligible student has the right to place a statement with the record commenting on the contested information in the record.

-- Generally, the school must have written permission from the parent or eligible student before releasing any information from a student's records. However, the law allows schools to disclose records, without consent, to the following parties:

- School employees who have a need-to-know;
- Other schools to which a student is transferring;
- Certain government officials in order to carry out lawful functions;
- Appropriate parties in connection with financial aid to a student;
- Organizations doing certain studies for the school;

400 MARYLAND AVE., S.W. WASHINGTON, D.C. 20202-4500

Our mission is to ensure equal access to education and to promote educational excellence throughout the Nation.

- Accrediting organizations;
- Individuals who have obtained court orders or subpoenas;
- Persons who need to know in cases of health and safety emergencies; and
- State and local authorities to whom disclosure is required by State laws adopted before November 19, 1974.

Schools may also disclose, without consent, "directory" type information such as a student's name, address, telephone number, date and place of birth, honors and awards, and dates of attendance. However, the school must tell parents and students of the information that is designated as directory information and provide a reasonable amount of time to allow the parent or eligible student to request the school not to disclose that information about them.

Schools must notify parents and eligible students of their rights under this law. The actual means of notification (special letter, inclusion in a PTA bulletin, student handbook, or newspaper article) is left to each school.

Schools must adopt a written policy about complying with FERPA. Schools must give the parent or eligible student a copy of the policy on request.

If you wish to see your child's education records, or if you are over 18 or are attending college and would like to see your records, you should contact the school for the procedure to follow.

If you have any questions about FERPA, or if you have problems in securing your rights under the Act, you may call (202) 732-1807 or TDD (202) 732-1854 or write to:

Family Policy Compliance Office
U.S. Department of Education
400 Maryland Avenue, S.W.
Washington, DC 20202-4605.

APPENDIX 4.3: CALIFORNIA STATE UNIVERSITY, FULLERTON EXAMPLES

California State University, Fullerton
Fullerton, California 92634-9480

Vice President for Student Services
(714) 773-3221

REQUEST TO PREVENT DISCLOSURE OF GENERAL DIRECTORY INFORMATION

TO: ALL STUDENTS:

You have the opportunity to indicate on your registration form whether you wish to be listed in the *Public Directory* which is available at several locations on campus, and contains name, address, telephone number, class level, and major field of study. This information is available to the general public on request. Commercial agencies may obtain access to this information.

In addition to the *Public Directory*, the university also maintains a *General Directory*. At its discretion the university may provide general directory information in response to legitimate inquiries, to include name, date and place of birth, major field of study, class level, dates of attendance, degrees and awards received, previous educational institutions attended, participation in officially recognized activities and sports, and weight and height of members of athletic teams. Under the provisions of the Family Educational Rights and Privacy Act of 1974, currently enrolled students have the right to withhold the disclosure of general information. Regardless of any request to withhold general directory information, you should know that information in your student records may be released to certain individuals or institutions under carefully controlled conditions as provided by law.

Please consider very carefully the consequences of any decision by you to withhold general directory information. Should you decide to inform the university not to release general directory information, any future requests for such information from non-institutional persons or organizations will be refused except as provided by law.

The university will honor your request to withhold general directory information, but cannot assume responsibility to get in touch with you for subsequent permission to release it. Regardless of the effect upon you, the university assumes no liability for honoring your instructions that such information be withheld.

I request that the university not disclose, except as provided by law, general directory information about me for the _____ semester, 19 ____

DATE _____ SIGNATURE _____

STUDENT NO._____ PRINT NAME _____

If this form is not received in the Office of the Vice President for Student Services (LH-810) prior to the close of late registration (the 10th day of instruction), it will be assumed that the above information may be disclosed until the close of late registration for the next academic semester. A new form for nondisclosure must be completed each academic semester.

Copies of the university's policy on privacy rights of student in education records may be obtained from either the Office of the Vice President for Student Services or the Office of Admissions and Records. Questions about the university's policy may be addressed to the Vice President for Student Services, Langsdorf Hall 810, (714) 773-3221.

/sks:June 1990

The California State University

PRIVACY RIGHTS

PRIVACY RIGHTS OF STUDENTS IN EDUCATIONAL RECORDS

The Family Educational Rights and Privacy Act, (a federal law referred to as FERPA), Sections 67100 through 67147 of the California Education Code and Executive Order 382 of the California State University, designate that a written institutional policy be established and that a statement of procedures covering the privacy rights of students be made available. These laws and Executive Order provide that the university will maintain the confidentiality of student education records.

ACCESS TO RECORDS POLICY

California State University, Fullerton accords all the rights under the law to currently or previously enrolled students at the university. The law does not apply to prospective students. No one shall have access to nor will the university disclose any information from student education records without the written consent of students except to 1) personnel within the university; 2) personnel within the California State University with a legitimate educational interest; 3) officials of other institutions in which students seek to enroll; 4) specified representatives of federal and state agencies in connection with legal requirements for federal and state supported education programs; 5) persons or organizations providing student financial aid; 6) institutions conducting studies to develop, validate, and administer predictive tests, or to improve instruction; 7) accrediting agencies carrying out their accreditation function; 8) persons in compliance with a judicial order or lawfully issued subpoena; and 9) persons in an emergency to protect the health and safety of students and other persons. All of these exceptions are permitted under the law. Records will be maintained where required of requests and disclosures of personally identifiable information as part of student education records, and shall include the names and addresses of the persons who requested the information and their legitimate interests in the information.

Within the university, only authorized members, individually or collectively, of the faculty, administration, professional and clerical staff, and others who manage student record information, and who on a demonstrated need to know act in students' educational interests, will have access to student education records. Normally these members include personnel in the offices of admissions and records, academic affairs, student affairs and academic personnel functioning within the limitations of their need to know.

DIRECTORY INFORMATION

The university maintains two categories of directory information:

- *Public directory*—the names, addresses, telephone numbers, class level, and major field of study of those students who respond affirmatively during registration each term are published in a public directory, available at several locations on campus. It should be noted that commercial agencies have access to this publication.

- *General directory*—at its discretion the university may provide general directory information, in response to legitimate inquiries, to include name, date and place of birth, major field of study, class level, dates of attendance, degrees and awards received, previous educational institutions attended participation in officially recognized activities and sports, and weight and height of members of athletic teams. Currently enrolled students may withhold general directory information each term by notifying the vice president for student affairs in writing within two weeks after the first day of instruction for each term.

STUDENT RIGHTS

The law provides students with the right to inspect and review information contained in their education records, to challenge the contents of their education records, to have a hearing of the outcome if the challenge is unsatisfactory, and to submit explanatory statements for inclusion in their files if they feel the decision of the hearing panel to be unacceptable. The right to a hearing under the law does not include any right to challenge the appropriateness of a grade determined by a instructor. The vice president for student affairs at California State University, Fullerton has been designated to coordinate the inspection and review procedures for student education records. Students wishing to review their education records must make written requests to the Vice President for Student Affairs, Langsdorf Hall 810. Records covered by the law will be made available within fifteen days of the request. In the event students cannot be present on campus to review their education records, copies may be made at prevailing rates, with the exception that copies will not be made of records for which a financial hold exists, or of transcripts of source documents that exist elsewhere.

TYPES OF RECORDS

The following types of education records are maintained by the university:

- *Academic information*—all records and documents pertaining to admission, enrollment, and academic progress are maintained in the office of the director of admissions and records.

- *Academic advising*—all records pertaining to academic advising are maintained either in the academic department of the student's major field of study or in the office of the dean of the school.

- *Financial aid information*—all records and documents pertaining to scholarships and financial aids applications and awards are maintained in the office of the director of financial aid.

- *Placement information*—all records and the documents pertaining to job placement purposes are maintained in the office of the director of the career development and counseling center.

- *Student affairs information*—all documents pertaining to special programs, student grievances and discipline are maintained by the office of the vice president for student affairs.

Education records are reviewed periodically to insure that information contained in them is accurate and appropriate. Removed material is destroyed in accordance with record retention policies of the California State University.

Education records do not include records of instructional, administrative and educational personnel, which are in the sole possession of the maker, and are not accessible or revealed to any individual except a temporary substitute. Records of the law enforcement unit, student health records, employment records or alumni records are also not included in the category of student records. Health records, however, may in most cases be accessed by students, or when such access would be detrimental to students' health, may be reviewed by physicians of the students' choosing.

Students may not inspect and review the following as outlined by FERPA: financial information submitted by their parents; confidential letters and recommendations associated with admissions, employment or job placement, or honors to which they have waived their rights of inspection and review; or education records containing information about more than one student, in which case the institution will permit access only to that part of the record which pertains to the inquiring student. The university is not required to permit students to inspect and review confidential letters and recommendations placed in their files prior to January 1, 1975, provided those letters are collected under established policies of confidentiality and were used only for the purposes for which they were collected.

CHALLENGE OF INFORMATION

Students who believe that their education records contain specific information that is inaccurate or misleading, or is otherwise in violation of their privacy or other rights, may discuss their problems informally with the vice president for student affairs. If the decisions are in agreement with the students' requests, the appropriate records will be amended, If not, the students will be notified within a reasonable period of time that the records will not be amended, and they will be informed by the vice president for student affairs of their right to a formal hearing. Student's requests for a formal hearing must be made in writing to the vice president for student affairs, who, within a reasonable period of time after receiving such requests, will inform students of the date, place, and the time of the hearing. Students may present evidence relevant to the issues raised and may be assisted or represented at the hearing by one or more persons of their choice, including attorneys, at the students' expense. The hearing shall be conducted by a hearing officer appointed by the president.

HEARINGS

Decisions of the hearing officer will be based solely on the evidence presented at the hearing, and will consist of written statements summarizing the evidence and stating the reasons for the decisions, and will be delivered to all parties concerned. The education records will be corrected or amended in accordance with the decisions of the hearing officer, if the decisions are in favor of the students, the students may place with the education records statements commenting on the information in the records, or statements setting forth any reasons for disagreeing with the decisions. The statements will be placed in the education records maintained as part of the students' records, and released whenever the records in question are disclosed.

Students who believe that the adjudications of their challenges were unfair, or not in keeping with the provisions of the law, may request in writing assistance from the president of the university. Further, students who believe that their rights have been abridged, may file complaints with The Family Educational Rights and Privacy Act Office (FERPA), Department of Education, Washington, D.C., 20201, concerning the alleged failures of California State University, Fullerton to comply with the Act.

Revisions and clarifications will be published as experience with the law and university policy warrants.

STSV
10/93

APPENDIX 4.4: UNIVERSITY OF HOUSTON EXAMPLE

U N I V E R S I T Y *of* **H O U S T O N**

Office of Registration and Academic Records   Houston, TX 77204-2161   713/743-1010

⊞H

TO: _____ DATE:_____

OFFICE: _____

UH MAILCODE: _____

Your request for access to the Student Information System RARSTU has been received and approved. A reservation has been booked for you to attend the following training session:

        DAY: _____

        DATE: _____

        TIME: _____

        PLACE: 111 Ezekiel W. Cullen Building

We recommend that you make arrangements to arrive about 10 minutes before the session is scheduled to begin. You may wish to bring a pencil or pen with you, however, all the material covered in the session will be available on each screen in the RARSTU application through the PF2 on-line documentation function.

We also recommend that if you just recently received your USERID and/or have not recently logged onto the system, you should log on the morning of your class to insure that you remember your USERID and PASSWORD. This will enable you to feel more comfortable logging on when you come to the training session.

If you are unable to attend the training session, please call _____ at ext. _____ at least 24 hours before the session is scheduled to set up another time. The Office of Registration and Academic Records holds training sessions each month, generally on the first Tuesday, enrollment activities permitting. Reservations must be made in advance as classes are restricted in size.

REQUEST FOR ACCESS TO RARMNT(RECORD MAINTENANCE)

I, _____, _____in my capacity as
   (Print full name)   (SSN)
_____in the department/college of _____

RM/BLDG_____UHMAIL CODE_____ EXT._____request access to RARMNT.

I realize that I am being given access to a record maintenance application which will be used to update student records in the University of Houston database and I will be responsible for insuring that any and all transactions I make to the students' records will be accurate and appropriate to the best of my ability.

I agree to abide by the procedures identified by University Support Services and the Office of Registration and Academic Records during training,   through on-line documentation, notices posted on database screens and any subsequent correspondence.   I agree that given the nature of the application that I will not allow anyone to use my USERID and PASSWORD to gain access to this application and will inform Registration and Academic Records if I know or suspect that someone has obtained unauthorized use of my access.   In addition, I understand that Registration and Academic Records may terminate or subsequently refuse my access to RARMNT at any time, with or without notification.

I understand and agree to abide by the information above.

Signature of applicant: _____USERID:_____DATE:_____

I agree that the employee applicant has an academic/administrative need to access the student information database and I will notify the Office of Registration and Academic Records in writing should the employee resign, transfer, or be terminated by this office.

Signature of supervisor: _____Title:_____DATE:_____

Signature of College Dean or
Administrative Officer:_____DATE:_____

REGISTRATION AND ACADEMIC RECORDS USE ONLY

RAR STAFF _____ APPROVED___ DISAPPROVED _____ TRAINING DATE _____

U N I V E R S I T Y *of* H O U S T O N

Office of Registration and Academic Records   Houston, TX 77204-2161   713/743-1010

REQUEST FOR ACCESS TO RARSTU(STUDENT INFORMATION INQUIRY)

I, _____, _____in my capacity as
   (Print full name)   (SSN)
_____in the department/college of _____

RM/BLDG_____UHMAIL CODE_____ EXT._____ request access to RARSTU.

I realize that most of the information within RARSTU is classified as confidential under the **Family Education Rights and Privacy Act of 1974.** Students' records are released only for use by faculty and staff for authorized campus related purposes on a need to know basis, i.e. advising or counseling of students. The release of records for off campus or non-academic department use occurs only with the student's knowledge and consent or where required by law or when subpoenaed.

I understand that public information on a record that may be released upon request includes name, address, telephone number, date and place of birth, classification, major, current class schedule, participating in officially recognized activities and sports, weight and height(athletes only), dates of attendance, degree(s) received, the most recent previous educational institution attended, or other similar information. Students who do not wish this information to be released are responsible for notifying the Office of Registration and Academic Records during the first week of classes. Display in RARSTU of the message **"Withhold Public Information"** indicates that no information regarding the student can be released without the student's permission.

I agree to abide by the procedures identified by University Support Services and the Office of Registration and Academic Records during training, through on-line documentation, notices posted on database screens and any subsequent correspondence. I understand that Registration and Academic Records may terminate or subsequently refuse my access to RARSTU at any time, with or without notification.

I understand and agree to abide by the information above.

Signature of applicant: _____USERID:_____DATE:_____

I agree that the employee applicant has an academic/administrative need to access the student information database and I will notify the Office of Registration and Academic Records in writing should the employee resign, transfer, or be terminated by this office.

Signature of supervisor: _____Title:_____DATE:_____

Signature of College Dean or
Administrative Officer:_____DATE:_____

REGISTRATION AND ACADEMIC RECORDS USE ONLY

RAR STAFF _____ APPROVED___ DISAPPROVED _____ TRAINING DATE _____

APPENDIX 4.5: FAMILY EDUCATIONAL RIGHTS AND PRIVACY ACT: RULE, THURSDAY, JANUARY 7, 1993

DEPARTMENT OF EDUCATION

34 CFR Part 99

RIN 1880–AA54

Family Educational Rights and Privacy

AGENCY: Department of Education.

ACTION: Final regulations.

SUMMARY: The Secretary amends the regulations for the Family Educational Rights and Privacy Act (FERPA). These amendments are needed to implement a disclosure provision of the Crime Awareness and Campus Security Act of 1990. Additionally, the amendments are needed to (1) reflect a change in the enforcement provisions of the existing regulations, including designation of a new review authority; and (2) incorporate a number of technical amendments. The principal change resulting from these regulations is establishment of another condition under which an institution of postsecondary education may, without prior consent, disclose information from an education record.

EFFECTIVE DATE: These regulations take effect either 45 days after publication in the **Federal Register** or later if the Congress takes certain adjournments. If you want to know the effective date of these regulations, call or write the Department of Education contact person. A document announcing the effective date will be published in the **Federal Register.**

FOR FURTHER INFORMATION CONTACT: Ellen Campbell, Family Policy Compliance Office, Office of Human Resources and Administration, U.S. Department of Education, 400 Maryland Avenue, SW., Washington, DC 20202–4605. Telephone: (202) 732–1807. Individuals who are hearing impaired may call the Federal Dual Party Relay Service at 1–800–877–8339 (in the Washington, DC 202 area code, telephone 708–9300) between 8 a.m. and 7 p.m., Eastern time.

SUPPLEMENTARY INFORMATION: The current FERPA regulations allow educational agencies and institutions to disclose personally identifiable information from a student's education records without the student's consent only under certain conditions. These final regulations allow institutions of postsecondary education to disclose the results of a disciplinary proceeding conducted by the institution against an alleged perpetrator of a crime of violence to the alleged victim of that crime without the prior written consent of the alleged perpetrator. This new condition was created by section 203 of

the Crime Awareness and Campus Security Act of 1990 (Public Law 101–542, title II, section 203; 20 U.S.C. 1232g(b)(6)), which amended FERPA to allow for this disclosure.

Additionally, these final regulations reflect changes in the enforcement provisions under 34 CFR part 99, subpart E. Specifically, FERPA provides that the Secretary shall designate a review board within the Department for the purpose of reviewing and adjudicating violations of FERPA. In the current regulations, the Education Appeal Board (EAB) serves as the designated review board. Because the EAB is being phased out, the Secretary designates the Office of Administrative Law Judges to act as the review board for the purpose of reviewing and adjudicating under FERPA.

Further, several amendments are included in these final regulations for reasons of clarification. A change has been made to the provision that describes the conditions under which an educational agency or institution must obtain prior consent in order to disclose information. The change will allow an educational agency or institution to disclose information from a student's education records if the parent or eligible student has provided written consent to the party seeking access to the records, rather than require that the educational agency or institution obtain written consent directly from the parent or eligible student.

These final regulations also include a definition of what is considered to be a "timely complaint" of an alleged violation of FERPA. Historically, the office designated to administer FERPA has had to determine on a case-by-case basis what it considered to be a "timely complaint." Based on this historical experience and comparison with similar limitation periods for filing complaints, the Secretary has determined that a complaint brought within 180 days of the alleged violation should be considered timely.

On August 11, 1992, at 57 FR 35964 the Secretary published a notice of proposed rulemaking (NPRM). Except for minor technical revisions, there are no differences between the NPRM and these final regulations.

Public Comment

In the NPRM the Secretary invited comments on the proposed regulations. Two parties submitted comments endorsing the proposed regulations. The only substantive comment the Secretary received suggested a change the Secretary is not legally authorized to

make under the applicable statutory authority.

Executive Order 12291

These regulations have been reviewed in accordance with Executive Order 12291. They are not classified as major because they do not meet the criteria for major regulations established in the order.

Paperwork Reduction Act of 1980

These regulations have been examined under the Paperwork Reduction Act of 1980 and have been found to contain no information collection requirements.

Assessment of Educational Impact

In the NPRM, the Secretary requested comments on whether the proposed regulations would require transmission of information that is being gathered by or is available from any other agency or authority of the United States.

Based on the response to the proposed rules and on its own review, the Department has determined that the regulations in this document do not require transmission of information that is being gathered by or is available from any other agency or authority of the United States.

List of Subjects in 34 CFR Part 99

Administrative practice and procedure, Education, Family educational rights, Parents, Privacy, Reporting and recordkeeping requirements, Students.

Dated: December 18, 1992.

Lamar Alexander,

Secretary of Education.

(Catalog of Federal Domestic Assistance Number does not apply.)

The Secretary amends part 99 of title 34 of the Code of Federal Regulations as follows:

PART 99—FAMILY EDUCATIONAL RIGHTS AND PRIVACY

1. The authority citation for part 99 is revised to read as follows:

Authority: 20 U.S.C. 1232g, unless otherwise noted.

2. Section 99.5 is amended by revising the section heading to read as follows:

§ 99.5 What are the rights of students?

*   *   *   *   *

§ 99.6 [Amended]

3. In § 99.6, paragraph (a)(5) is amended by removing "maintained" and adding, in its place, "maintained".

4. Section 99.30 is amended by revising the section heading and paragraph (a) to read as follows:

§ 99.30   Under what conditions is prior consent required to disclose Information?

(a) The parent or eligible student shall provide a signed and dated written consent before an educational agency or institution discloses personally identifiable information from the student's education records, except as provided in § 99.31.

* * * * *

5. Section 99.31 is amended by adding a new paragraph (a)(13), revising paragraph (b), and revising the authority citation to read as follows:

§ 99.31   Under what conditions is prior consent not required to disclose information?

(a) * * *

(13) The disclosure is to an alleged victim of any crime of violence, as that term is defined in section 16 of title 18, United States Code, of the results of any disciplinary proceeding conducted by an institution of postsecondary education against the alleged perpetrator of that crime with respect to that crime.

(b) This section does not forbid an educational agency or institution to disclose, nor does it require an educational agency or institution to disclose, personally identifiable information from the education records of a student to any parties under paragraphs (a)(1) through (11) and (13) of this section.

(Authority: 20 U.S.C. 1232g(a)(5)(A), (b)(1), (b)(2)(B) and (b)(6))

6. Section 99.60 is amended by revising the heading and paragraphs (a) and (c) to read as follows:

§ 99.60   What functions has the Secretary delegated to the Office and to the Office of Administrative Law Judges?

(a) For the purposes of this subpart, "Office" means the Family Policy

Compliance Office, U.S. Department of Education.

* * * * *

(c) The Secretary designates the Office of Administrative Law Judges to act as the Review Board required under the Act to enforce the Act with respect to all applicable programs. The term "applicable program" is defined in section 400 of the General Education Provisions Act.

7. Section 99.63 is revised to read as follows:

§ 99.63   Where are complaints filed?

A person may file a written complaint with the Office regarding an alleged violation under the Act and this part. The Office's address is: Family Policy Compliance Office, U. S. Department of Education, Washington, D.C. 20202–4605.

(Authority: 20 U.S.C. 1232g(g))

8. Section 99.64 is amended by adding new paragraphs (c) and (d) to read as follows:

§ 99.64   What is the complaint procedure?

* * * * *

(c) A timely complaint is defined as an allegation of a violation of the Act that is submitted to the Office within 180 days of the date of the alleged violation or of the date that the complainant knew or reasonably should have known of the alleged violation.

(d) The Office extends the time limit in this section if the complainant shows that he or she was prevented by circumstances beyond the complainant's control from submitting the matter within the time limit, or for other reasons considered sufficient by the Office.

9. Section 99.65 is revised to read as follows:

§ 99.65   What is the content of the notice of complaint issued by the Office?

(a) The Office notifies the complainant and the educational agency or institution in writing if it initiates an investigation of a complaint under § 99.64(b). The notice to the educational agency or institution—

(1) Includes the substance of the alleged violation; and

(2) Asks the agency or institution to submit a written response to the complaint.

(b) The Office notifies the complainant if it does not initiate an investigation of a complaint because the complaint fails to meet the requirements of § 99.64.

(Authority: 20 U.S.C. 1232g(g))

10. Section 99.67 is amended by revising paragraph (a) and the authority citation to read as follows:

§ 99.67   How does the Secretary enforce decisions?

(a) If the educational agency or institution does not comply during the period of time set under § 99.66(c), the Secretary may, in accordance with part E of the General Education Provisions Act—

(1) Withhold further payments under any applicable program;

(2) Issue a compliant to compel compliance through a cease-and-desist order; or

(3) Terminate eligibility to receive funding under any applicable program.

* * * * *

(Authority: 20 U.S.C. 1232g(f); 20 U.S.C. 1234)

[FR Doc. 93–133 Filed 1–6–93; 8:45 am]
BILLING CODE 4000-01-M

REFERENCES

Alexander, G. 1988. Should students permit the registrar to access their records? *CAUSE/ EFFECT* (Winter): 47–50.

Barr, Margaret J., et al. 1988. *Student Services and the Law*. San Francisco: Jossey-Bass.

Berman, J., and Goldman, J. 1989. *A Federal Right of Information Privacy: The Need for Reform* (4). Washington, DC: Benton Foundation.

CAUSE and AACRAO. 1997. *Privacy and the Handling of Student Information in the Electronic Networked Environments of Colleges and Universities*. Denver, CO: CAUSE and AACRAO.

Cavanaugh, P. 1994a. *Access to the Student Information Inquiry System*. University of Houston, Office of Registration and Academic Records, April 12.

———. 1994b. *RARSTU Training Session*. University of Houston, Office of Registration and Academic Records, April 12.

———. 1994c. *Request for Access to RARMNT (Record Maintenance)*. University of Houston, Office of Registration and Academic Records, April 12.

Compliance Agency: Director, Family Policy Compliance Office, U.S. Department of Education, 400 Maryland Avenue, SW, Washington, DC 20202–4500; (202) 732–1807.

Curran, R., 1989. Student privacy in the electronic era: Legal perspectives. *CAUSE/ EFFECT* (Winter).

DeLoughry, T.J. 1989. Computerization makes student records accessible, but raises issues of security and confidentiality. *The Chronicle of Higher Education* (May 10).

Fry, B. 1994. *Responsibility of McMurry Computer Users regarding Confidentiality of Student Information*. Abilene, TX: Office of the Registrar, McMurry University.

Harris, V. 1993. Educating the educators (who was Buckley anyway?) [summary]. *Proceedings Bulletin of the 72nd Annual Conference of the Texas Association of Collegiate Registrars and Admissions Officers*, November, 24–25.

Hyman, Ursula H. 1982. The Family Educational Rights and Privacy Act of 1974 and college record systems of the future. *Computer/Law Journal* 3(4).

McKinney, R.L., Schoot, J.S., Teeter, D.J., and Mannering, L.W. 1986. The role of institutional research in data administration and management. Paper presented at the Twenty-Sixth Annual AIR Forum, Orlando, FL, June.

Privacy Rights of Students in Educational Records. 1993. California State University, Fullerton. Dr. Charles W. Buck. Office of the Vice President for Student Affairs. Fullerton, CA 92634. October.

Request to Prevent Disclosure of General Directory Information. 1990. California State University, Fullerton. Dr. Charles W. Buck. Office of the Vice President for Student Affairs. Fullerton, CA 92634. June.

Trubow, G. 1989. *Watching the Watchers: The Coordination of Federal Privacy Policy*. (5). Washington, DC: Benton Foundation.

U.S. Department of Education. 1974. Fact sheet: Family Educational Rights and Privacy Act of 1974. (Available from U.S. Department of Education, 400 Maryland Avenue, SW, Washington, DC 20202–4500.)

U.S. Department of Health, Education, and Welfare. 1993. Privacy act issuances; rules and regulations. *Federal Register* 58(4).

———. 1991. Privacy act issuances; 1991 compilation. *Federal Register* 1.

———. 1988. Privacy act issuances; final regulations. *Federal Register* 53(69).

Webster, S. 1989. Ethics in the information age: After rules and locks, what do we do? *CAUSE/EFFECT* (Winter): 51.

Weeks, Kent M. 1993. *Complying with Federal Law: A Manual for College Decision Makers*. Nashville, TN: College Legal Information.

Westin, A.F., and Baker, M.A. 1972. *Databanks in a Free Society: Computers, Record-keeping and Privacy. Report of the Project on Computer Databanks of the Computer Science and Engineering Board. National Academy of Sciences*. New York: Quandrangle Books.

5

Managing Enrollments of Individuals with Disabilities

James F. Menzel and Sally S. Scott

INTRODUCTION

On July 29, 1990, President George Bush signed into law the Americans with Disabilities Act (ADA) and ensured equal rights to over 43 million individuals with disabilities. The ADA is a significant and wide-reaching piece of civil rights legislation that reiterates and reinforces existing federal mandates prohibiting colleges and universities from discriminating against individuals with disabilities. Assurances for nondiscrimination include equal opportunities for admission to colleges and, if admitted, equivalent access to the educational experience for students with disabilities.

The number of students with disabilities on college campuses has grown significantly in the years since the Rehabilitation Act of 1973 originally established a mandate for nondiscrimination. In 1978, 2.6 percent of first-time, full-time freshmen self-reported as having a disability. By 1991, this figure had tripled, reaching 8.8 percent (Henderson, 1992). Other sources note incidence figures as higher, citing 10.5 percent, or one and one-third million students with disabilities enrolled in postsecondary education during the 1988–89 academic year (Wilson, 1992). Disability categories showing the greatest increases on college campuses are the "invisible" disabilities such as learning disabilities, health impairments, and hearing impairments (Henderson, 1992). Projections of future numbers of individuals with disabilities planning to attend postsecondary institutions vary. Among students with learning disabilities, the fastest growing group on college campuses (Henderson, 1992), estimates reach as high as 67 percent (White et al., 1982).

This growing presence of students with disabilities on college campuses is occurring for several reasons. Federal law established special education services in the K–12 school system in 1975, resulting in earlier identification of disabilities and individualized plans for education and support services. Traditional-age students now applying to college have potentially reaped the benefits of these services throughout their educational experiences. Medical and technological advances have promoted greater independence needed for entrance and success on college campuses. Federal legislation, specifically, the ADA, has reinforced and expanded the rights of individuals with disabilities and greatly enhanced the awareness of advocacy groups, including parents and students, that college is a possibility for individuals with disabilities.

In keeping with the American Association of Collegiate Registrars and Admissions Officers' (AACRAO) long-standing commitment to developing access for an increasingly diverse student population, it is important to address proactively the issues that arise in considering college admission practices for individuals with disabilities. To lay the groundwork for establishing a nondiscriminatory admission policy, we first examine the requirements of federal law. Next we consider how disputes over federal requirements are being interpreted in case law and examine current practices in college admission activities. From this foundation, specific guidelines are proposed for implementing "ADA-friendly" practices on your campus.

FEDERAL LAW

Section 504 of the Rehabilitation Act of 1973 states, "No otherwise qualified individual with disabilities in the United States shall solely by reason of his/her disability be excluded from the participation in, be denied the benefits of, or be subjected to discrimination under any program or activity receiving federal financial assistance." Receipt of federal moneys by any department within a postsecondary institution triggers the accountability of the entire institution under Section 504 (Civil Rights Restoration Act of 1987). Federal financial assistance has been clarified as including student financial aid (*Grove City College v. Bell*, 1984). Hence, few institutions of higher education are exempt from Section 504 mandates.

The Americans with Disabilities Act of 1990 is based on the same principles and beliefs as Section 504 and, in fact, duplicates much of its terminology. However, the ADA extends the nondiscrimination mandate beyond merely federal financial recipients and applies to most public and private establishments. In most instances, if a postsecondary institution is in compliance with Section 504, it will be nondiscriminatory under the ADA as well. However, where ADA standards are more stringent and provide greater protection for individuals with disabilities, institutions of higher education must comply with the ADA (Jarrow, 1993; Kincaid and Simon, 1994).

Terminology

Both Section 504 and the ADA contain several key terms warranting definition. An *individual with a disability* is someone who has a physical or mental impairment that substantially limits a major life activity, has a record or history of such an impairment, or is regarded as having such an impairment. Major life activities include walking, seeing, hearing, speaking, breathing, learning, working, caring for oneself, and performing manual tasks. Some examples of disabilities include all elementary and secondary school special education classifications (such as learning disabilities, physical disabilities, or serious emotional disturbances), AIDS, cancer, alcohol or drug addiction (excluding current users of illegal drugs), attention deficit disorders, and so forth.

Institutions of higher education are required to provide admission only to those individuals with disabilities who are otherwise qualified. An *otherwise qualified* individual with a disability is one who can meet the academic and technical standards for admission to the institution with or without accommodation. *Technical standards* refer to all nonacademic criteria used for admission to, and participation in, a program. These may include physical requirements if they are essential to the program and applied equally to all applicants (*Davis v. Southeastern Community College*, 1979).

Institutions must provide reasonable accommodations to college applicants and, if admitted, in general student treatment. A *reasonable accommodation* is not a standard formula but rather entails a reasoning process in which requirements of the institution, individual student abilities, and possible accommodations are considered. Reasonable accommodations may be straightforward, such as providing recruitment literature and application forms in accessible formats (such as large print) or holding interviews in wheelchair-accessible locations. They may also become more complex in such situations as considering the scores from standardized tests given under nonstandard administration or weighing high school grades earned in special education classrooms. Case law has helped clarify some parameters in weighing accommodations requests and is discussed in more detail later in the chapter.

Implementing Regulations

In addition to these broad principles of nondiscrimination, the implementing regulations of federal law provide specific guidance in the area of admissions and recruitment considerations. They clarify that institutions of higher education (1) may not limit the number or proportion of individuals with disabilities admitted to the institution or program (Section 104.42 (b)(1)); (2) are prohibited from using any test or criterion for admission that has a disproportionate, adverse effect on individuals with disabilities unless the criterion is a validated predictor of success (Section 104.42 (b)(2)); (3) must select and administer admissions tests that reflect the applicant's aptitude or achievement level rather than disability (Section 104.42 (b)(3)); (4) may not make preadmission inquiry about the presence of a disability (Section 104.42 (b)(4)); and (5) must conduct periodic validity studies assessing overall success in the program (Section 104.42 (d)). (See Mazzeo and Hartman, 1994, for a discussion, suggested strategies, and campus checklist for each of these activities.)

Once again, though general areas of nondiscrimination are articulated in the implementing regulations, application to individuals on the case-by-case basis required by law entails a reasoning process. Case law has served to clarify how the courts will consider disputes in implementation.

CASE LAW

As of the mid-1990s, only one Supreme Court ruling was available to guide the implementation of nondiscriminatory practices on college campuses. This ruling, *Davis v. Southeastern Community College* (1979), entailed an admissions issue. Frances Davis, a licensed practical nurse with a hearing impairment, was denied admission to the registered nursing program at Southeastern Community College because the college felt she would require extensive individual supervision in the clinical phase of the nursing program to ensure patient safety. Davis brought suit under Section 504, alleging that she had been discriminated against and denied admission solely on the basis of her disability. The Supreme Court, in ruling for the institution, found that a qualified person with a disability must be able to meet all of a program's requirements in spite of the disability.

The reasoning process used by the Court in weighing the admissions decision is instructive. First, the nature and requirements of the registered nursing program were examined. As reiterated in later case law, admissions standards (both academic and technical) must be legitimate, rationally related to the goals and objectives of the program, and applied in a nondiscriminatory way (e.g., *Davis v. Southeastern Community College*, 1979; *Doe v. New York University*, 1981; *Pushkin v. Regents of the University of Colorado*, 1982). Next, the Supreme Court examined Davis' physical and mental abilities, as they related to the program. General assumptions about the capabilities of a person with a disability are not permissible (*School Board of Nassau County v. Arline*, 1987). Decisions must be made on a case-by-case basis after examining the specific abilities and disabilities of the individual and the demands of the particular setting in question. Finally, the Court considered a range of accommodations that might permit safe participation in the program. Reasonable accommodations do not require a fundamental alteration of standards. The burden of proof that a standard is essential to a course or program lies with the institution and must consist of clear and convincing evidence to support decisions to deny accommodation (*Wynne v. Tufts University School of Medicine*, 1991). A reasonable accommodation does not entail an undue financial or administrative burden. Though this defense has never been used successfully in court, Rothstein (1993) noted that the overall size of the program and type of operation might be considered in this defense. Finally, a reasonable accommodation does not pose an appreciable threat to personal or public safety. Jarrow (1993), however, cautioned that health-related training programs need to apply this standard carefully and not interpret it as a mandate to deny individuals with disabilities an opportunity to train in these fields.

Federal law and case law clearly state that accommodation must be made in considering the admission of students with disabilities. How are admissions officers currently applying the principles of determining essential requirements, examining individual abilities, and providing reasonable accommodations?

CURRENT PRACTICE

The literature contains scant information on how college admissions officers are actually weighing accommodation considerations for applicants with disabilities. Existing studies focus on dilemmas surrounding candidates with learning disabilities.

Spillane, McGuire, and Norlander (1992) conducted a survey of admissions personnel in 66 state universities and colleges in the Northeast to examine the academic and nonacademic criteria used in assessing the eligibility of undergraduate applicants with learning disabilities. High school grade point average (GPA) and class rank were cited as very important or the single most important factor in the admissions process by 85 percent of respondents. Admission test scores were emphasized to a lesser extent, with 39 percent of respondents indicating them as very important or the single most important factor.

Nonacademic criteria considered very important were interviews (33 percent), letters of recommendation (15 percent), intelligence test scores (19 percent), personal qualities of motivation (62 percent), and commitment to becoming an independent learner (54 percent). Spillane et al. concluded that admission standards were generally the same for applicants both with and without learning disabilities. The match of a candidate's need for support and the institution's available services was regarded as an important factor.

Yarwood (1988) surveyed college admission personnel at 90 institutions of higher education in Pennsylvania regarding admission practices for candidates with learning disabilities. In concurrence with Spillane et al. (1992), high school achievement was weighted more heavily than standardized test scores. Private institutions reported considering individualized education plans, recommendations, campus visits, and extracurricular activities significantly more often than public institutions.

Bursuck, Rose, Cowen, and Yahaya (1989) surveyed a national sample of college disabled student services staff. Twenty-three percent of respondents reported that their institution involved the campus service providers in a cooperative admission decision process. (See Mazzeo and Hartman, 1994, for recommended strategies.)

It is apparent that little information is yet available on how admissions officers are currently accommodating students with disabilities. The literature contains indicators of possible efforts to accommodate applicants with disabilities, but specific, proactive procedures to comply with federal law do not appear widespread. Colleges sometimes mistakenly take the stance in dealing with students with disabilities that accommodation is provided on a case-by-case basis and thus need not be reflected in college policy. However, case law has clarified that it is prudent to have clearly established procedures and policies in place for considering the individual needs of students with disabilities (*Brown v. Washington University*, 1990; *Dinsmore v. Pugh and the Regents of the University of California at Berkeley*, 1989).

INSTITUTIONAL POLICY DEVELOPMENT: GETTING STARTED

The job of putting in place those policies and procedures so often cited in case law and in the ADA itself frequently comes under the jurisdiction of the admissions officer and the registrar. These campus administrators have a legal, professional, and ethical responsibility to ensure access to higher education for individuals with disabilities. However, no matter how thorough their understanding of the law or how deep their moral commitment to its purpose, admissions officers and registrars also need to consider how to make such access become a reality on their campus. They are the ones expected to implement and clarify the necessary policies and procedures. Often, these administrators are given the task to galvanize into action the mandates of the ADA.

In order for the admissions officer and the registrar to initiate this task on their campus, they should start with a program of self-education. Their first textbook should be the *ADA Handbook*, published by the Equal Employment Opportunity Commission and the U.S. Department of Justice (EEOC-BK-19). In addition to studying this handbook, they should seek out and attend workshops devoted to ADA training. Often their own campus office of human resource management provides this training; sometimes training opportunities are offered regionally. AACRAO now includes information and training sessions on the ADA at the annual meeting, and many state and regional associations sponsor similar workshops.

It is recommended that the institution's chief executive officer establish a campus committee and formally charge it with the responsibility to develop the overall program of campus compliance with both the spirit and the law of the ADA. The ideal committee for this task is large in size and wide in composition. It should include representative faculty members, a student (or faculty member) with a disability, a person familiar with the ADA who is also responsible for campus compliance, someone who can evaluate and authorize accommodations and implement them, a person who can evaluate the accuracy of a diagnosis of a disability made by an outside specialist, the institution's legal counsel, the admissions officer, the registrar, and the institution's enabler for persons with disabilities.

The initial task of this committee may well be to define those curricular requirements that are essential for applicants and students to master if they are to be successful in the educational programs offered by the institution. Such requirements include those fundamental and essential skills, abilities, knowledge, and behaviors that all applicants and students must demonstrate at each stage of their enrollment in order to be successful in their educational program. For instance, a student in nursing will be expected to be able to read (with or without accommodation) a manometer, a chart, a computer screen, digital print-outs, labels, and gauges. Note, however, that while a nursing applicant might not have to lift 50 pounds, this ability might very well be a physical requirement for any student who expects to complete a physical therapy program.

Faculty involvement and support are important to the successful development and implementation of the institutional ADA compliance policies. It is critical that representative faculty participate actively in defining essential program requirements; they are most familiar with those essentials for successful academic performance and job placement. Also, the faculty will be expected to direct admission decisions and handle many of the classroom accommodations for individuals with disabilities (e.g., front-row seating, extended test-taking time). Faculty are renowned for their concerns as to whether students are qualified, and they need to be included in all discussions that address the qualifications of applicants and students. It is essential that the faculty understand and support the goals of the institution equally to admit, enroll, and graduate qualified individuals regardless of disabilities. They should also understand that the ADA does not serve as an affirmative action program: it does not dictate that preference be given to individuals with disabilities over those who have no disclosed disabilities when all other things are equal.

The faculty and other interested members of the committee can first assist the admissions officer and the registrar by compiling a list of all the essential requirements that come to mind as members review their curricula. The ADA does not in any way require the institution to alter its academic standards, course requirements, or functional levels in order to accommodate persons with disabilities. Therefore, the committee can proceed with the knowledge they already have of the current requirements that all applicants and students must meet in order to be successful in their educational program.

It is recommended that the committee develop two lists of requirements: one list should reflect the requirements that *all* applicants and students must meet to be considered eligible; the second list should expand upon the first list so that it reflects the technical standards required by each of the specific programs of the institution. For example, all eligible applicants and enrolled students might need to be able to search for, and evaluate, information, but a history major might not have to meet the same technical standards required of a studio art major (such as possession of manual dexterity). A hard-of-hearing student could perhaps complete the requirements of all biology majors but not of students seeking to become firefighters (who need to hear cries for help).

Examples of the types of requirements that the faculty of one of the authors' institutions considered essential for all of their students to fulfill with or without accommodation include the ability to:

- make proper assessments and lawful judgments
- prioritize
- communicate effectively
- interpret data
- participate in classroom discussion
- complete reading assignments and search literature
- solve problems
- use a computer for searching, recording, storing, and retrieving information

This same faculty went on further to identify requirements that are specific to each of the institution's educational programs. Examples of these more specific requirements, collected from among the numerous campus majors, included manual dexterity in both wrists and the ability to:

- conduct experiments in the field (rough terrain)
- operate manual and power tools (each tool defined)
- grasp and hold
- explain procedures
- calibrate equipment
- distinguish primary colors

These two lists are by no means exhaustive, and they are intended only as examples. Each institution will define lists appropriate to its own educational programs, both general and specific.

In all instances, however, when the faculty present such a list of requirements, they must be able to defend it. For instance, faculty must be able to justify the reason they require their students to have manual dexterity in both wrists and that this requirement would alter the standards of the curriculum or present a safety threat if it were removed. It should also be clear whether such requirements can or cannot be met with reasonable accommodation.

Once the faculty on the committee have helped to define a preliminary list of requirements, it is time for the admissions officer and the registrar to turn to the rest of the faculty and to the administrators (especially the deans) for further input. One method to get this input is to provide department chairpersons with a checklist of all of the potential requirements and ask them to mark the ones that apply to their programs, add others that are not already on the list, and correct the terminology of any items not adequately described.

After the lists are returned, it is a clerical matter to tabulate the results and create the two lists mentioned earlier. However, at this time it is critical for the lists to be reviewed by the committee and, in particular, by the institution's legal counsel. Because a number of admission and progression decisions are likely to be made according to the degree to which an applicant or student successfully meets the program requirements stipulated on the lists, it is in the best interest of the institution that each of these listed requirements be defensible.

THE ADMISSION PROCESS

Following approval by the institution's legal counsel, the lists (and any other general information about the institution's commitment to the ADA) should be integrated into the admission process. This might effectively begin with the list of requirements applicable to all applicants and students being bound into the admission application or inserted into the packet as a flyer. The purpose in doing this at this time is to announce clearly to all applicants that the institution is ADA-friendly and wishes to advise all potential applicants of those physical and mental requirements that it considers essential.

Even though the institution may include with the application for admission statements of its intention to comply with the ADA and a list of requirements it considers essential, the institution may not include on the application form itself any questions about the applicant's disability status, whether the applicant has previously requested an accommodation, or whether he or she has ever received an accommodation because of a disability. Nonetheless, provided *all* applicants are asked this same question, the institution may ask applicants whether or not they can fulfill, with or without reasonable accommodation, those essential functions identified on the list of educational requirements.

This last question opens the door for persons with disabilities to make known to the institution for the first time their special needs as an applicant, such as their need for an interpreter to help with a tour of the campus. This may also be the first time the institution considers making an accommodation for the applicant. It would be unusual for the institution to require proof of the disability at this time, unless the accommodation requested by the prospective applicant is unreasonable (such as extremely costly or disruptive). However, persons with disabilities shall by law be provided equal opportunity to participate in the application for admission process and shall be eligible to be considered for enrollment.

It is always the responsibility of the person with a disability to make known and to substantiate the disability if accommodation is sought. For example, the institution is not expected automatically to provide interpreters to assist with campus tours just in case an applicant taking the tour turns out to be hard of hearing. Yet admission officers are advised of their responsibility to provide accommodations that are universally considered reasonable, such as a large-print application or a physically accessible location where the applicant with a mobility impairment can pick up application materials.

When face-to-face interviews are part of the application process, the interview itself presents multiple and problematic opportunities for aborting the access of persons with disabilities. Without proper training of the interviewers, inappropriate and unlawful questions might be asked during the interview. For example, interviewers should be instructed that they may not ask an applicant who is in a wheelchair to disclose anything about the disability, even though it is obvious that a disability exists. It is imperative that the admissions officer orient interviewers to the ADA and to the institution's responsibility to admit persons with disabilities who are otherwise qualified.

Once participation in the recruitment, application, and interview process is ensured for persons with disabilities, the admissions officer must give particular attention to eligibility criteria. At this time, it is critical for the admissions officer to have a clear delineation of those essential functions required for successful participation in the educational program. This information is important for both the applicant and the institution. Applicants with disabilities should know in advance what is required of them and whether they can fulfill these essential functions (preferably prior to the time they seek and accept admission). Further, institutions need to stipulate the fundamental performance standards that are a condition of successful participation in, and completion of, the educational program. In many cases, this information will be exchanged without the institution's knowing of the applicant's disability.

Within the context of the ADA, applicants or students eligible to participate in an educational program must be able to meet prerequisites and fulfill the requirements of that program. It does not matter whether they use assistance devices or services, so long as they fulfill the requirements. However, applicants with disabilities are not guaranteed special admission status, nor are they to be given preference.

REASONABLE ACCOMMODATIONS FOR APPLICANTS AND STUDENTS

If an applicant or student does request accommodation, what is the obligation of the institution to provide it? What procedures should be followed? What constitutes reasonable accommodation?

Initially, it is the duty of the individual to disclose the disability, to provide diagnosis of the disability written by a doctor or therapist, and then to request accommodation. It is next the duty of the institution to validate the claim of disability and to determine how and to what extent it will make accommodation.

It is suggested that the institution routinely provide all students with an accommodation request form, perhaps even as part of the admission application packet. Such an accommodation request form would guide the student and the institution through a basic process. The form might clarify whether it will apply in general or only to a specific course (or courses).

At the institution of one of the authors, for example, the student is required to identify himself or herself and the nature of the disability, attach documentation of the disability, describe for what requirements accommodation is being requested, describe how this accommodation will enable successful performance as a student, and submit the form to the appropriate institutional representative.

Next, the institution's ADA representative reviews the request, makes written comments and recommendations regarding the request (including any suggested modifications or changes to the request), writes a statement describing the accommodation that the institution can make, signs and dates the form, and returns the form to the applicant/student.

Finally, the student acknowledges that the proposed accommodation is or is not acceptable and signs, dates, and returns the form to the institutional representative.

If the accommodation is not accepted, the institution should expect the student to press forward and should expect to have to negotiate further. However, if the individual refuses the accommodation when it is generally recognized that it is reasonable (such as extended test-taking time), then the person seeking accommodation can no longer be considered a qualified individual with a disability. It is important for everyone involved to maintain complete written records of all interactions, but all documents regarding the disability of the student must be kept apart from the academic records of that person. It may also be good practice for the institution to establish a campus review board that is charged with the job of handling all challenges to conditions of accommodation.

The accommodation itself must be made only for disabilities that have been identified by the applicant or student. Also, while accommodation is made on a case-by-case basis for individual students, accommodations universally considered reasonable for students with disabilities include teaching aids, readers, sign-language interpreters, extension of test-taking time, and modification or adjustment of equipment or devices. It should be known that the institution is obligated under the law to provide only that accommodation that enables educational access; it is not obligated to provide the newest, best, or most expensive accommodation if the one chosen by the institution is effective.

What is considered reasonable in terms of the time it takes an institution to review a request, validate the disability, and provide the accommodation has not been prescribed in the ADA. However, timelines might be negotiated as part of the accommodation request form. "Timeliness" has been addressed in case law not with regard to when the institution must respond but as to when the request for accommodation is made. For example, it has been decided that former students academically dismissed need not be readmitted because their failure was due to lack of accommodation that they did not request prior to failure. Similarly, if a dismissed student finds out later that he or she is disabled and that the disability accounts for the failure, the institution is not bound to readmit the student on that basis. Nonetheless, the institution might want to weigh other considerations (such as why the student had not previously disclosed the disability) in its decision whether or not to readmit and accommodate.

Institutional responsibility for providing accommodation stops whenever an applicant or student refuses the accommodation, drops out, graduates, or transfers or when the accommodation would put others at risk.

The potential for academic dismissal of a student with a disability may be of special concern for the registrar. Clearly, however, the institution can dismiss a student with an accommodated disability if the student has not fulfilled the requirements of the program. (This again points to the need to define closely all requirements of the educational program.) The institution can also, in fact, change its requirements (which might result in a student with a disability becoming ineligible to continue successfully) so long as the changes are applied equally to all students, are announced in time for students to come into compliance, are not capricious, and are based on defensible academic criteria that address a demonstrable need for the change.

SUMMARY

What measures can the admission officer and the registrar have in place ahead of time to help out if their institution is ever accused of violating the ADA? First, they should ensure that a grievance procedure is installed at the campus level, but they should also know that an applicant or student can file suit in federal court and complain to the Office of Civil Rights. Second, they can anticipate that an accusation is likely to be based on charges already popular in the courts: failure to provide reasonable accommodation, insistence that an individual with a disability comply with a standard institutional policy not educationally relevant, excessively evaluating the eligibility of the applicant or student above and beyond what is normally done, or treating the individual with a disability differently because of the disability. The registrar and admissions officer should take proactive steps to strengthen their institution's compliance with the ADA. Such steps might include the following:

- Educate the entire campus community about ADA
- Define educational program requirements
- Write policies and procedures about accommodation
- Create an ongoing ADA committee to ensure
  —compliance with the law
  —grievance procedures
  —proper assessment of evidences of disability (especially of learning disabilities)
- Identify a campus ADA spokesperson
- Assure that complete records related to the disability are maintained but are kept separate from the academic file
- Perform a campus self-evaluation to determine whether
  —physical barriers exist that prohibit access
  —there is justification for any requirements that cannot be accommodated

—the campus communicates as well with any of its public who are disabled as it does with those who are not

—auxiliary aids are readily available and provided

—persons with disabilities on campus are able to be evacuated safely in emergencies

—new construction complies with the law

The purpose is not only to protect the institution from charges of discrimination but also to create an ADA-friendly campus environment. These two purposes are aspects of the same goal: to ensure and enhance access to educational programs by individuals with disabilities.

REFERENCES

Americans with Disabilities Act. 1990. P.L. 101-336, 42 U.S.C. Sec. 12101.

Americans with Disabilities Act. 1991. Washington, DC: Equal Employment Opportunity Commission.

Brown v. Washington University, CA No. 88-1907-c-5 (settled May 11, 1990).

Bursuck, W., Rose, E., Cowen, S., and Yahaya, M. 1989. Nationwide survey of post-secondary education services for students with learning disabilities. *Exceptional Children* 56: 236–245.

Carey, J.H. *The Americans with Disabilities Act.* 1992. Baltimore: Venable, Baetjer, and Howard.

Civil Rights Restoration Act of 1987, P.L. 100-259, 29 U.S.C. Sec. 794 (a)(2)(A).

Davis v. Southeastern Community College, 442 US 397 (1979).

Dinsmore v. Pugh and the Regents of the University of California at Berkeley (settled 1989).

Doe v. New York University, 666 F. 2d 761 (2d Cir. 1981).

Grove City College v. Bell, 465 US 555, 104 S. Ct. 1211 (1984).

Hansen, M. 1993. The ADA's wide reach. *ABA Journal* 79 (December): 14.

Henderson, C. 1992. *College Freshmen with Disabilities: A Statistical Profile.* Washington, DC: American Council on Education, HEATH Resource Center.

Henry, K.D. 1989. Civil rights and the disabled: A comparison of the Rehabilitation Act of 1973 and the Americans with Disabilities Act of 1990 in the employment setting. *Albany Law Review* 54: 123–140.

Hill, W.A., Jr. 1992. Americans with Disabilities Act of 1990: Significant overlap with Section 504 for colleges and universities. *Journal of College and University Law* 18: 389–417.

Jarrow, J. 1993. *Subpart E: The Impact of Section 504 on Postsecondary Education.* Columbus, OH: Association of Higher Education and Disabilities.

Kincaid, J., and Simon, J. 1994. *Issues in Higher Education and Disability Law.* Columbus, OH: Association of Higher Education and Disabilities.

King, W., and Jarrow, J. 1992. *Testing Accommodations for Persons with Disabilities; A Guide for Licensure, Certification, and Credentialing.* Columbus, OH: Association of Higher Education and Disabilities.

Mangrum, C., and Strichart, S. 1988. *College and the Learning Disabled Student.* Orlando, FL: Grune and Stratton.

Mazzeo, K., and Hartman, R. 1994. *Recruitment, Admissions and Students with Disabilities: A Guide for Compliance with Section 504 of the Rehabilitation Act of*

1973 and Amendments of 1992 and the Americans with Disabilities Act of 1990. Washington, DC: HEATH Resource Center, American Council on Education, and American Association of Collegiate Registrars and Admissions Officers.

Pushkin v. Regents of the University of Colorado, 689 F. 2d 742 (7th Cir. 1982).

Redden, M., Levering, C., and Guthrie, C. 1985. *Recruitment, Admissions and Handicapped Students: A Guide for Compliance with Section 504 of the Rehabilitation Act of 1973.* Washington, DC: HEATH Resource Center, American Council on Education, and American Association of Collegiate Registrars and Admissions Officers.

Regulations to Implement the Equal Employment Provisions of the Americans with Disabilities Act, 29 CFR Part 1630.

Rehabilitation Act of 1973, Section 504, P.L. 93-112, 29 U.S.C. Sec. 794 (1977).

Rothstein, L. 1993. Legal issues. In S. Vogel and P. Adelman, eds., *Success for College Students with Learning Disabilities.* New York: Springer-Verlag, 21–35.

School Board of Nassau County v. Arline. 480 US 273 (1987).

Spillane, S., McGuire, J., and Norlander, K. 1992. Undergraduate admission policies, practices, and procedures for applicants with learning disabilities. *Journal of Learning Disabilities* 25: 665–670.

Thrasher, F. 1992. *The Impact of Titles II and III of the Americans with Disabilities Act of 1990 on Academic and Student Services at Colleges, Universities and Proprietary Schools.* Washington, DC: National Association of College and University Attorneys.

U.S. Equal Employment Opportunity Commission. Americans with Disabilities Act. 1992. *A Technical Assistance Manual on the Employment Provisions (Title I).* Washington, DC: Equal Employment Opportunity Commission.

White, W., Alley, G., Deshler, D., Schumaker, J., Warner, M., and Clark, F. 1982. Are there learning disabilities after high school? *Exceptional Children* 49: 273–274.

Wilson, D. 1992. New federal regulations on rights of the handicapped may force colleges to provide better access to technology. *The Chronicle of Higher Education* 38(1): 1, 21–22.

Wynne v. Tufts University School of Medicine, 932 F. 2d 19 (1st Cir. 1991).

Yarwood, W. 1988. Perceptions of college admissions decision makers concerning students with learning disabilities. Ed.D. diss., Temple University, Philadelphia.

6

Certifying Academic Eligibility for Athletic Participation

John F. Demitroff and Sara N. McNabb

INTRODUCTION

Registrars and admissions officers increasingly are being asked to certify the academic records, admission, and enrollment of students, usually for the purpose of determining the eligibility of students to participate in the activities or programs of the institution, organization, firm, or agency that is requesting the certification (bank loan deferments, insurance rebates, memberships, etc.). This chapter discusses the general issues registrars and admissions officers should address in the processes of certifying academic eligibility for participation in intercollegiate athletics.

It is not possible, nor would it be desirable, to attempt to define the rules of the various athletic associations within the confines of this chapter. Rule books already exist for the athletic associations; duplication of that information would serve no useful purpose. Because rules of the associations differ and because the rules of any association change from year to year, the discussion that follows is based on commonalities among academic eligibility concepts rather than on the specific rules of the individual associations. The reader should not consider the discussion that follows to be all that is needed for certifying athletic eligibility at his or her particular institution. Rather, the information should be viewed as a road map, providing directional indicators and signposts that should alert the reader to explore issues further.

ROLE OF THE REGISTRAR AND ADMISSIONS OFFICER

In many institutions, registrars and admissions officers have no responsibility for certifying academic eligibility for athletic participation. Consequently, the function is often assigned to staff at the institution who do not have the background or expertise to properly interpret academic documents or who, unfortunately, may have a conflict of interest. It is strongly suggested that those registrars and admissions officers not currently involved in certifying academic eligibility for athletic participation review and reconsider their role in this matter.

In November 1989, the American Association of Collegiate Registrars and Admissions Officers (AACRAO) published the *Guide to NCAA Eligibility*, a handbook for registrars and admissions officers of the National Collegiate Athletic Association (NCAA) Division I and Division II institutions. In that handbook, the following statement was included in the Foreword and bears repeating:

The importance of the involvement of the registrar and the admissions officer in these processes cannot be overstated. The institution is obligated to assure the participation in intercollegiate athletics only of those students who have satisfied academic requirements. Those officers of the college or university who normally interpret the criteria for admission, enrollment, and academic progress must be involved. It is the recommendation of this Committee and the Executive Committee of AACRAO that registrars and admissions officers should take a leading role in interpreting the applicable academic rules and certifying that their institutions' athletes satisfy those academic requirements for eligibility.

BASIC GUIDELINES

There are a number of practical guidelines (defined in AACRAO *Guide to NCAA Eligibility*) to follow in establishing an effective system of certifying academic eligibility for athletic participation. Specifically, a registrar or admissions officer:

1. Must know and understand applicable rules of the association, athletic conference, and the institution and must remain current in that knowledge through review of appropriate publications, attendance at seminars and workshops at professional meetings, and contact with knowledgeable representatives of the associations and athletic conferences.

2. Must have access to, and be able to use and interpret, official academic records that are related to, and required for, certifying eligibility.

3. Must develop a procedures handbook for certification of academic eligibility and must make that handbook available to appropriate members of the staff of the institution's department of athletics.

4. Should volunteer to conduct or participate in training seminars for coaches and other staff members of the department of athletics.

5. Should develop a system of communication with a single member of the staff of the department of athletics rather than attempt to respond to all coaches and other personnel from the department of athletics.

ASSOCIATION, CONFERENCE, AND INSTITUTIONAL ELIGIBILITY REQUIREMENTS

Four primary athletic associations in the United States govern participation in intercollegiate athletics. The National Junior College Athletic Association (NJCAA) certifies 26 separate men's and women's sports for approximately 550 member two-year institutions. The National Association of Intercollegiate Athletics (NAIA) membership is composed of approximately 400 fully accredited four-year colleges, upper-level two-year colleges, and universities throughout the United States and Canada and offers championship competition in eighteen men's and women's sports. The National Christian College Athletic Association (NCCAA), founded in 1966, comprises approximately 100 Christian colleges that sponsor nine men's and women's sports. The National Collegiate Athletic Association (NCAA) is composed of nearly 900 colleges and universities in the United States. The three divisions in the NCAA, which are based on level of competition and awarding of athletic scholarships, offer competition in 21 sports for men and women.

These associations operate independently of one another, and each is governed by the collective votes of its member institutions. As might be expected, the academic requirements for student eligibility to participate differ, oftentimes significantly, among the associations (requirements are quite different even among the three divisions of the NCAA).

Eligibility standards also may be established by conferences and the individual institution. Many colleges and universities are members of athletics conferences, joining together institutions with similar academic and athletic goals. The conferences and their member institutions are required to adhere to the minimum regulations of their associations but are free to enact and enforce regulations that are more stringent than those imposed by the associations. Likewise, an institution that is a member of a conference and an association may establish its own guidelines, rules, or policies related to academic eligibility provided they are consistent with, and in addition to, the minimum standards established by the conference and the association.

The following discussion of the basic concepts of academic eligibility must, of necessity, be limited to a broad sweep of existing regulations for the four major athletics associations. It is imperative that the person responsible for certifying academic eligibility for an institution have available the specific rules of the conference and the association to which the institution belongs and also be aware of any institutional academic policy for athletes.

BASIC CONCEPTS

As indicated earlier, this chapter does not define the specific rules of the athletic associations that govern academic eligibility. Such rules vary considerably among the associations and change often, generally on an annual basis.

What follows is a brief discussion of the basic concepts of academic eligibility as defined by the current rule books of the four primary associations. Specific details related to these requirements may be found in the eligibility manuals of the associations.

1. *Initial Eligibility*

    a. First-year students are those who come to an institution from high school with no intervening collegiate experience. All of the associations permit these students to participate in intercollegiate athletics in their first year if certain requirements are met. The NJCAA requires high school graduation or successful completion of the General Educational Development (GED) examination of high school equivalency or successful completion of a conditional full-time semester at the two-year institution. The NAIA and NCCAA stipulate that a student must meet two of three requirements for initial eligibility; these requirements include a specified score on either the Scholastic Aptitude Test (SAT) or the American College Test (ACT), a defined high school grade point average, or a class rank at the time of graduation from the high school that would place the student in the upper half of the class.

    Divisions I and II of the NCAA require a student to (1) be a high school graduate, (2) achieve a defined average in a core curriculum, and (3) score at a specified level on the SAT or the ACT examinations. Eligibility of first-year student athletes in Divisions I and II of the NCAA must be certified by the NCAA Initial Eligibility Clearinghouse. Currently, in Division III of the NCAA, a student who meets institutional standards for admission is immediately eligible to participate.

    b. Transfer students are those who began their college education at a postsecondary institution other than the one they are currently attending. These students are required to fulfill additional requirements to be certified immediately eligible for athletic participation. These requirements typically are determined by the following general considerations:

- The type of institution from which the student athlete transferred, for example, two-year or four-year.

- The athletic participation and eligibility status from the previous institution(s).

- The athletic association/conference by which the former institution is governed.

- The student's high school academic credentials prior to initial college enrollment at any postsecondary institution.

- The academic record at the former institution(s), for example, progress toward a degree, type of degree awarded (if required), and so on.

- Applicability of the transfer credits to degree programs at the receiving institution.

2. *Satisfactory Progress and Continuing Eligibility*

All of the associations require that an athlete participating in intercollegiate competition be enrolled as a full-time student with a specified minimum number of credit hours. A few exceptions to this requirement allow part-time students to qualify for a waiver and compete while enrolled for fewer than the specified minimum number of credits. All of the associations state that a student must be in good academic standing according to the institution's standards. Each of the associations has specific regulations that require that a student make satisfactory progress toward an approved degree program. One exception is that Division III of the NCAA has no specific satisfactory progress requirement other than that the student must be in good academic standing according to institutional standards. The NJCAA requires its institutions to verify satisfactory progress on a semester-by-semester basis; the NAIA, NCCAA, and the NCAA certify eligibility from year to year. The NAIA, NCCAA, and Divisions II and III of the NCAA require that students complete their four years of eligibility in ten semesters (twelve quarters), whereas the NCAA Division I specifies that the four years of eligibility must be completed within five calendar years. Each of the associations sets a specified minimum number of credits to be earned each year and establishes grade point average requirements.

3. *Reporting*

Currently, the NCAA has an extensive graduation rates-reporting requirement that applies to all three divisions of the association. This requirement has been in effect since 1986 for Division I institutions and since 1993 for Divisions II and III. Basically, NCAA institutions are required to report graduation rates for students who were awarded athletically related financial aid. These rates must be provided to all potential student athletes being recruited by the institution. While the reporting requirements are based, for the most part, on the U.S. Department of Education's (DOE) rules for implementing the Student-Right-to-Know Act, the Division I report requests other information that is deemed important by the NCAA. All postsecondary institutions will have similar basic reporting requirements as specified by the law according to rules recently issued by DOE.

SYSTEMS FOR MONITORING ACADEMIC ELIGIBILITY FOR ATHLETIC PARTICIPATION

Manual systems for monitoring academic eligibility of athletes have been developed and can be reasonably effective for some institutions. However, if an institution has a computerized data system for some or all of the major functions related to admissions, financial aid, student enrollment, and academic records, the registrar and the admissions officer should strive to get some or all of the academic eligibility processes incorporated in the records system. All that is needed is a way to identify a student as an athlete and computer programs that will pull data from the records system's file for those students so identified.

The identifier can be as simple as a one-digit code; that digit could identify the sport in which the student is participating. If a second digit is available, that could define the athlete's eligibility status (eligible, ineligible, pending eligibility, dropped from the sport). A third digit, if available, could identify the athlete as a scholarship recipient or as a recruited athlete. Still another digit could describe the number of years or semesters of eligibility that remain for the student. If desired, it is possible to collect and maintain considerable amounts of other information relating to the athlete's background and athletic experience while a student at your college or university; however, the more data that are collected, the more that will need to be reviewed, maintained, and updated. Each institution has to determine if the additional data are worth the effort to collect and maintain.

The identifier is the key; if the athletes cannot be identified, it is not possible to monitor their enrollment or their progress. The system does not have to be elaborate; it can be very simple and yet be effective. If the identifier is recorded, weekly or twice-weekly checks on full-time enrollment are possible and simple (daily exception reports that identify those who drop below full-time are even better), data are available for checking satisfactory progress (use a degree audit system for this if one is available), and, of course, all of the information needed to satisfy reporting requirements should be readily available and accessible.

Many resourceful registrars and admissions officers have developed excellent systems for monitoring academic eligibility for athletes. Most of these professionals are happy to share their experience with other registrars and admissions officers; one should never hesitate to ask for help.

RELATIONSHIPS AND ETHICAL ISSUES

The person responsible for certifying academic eligibility for participation in intercollegiate athletics must be dedicated to professional standards; his or her honesty and integrity must be unquestioned. In addition, that person's first loyalty must be to the institution and not to individuals or groups of individuals within it.

These statements must set the tone for the relationships among the certifying officer (admissions officer, registrar), members of the athletics department, and the faculty athletics representative. Many registrars and admissions officers can attest to the pressure that can be applied by coaches and other members of the athletics department to admit a student who is well below the institution's normal admission standard or to bend an institutional, conference, or association rule to certify an athlete who has not satisfied regulations related to academic requirements.

Generally speaking, the relationship between the registrar or admissions officer and the members of the athletics department should be reasonably limited to professional responsibilities. The director of athletics, the athletic department staff, and all of the coaches must know of, and respect, the integrity of the admissions officer and the registrar and must recognize that that integrity will not be sacrificed, even for a national championship. It is suggested that each of the involved departments (admissions, registrar, athletics) designate one person who will officially represent the department in those interactions that occur on a daily basis. Such an arrangement, if agreed to by all parties, will reduce considerably the number of contacts between and among the departments and will eliminate the pressures of responding to those individuals whose primary interest is the athletic, rather than the academic, prowess of a student.

HELP IS AVAILABLE

Regardless of the athletic association with which an institution is affiliated, it is reasonable to say that the regulations governing academic eligibility to compete in intercollegiate athletics are complex and, in some cases, not altogether clearly defined. In addition, the eligibility of a student to compete may be discussed publicly in the media, adding still more pressure to the person who is designated as the certifying officer. This particular role, as certifying officer for the institution, is not an easy one, and it is understandable that a registrar or an admissions officer, given a choice, would rather not have the responsibility.

Fortunately, help is available for registrars and admissions officers who must certify academic eligibility for athletic participation. Each year at its annual meeting, the American Association of Collegiate Registrars and Admissions Officers (AACRAO) presents numerous workshops and program sessions for its members. In addition, state and regional associations of AACRAO often sponsor similar program sessions at their annual conferences. AACRAO has designated interassociation representatives to three of the primary athletic associations; the interassociation representatives' primary responsibilities are to represent AACRAO and the interests of its members in their relationship with the athletic association and to keep AACRAO members informed about activities of the athletic associations that might have an impact on the work of the membership.

But AACRAO is not the only source of help. Staff in the offices of the athletic associations generally are very knowledgeable and helpful and will readily respond to questions. Athletic conferences with a central office usually have staff members who are available to provide assistance that may be needed. The athletic associations and the conferences often sponsor seminars to help members better understand the rules related to academic requirements. In addition, all of the associations produce and distribute publications that are very helpful. At a minimum, certifying officers should possess the manual of rules for the appropriate association and conference. Additionally, newspapers from the NCAA and the NJCAA are available on a subscription basis. Addresses of the four associations identified earlier are listed in the following Appendix.

Finally, a registrar or admissions officer in need of help should never underestimate the value of a telephone call to a knowledgeable colleague. Many well-informed registrars and admissions officers throughout the country welcome the opportunity to discuss athletic eligibility issues with others. It is most helpful to build and maintain a network of registrars and admissions officers with whom to interact as questions and problems arise.

APPENDIX 6.1: ADDRESSES OF THE ATHLETICS ASSOCIATIONS

Manuals from each athletic association are produced annually. Contact the specific association to obtain the most current version.

National Junior College Athletic Association
PO Box 7305
Colorado Springs, CO 80933–7305

National Association of Intercollegiate Athletics
1221 Baltimore Avenue
Kansas City, MO 64105

National Christian College Athletic Association
PO Box 1312
Marion, IN 46952

National Collegiate Athletic Association
6201 College Boulevard
Overland Park, KS 66211–2422

REFERENCE

American Association of Collegiate Registrars and Admissions Officers (AACRAO). 1989. *Guide to NCAA Eligibility*. Washington, DC: AACRAO. The address is One Dupont Circle, NW, Suite 520, Washington, DC 20036–1171.

7

Veterans Certifications

David Guzman

The Department of Veterans Affairs (DVA) administers a variety of educational benefit programs for veterans and their dependents. In assisting these individuals to ensure that they receive their earned benefits, institutions of higher learning (IHL) and technical and vocational institutions must process enrollment certifications to the DVA regional office responsible for adjudicating and paying VA educational benefit claims. Many believe that educational institutions have a moral and civic obligation to society to provide such certifications to the DVA. Included among these obligations is the responsibility to administer the certification of veteran enrollments in educational programs to the Department of Veterans Affairs for educational benefits earned by veterans for either themselves or their dependents in accordance with regulations and policy outlined by the U.S. Departments of Veterans Affairs, Education, and Defense. These duties include, but are not limited to, processing applications for VA educational benefits and certifying enrollment for courses leading to standard undergraduate degrees, graduate or advanced professional degrees, certificates of training, or other programs as prescribed by the DVA or Department of Defense (DOD).

Education benefits for veterans date back to the passage of the Rehabilitation Act of 1919. However, not until the Servicemen's Readjustment Act of 1944 (GI Bill of Rights) did education really become the focal point of congressional legislation for veterans benefits. Passage of the GI Bill is considered the single most important event that gave impetus to the growth of higher education following World War II (Quann, et al., 1987).

Since that time, the GI Bill of Rights has given birth to other legislation that has benefited veterans' education and training. Several legislative packages have expanded veterans' educational benefits. The single most noteworthy of these is the Montgomery GI Bill (the All-Volunteer Force Educational Assistance Program of 1984). This act, originally a test program and since made permanent, is continually being refined to meet the changing needs of service members and their dependents.

This chapter addresses veterans' educational benefit programs since enactment of the original GI Bill in 1944. Also included are references on correct procedural processes to ensure compliance with DVA guidelines regarding service to the veteran and the institution as well as institutional liability.

Specific criteria and eligibility requirements differ from program to program. Benefit amounts vary depending on branch of service and length of service, as does the amount of bonuses, if any, offered by a specific service.

There are six major VA educational programs:

1. Vocational Rehabilitation Program (Chapter 31)
2. Veterans Educational Assistance Program (VEAP—Chapter 32)
3. Educational Assistance Test Programs (Sections 901 and 903)
4. Survivors' and Dependents' Educational Assistance Program (Chapter 35)
5. Montgomery GI Bill for Active Duty Personnel (Chapter 30)
6. Montgomery GI Bill for Selected Reserve (Chapter 1606)

Each of these is described briefly in the following pages.

HOW VETERANS ENROLL IN SCHOOLS/INSTITUTIONS OF HIGHER LEARNING

Veterans are admitted to institutions of higher learning based on those institutions' entrance qualifications as applicable to all students.

The Concurrent Admissions Program (ConAP), a relatively new program, allows men and women who are postponing college, usually for financial reasons, to gain admission to college at the same time they enlist in the U.S. Army and U.S. Army National Guard or U.S. Army Reserve. The participating ConAP college admits the soldier and defers enrollment in class until the enlistment or active duty training period is completed. ConAP colleges are also members of Servicemembers Opportunity Colleges (SOC).

One of the many benefits of the ConAP and SOC programs is transfer of credit for educational experiences in the army, granted by a "home college." Colleges that participate in ConAP/SOC often can increase their enrollment of veterans. Veterans are traditionally mature, motivated students who have both job experience and funds for education, such as Montgomery GI Bill education benefits (discussed later). ConAP/SOC helps veterans transfer credits from other colleges, thereby minimizing credit loss and avoiding course duplication. Veterans receive appropriate credit for their military training courses and may be granted credit for their occupational experience while in the service. They may also receive credit for learning that was achieved in nontraditional settings and from nationally recognized testing programs. There are over 1,000 ConAP/SOC colleges. Institutions desiring to participate in ConAP/SOC should contact the Servicemembers Opportunity Colleges, One Dupont Circle, Suite 680, Washington, DC 20036–1117, or call (202) 667–0079 or (800) 368–5622.

CHAPTER/SECTION ELIGIBILITY

This section discusses eligibility for each chapter of the VA educational benefits listed earlier for veterans and dependents of veterans. Refer to the American Association of Collegiate Registrars and Admissions Officers (AACRAO)'s *Certification of Students under Veterans' Laws* (Publication 89), as revised, for a detailed discussion of enrollment certification processing and completion of required forms.

Vocational Rehabilitation Program (Chapter 31)

Veterans found to have a service-connected disability may be eligible for vocational rehabilitation (Chapter 31) educational benefits. Disabled veterans should submit VA Form 28–1900, Disabled Veterans Application for Vocational Rehabilitation, for a determination of eligibility by the appropriate VA regional office, Vocational Rehabilitation and Counseling (VR&C) Division.

If it is determined that the veteran meets the criteria for training under this program, all tuition and fees, books, and reasonably necessary supplies will be paid by the DVA. A monthly stipend will be paid to the veteran as well, based on training time with the institution as authorized for veterans' benefits by the state approving agency.

Certification of enrollment for students approved for training under the vocational rehabilitation program is made directly to the VR&C Division of the regional VA office servicing the school by endorsing VA Form 28–1905, Authorization and Certification of Entrance or Reentrance into Rehabilitation and Certification of Status, as appropriate.

Veterans Education Assistance Program (Chapter 32)

The Veterans Education Assistance Program (VEAP) is a post–Vietnam-era contributory VA educational assistance program. It is the first contributory matching program approved by Congress. Under the provisions of this program, veterans could contribute between $25 and $100 per month while on active duty, up to a maximum of $2,700. The VA matching benefit is two for one.

VEAP applies only to those veterans who entered active duty between January 1, 1977, and July 1, 1985, and served for a continuous period of 181 days or more (not for training). Eligibility may be established after fewer than 181 days of service if the participant was discharged because of a service-connected disability.

While VEAP was a recruitment enhancement tool, some services have added bonuses or "kickers" for those who enlist in hard-to-fill specialties or specialties where there is an immediate need for new recruits. These kickers, service-unique recruiting incentives, pay monthly benefits above and beyond the VEAP base rate of $300. Kickers can vary in amount, and many veterans will receive different monthly amounts in VA educational assistance under this program.

Educational Assistance Test Programs (Sections 901 and 903)

Two educational assistance "noncontributory VEAP" programs were enacted into law under PL 96–342, the Department of Defense Authorization Act of 1981. These programs were extremely limited in nature and therefore apply to only a small population of veterans who qualified merely by being at the right recruiting office at the right time. Unique to these programs is the ability of the veteran to transfer his or her entitlement in whole or part to a spouse or child. Please refer to AACRAO's *Certification of Students under Veterans' Laws* (Publication 89), for eligibility criteria and processing instructions.

Survivors' and Dependents' Educational Assistance Program (Chapter 35)

Educational assistance benefits are available to eligible spouses and children of veterans who died or are permanently and totally disabled as the result of a disability arising from active service in the armed forces. Assistance is also available to qualifying dependents of a serviceperson who is currently missing in action or has been captured in the line of duty by hostile force and to servicepersons presently detained or interned in the line of duty by a foreign government or power.

Eligible dependents may receive up to 45 months of education or training (or the equivalent in part-time training) provided the program being pursued has a defined educational or training goal.

In addition to Chapter 35, Title 38, USC, educational benefits, surviving spouses and schoolchildren (between the ages of 16 and 22) may be eligible for the Restored Entitlement Program for Survivors (REPS), also referred to as the "Quayle Amendment," under Section 156, Public Law 97–377. Eligibility criteria and application-processing procedures are contained in AACRAO's *Certification of Students under Veterans' Laws* (Publication 89).

Montgomery GI Bill for Active Duty Personnel (Chapter 30)

The Montgomery GI Bill (MGIB) is a contributory program, named for its sponsor in Congress, Representative G.V. "Sonny" Montgomery (D–MS), which establishes three groups of benefit recipients based on individual active service:

Category I. Must have military service on or after July 1, 1985.

Category II. Must have military service on or after July 1, 1985, and be eligible to receive Chapter 34, Vietnam-era GI Bill and must have remained on active duty between October 19, 1984, and July 1, 1985, and continued on active duty without a break in service for three consecutive years, or must have served two continuous years on active duty after July 1, 1985, followed by four years in the Selected Reserves and received an honorable discharge or retirement.

These veterans are referred to as "Chapter 34/30 roll-over" and did not contribute to the MGIB in order to receive the benefits. Educational entitlement is 36 months of MGIB at the base rate and one-half of the Chapter 34 rate to include dependent eligibility apportionment; then, the remaining months (up to a maximum of 45 months total) at one-half of the Chapter 34 entitlement only.

Category III. In 1990 Congress provided certain individuals who were separated from the services as a result of downsizing of the military forces, who were not otherwise eligible, the opportunity to elect Chapter 30 based on a lump sum contribution of $1,200. Criteria for these conditions are lengthy and contained in AACRAO's *Certification of Students under Veterans' Laws* (Publication 89).

An additional benefit of Chapter 30 is that students who have insufficient entitlement remaining to complete a term will, nonetheless, be paid benefits through the end of the term. In addition to the specific criteria described earlier, in order to be eligible for the Montgomery GI Bill, the service member must have had a high school diploma prior to entering into agreement for the program, and he or she must be separated with an honorable discharge.

Montgomery GI Bill—Selected Reserves (Chapter 1606; formerly Chapter 106, Title 10, USC)

Members of the Selected Reserve and National Guard are eligible for this program, which is funded by the Department of Defense, if they meet the following criteria:

1. They are on active duty on or after July 1, 1985, and they enlist, reenlist, or extend their enlistment so that their obligated period of service is not less than six years;

2. They completed the requirements of a secondary school diploma (or equivalency) before completing the initial active duty for training (IADT) on or before completing a reenlistment or extension in order to establish eligibility; and

3. They have completed IDAT, are satisfactorily participating in the Selected Reserve, and have enlisted, reenlisted, or extended an enlistment for six years on or after October 1, 1990, for pursuit of programs at other than institutions of higher learning.

Eligible selected reservists are entitled to a maximum of 36 months of educational assistance based on full-time training.

ADDITIONAL PROGRAMS, BENEFITS, AND REQUIREMENTS

Advance Pay/VA Reporting Fees

Students eligible for VA educational benefits who enroll at a half-time rate or more may apply for advance pay. Applications may be submitted as early as 120 days, but no later than 30 days, prior to the beginning of the term provided there is at least a month break between terms, or it is the student's initial enrollment.

The Department of Veterans Affairs pays institutions that certify enrollments an annual reporting fee. At present, this fee is paid at a rate of seven dollars per enrolled veteran, except for those veterans who apply for advance pay, for whom a reporting fee of eleven dollars is paid.

Limitations

All veterans have ten years following separation, discharge, or retirement from active duty to use their entitlement. Delimiting dates are established by adding ten years to the veteran's last period of active duty. In rare instances, extensions have been granted due to circumstances such as physical or mental disabilities.

A maximum of 48 months of educational benefits under any combination of chapters has been established, and a claimant cannot receive benefits under more than one chapter at any given time. Additionally, a veteran cannot earn entitlement under Chapters 32 and 1606, or Chapters 30 and 1606, based on the same period of service.

Work-Study

VA work-study benefits are paid to eligible veterans, dependents, and selected reservists who are in pursuit of educational goals and training under one of the previously described programs at least three-quarters time. Students are paid for the first 50 hours in advance of commencing each work-study contract, or 40 percent of the amount specified in the work-study agreement, or an amount equal to 50 times the applicable minimum wage, whichever is less. Under this program, students may perform outreach services under the supervision of a VA employee or the institution's VA certifying official.

Institutional Liability

By signing VA enrollment certification forms as prescribed in *Certification of Students under Veterans' Laws*, institutions of higher learning are certifying that the institution has exercised reasonable diligence in meeting all applicable requirements of Title 38, US Code. Failure by the institution to meet any requirements of the law can subject the institution to liability for any overpayments made to veterans, as well as other damages as may be deemed appropriate in a court of law. Periodic surveys are conducted by the DVA at educational institutions to ensure compliance with laws governing certification of veterans as well as compliance with DVA policy.

Measurement of Pursuit

Normally, training time is measured as prescribed for undergraduates and graduate students in the institution's bulletin. When a term is not standard, that is, quarter or semester, the DVA will determine the training time. Appendix C of *Certification of Students under Veterans' Laws* contains decision logic tables to assist IHLs in determining credit-hour training time.

Tutorial Assistance

Tutorial assistance is another benefit available to eligible students training under the chapters of VA educational programs described earlier. In order to be eligible for tutorial assistance, students must be enrolled in postsecondary educational programs on at least a half-time basis and must have a deficiency in a subject required for, or prerequisite to, the satisfactory pursuit of their approved program. Tutorial assistance may be authorized only for tutoring given during the student's enrollment period. Application and certification procedures are detailed in *Certification of Students under Veterans' Laws*, Subpart II—Supplemental Educational Benefits. It should be noted that this program has been extremely beneficial to students who have had difficulty passing a course and has been credited with saving many students from dropping out or failing in their studies. Also, overpayment can be significantly reduced if the veteran can receive needed assistance early, rather than drop a class or withdraw from the institution. The earlier a student is identified for this program, the better for the student, the institution, and the DVA.

Enrollment Certification

The enrollment certification process is quite simple and involves completion of VA Form 22-1999, Enrollment Certification, or VA Form 28-1905 for Chapter 31, Vocational Rehabilitation students. The basic identification data are entered in Section I, Identifying Data. Care should be taken to mark section 4b, Change of Address, when this occurs. General Information, Section II, is self-explanatory; however, credit allowed for previous civilian or military training and experience must be reported to the VA within a reasonable period of time, usually within 30 days of enrollment.

Section III, Enrollment Data, must reflect beginning and ending dates of the school term. Two or three terms may be reflected in this section; however, the certifying official must again be sure to report changes of enrollment data within 30 days of occurrence. For IHLs, standard class sessions need not be reported in item 11B.

THE PLACEMENT AND ROLE OF THE INSTITUTIONAL VETERANS AFFAIRS COORDINATOR

Veterans affairs coordinators are most often located within the office of the registrar. Since this office is typically responsible for the function of enrollment certifications of other students, it appears to be a natural place to assign the office of veterans affairs. While some institutions have placed the veterans certification process in other areas (usually within student affairs) without degradation of service to veterans, compliance surveys conducted by the DVA will require that VA enrollment documents be verified against the student's transcript. Thus, the most natural placement of the veterans affairs coordinator appears to be within the office of the registrar.

Some institutions or states have defined the duties and responsibilities of the veterans affairs coordinator as program assistants, advisers, or coordinators, to name just a few of the job titles commonly used. Regardless of the classification name, many veterans affairs personnel within institutions of higher learning have typically taken on responsibilities as broad as their institutions have dared to give them. For example, the U.S. Department of Education, Office of Postsecondary Education, reported in 1989 that exemplary programs included strong counseling and referral programs by highly qualified, competent, and dedicated staff. It is also very desirable for institutional Veterans Affairs offices to establish strong linkages with organizations and resource agencies that provide meaningful assistance to veterans, such as mental health agencies; veteran organizations such as the Veterans of Foreign Wars (VFW) and American Legion; employment services; small business assistance; legal assistance; literacy programs; and health agencies. Many veterans affairs personnel at colleges and universities publish information to assist veterans in transition to college and help maintain positive awareness through handbooks, handouts, brochures, and newsletters. Technology, veterans clubs, and organizations on campus, as well as outreach programs, are often employed to help veterans achieve their goals in higher education. The services provided by many veterans affairs offices with institutions of higher learning are limited only by the imagination of the coordinator. College and university presidents and deans have typically been extremely supportive in past initiatives by coordinators to serve this segment of the student population. As we approach the year 2000 and beyond, we anticipate the number of veterans utilizing their VA educational assistance to increase significantly. We must prepare now to serve this group effectively in the future.

EVALUATION OF MILITARY CREDIT

This section discusses the hows and whys of evaluating military service schools and experience. *The Guide to the Evaluation of Educational Experiences in the Armed Services*, published annually by the American Council on Education (ACE), is the primary reference tool.

The ACE guide contains course evaluations for approximately 60 percent of all military courses currently offered by the armed services. The remaining courses cannot be evaluated for various reasons. However, ACE continually updates the guide and incorporates new courses as they are developed, provided they have a "servicewide" applicability.

Admissions staff transfer credit evaluators should take care to ensure that only those courses that will contribute to the veteran's pursuit of his or her current educational program are evaluated for credit. The Veterans Administration will take into consideration the number of transfer credits when making a determination on payment of benefit. Thus, it may actually prove harmful to grant excessive credit that does not apply to the individual's degree program.

ADDITIONAL SUGGESTIONS FOR VETERANS AFFAIRS COORDINATORS

Like most students, veterans seem continually to move. It is extremely important to ensure that the veteran's address is correct at all times to preclude a benefits check from being misrouted or returned. A monthly newsletter produced by the veterans affairs office staff (often a VA work-study person) will go a long way in keeping veterans and dependents informed of deadlines, changes to VA policy, and current events affecting students. A newsletter can also serve as a source to place reminders about notifying the veterans affairs office and the institution of any changes of mailing address.

Many veterans affairs coordinators have joined regional and/or national organizations as a means of networking. This can be extremely helpful when situations arise that require the expertise of seasoned coordinators. Some regional groups meet on a monthly basis to discuss various issues affecting veterans and to identify methods to address potential problem areas.

For example, one such group consists of veterans program administrators from federal and state Departments of Veterans Affairs as well as representatives from local military installations, employment security offices, the Small Business Administration, the VA Medical Center, county veterans services, and local colleges and universities. This group meets on a monthly basis to discuss methods for assisting veterans and their dependents and acts as a resource for networking and referral. A guest speaker is invited to give the group an outside perspective on various issues that may have an impact on their constituency. These groups have been very successful in staying abreast of the ever-changing service climate and have remained current in the various programs available to veterans.

For more information about such groups in your area, contact a representative of the National Association of Veterans Program Administrators in your region or state.

REFERENCES

American Association of Collegiate Registrars and Admissions Officers (AACRAO). 1989. *Certification of Students under Veterans' Laws*. Washington, DC: AACRAO, April.

Buckley, Benjamin C., Director. Concurrent Admissions Program, Servicemembers Opportunity Colleges. Memo dated April 14, 1995.

Quann, C. James, et al. 1987. *Admissions, Academic Records, and Registrar Services*. San Francisco: Jossey-Bass.

U.S. Department of Education. 1991. *Veterans Education Outreach Program, Exemplary Projects*. Washington, DC: U.S Government Printing Office (289-004/56061).

U.S. Department of Veterans Affairs. 1993. Federal benefits for veterans and dependents. VA Pamphlet 80-93-1.

8

Foreign Educational Credentials

James S. Frey and Kenneth P. Warren

INTRODUCTION

The development of an orderly process for obtaining and reviewing foreign educational credentials ensures that such documentation represents a complete and authentic record of the foreign-educated applicant's academic achievement. The purpose of this chapter is to assist admissions officers and registrars in developing guidelines and procedures for the evaluation of foreign educational credentials that provide a high level of quality assurance.

The term "educational credential" is used in this chapter to refer to the broad array of documentation received by students as they pass through the various levels of an educational system. This term includes transcripts, grade reports, mark sheets, and score reports, as well as affidavits, certificates, diplomas, or degrees.

University officials charged with the task of reviewing educational credentials from other countries know that the task can be a daunting, confusing, and often completely frustrating experience. In addition to differences in language, format, and content, one must also wrestle with strange terminology and with the strange use of familiar terminology. One must also guard against accepting documentation that has been forged, altered, or counterfeited.

In addition to a basic knowledge of foreign educational systems, common sense, prudence, and careful attention to detail are required. Proficiency in many foreign languages is desirable, but that qualification is infrequently found in university and college staff members in the United States. As a substitute, one can develop enough familiarity with each foreign language to be able to identify falsified decuments and to spot-check English translations for accuracy. For example, one can learn enough written Chinese in one day to identify Chinese documents and to check the English translations.

Admissions officers and registrars can develop policies and procedures that assure a consistent, fair, and reasonable treatment of foreign-educated applicants. Such guidelines serve to protect the institution from falsified documents and ensure that they do not unfairly discriminate or violate an applicant's rights. The goal should be to treat foreign-educated applicants with the same consistent and conscientious treatment that applicants educated in the United States receive.

The following topics are covered in this chapter:

- What is an official educational credential?
- What is an original educational credential? Why does one need to work with original credentials?
- What are acceptable sources for educational credentials? Which documents should be accepted from an applicant? Which documents should be obtained directly from a foreign educational institution?
- How can one determine whether an educational credential is authentic or fraudulent?
- What is an appropriate use of English translations of foreign educational credentials? Who can prepare an acceptable English translation?
- What are the best procedures for reviewing foreign educational credentials?
- What resources are available?

These topics will be treated from two points of view:

- What will work with the majority of foreign educational credentials, regardless of country of origin or level of education.
- Major exceptions to the general guidelines.

In addition to the basic guidelines, several techniques are described that can be used to make the credential evaluation process user-friendly and to produce admissions and transfer of credit decisions in a consistent and timely manner.

WHAT IS AN OFFICIAL EDUCATIONAL CREDENTIAL?

An official educational credential is issued by the agency, institution, or department with jurisdictional authority over that particular type of academic document. In the United States, for example, an official university transcript is issued by a university registrar, not by a dean of engineering or a professor of mathematics or a state department of education. Similarly, an official ACT, SAT, or Graduate Record Examination (GRE) score report is issued by the respective examination board, not by a high school counselor or a university testing center. In other countries, however, the relevant educational authority can be very

different from the equivalent U.S. authority, In addition, the criteria for determining what constitutes an official educational credential are country-specific,
because educational institutions are governed differently in different countries.

In some countries, the educational institution itself issues the official credentials. In other countries, official educational credentials are obtained from a division of the national government. Usually this is the Ministry of Education,
but in some cases it could be the Ministry of Defense, Health, Interior, or Social
Welfare.

The level of education involved also has some bearing on the issuing of
educational credentials. In most countries, primary and secondary school credentials are issued by officials external to the teaching institution (e.g., by a
ministry or an examinations board), whereas university credentials are usually
issued by the teaching institution (e.g., by the dean of the faculty involved or
the university registrar). In the case of tertiary nonuniversity institutions (e.g.,
art schools, music conservatories, teachers colleges, and institutions offering
programs in only one academic field such as engineering, journalism, nursing,
and social work), educational credentials might be issued by either the institution
or a ministry.

Resource materials published by two professional associations and three private credential evaluation services contain information concerning the responsibility for issuing educational credentials in various countries. For further
information, see the section on resources at the end of this chapter.

The mode of issuing educational credentials also varies from country to country. In the United States, it is possible to transmit educational credentials electronically. However, this would not be the case in a country such as India or
Portugal. Institutions in Canada are likely to issue computer-generated grade
reports and diplomas, but institutions in Albania and Poland may issue pre-
printed credentials with handwritten entries. Due to scarcity of resources and
technology, handwritten copies of credentials are common in the countries of
the former Soviet Union for students who graduated in earlier years.

WHAT IS AN ORIGINAL EDUCATIONAL CREDENTIAL?

An original educational credential is one that is issued by an educational
authority, either at the time that the credential was awarded or after the award
at the request of the student. An original educational credential has one or more
original signatures and one or more embossed or inked seals. It might also have
an official revenue stamp affixed to it.

It is important to note that an educational credential can be original without
being official. For example, a grade report issued to a student without the signatures or seal of the issuer is an original, but it is not official. The same is true
of original documents issued by unauthorized persons.

Alternatively, it can be official without being original. For example, a carbon copy or photocopy of a grade report that bears original signature(s) and seal(s) is an official document, even though it is not individually typed or printed.

In most cases, an educational credential should be both official and original if it is to be used for an admission or transfer of credit decision in the United States. Exceptions can be made when an admissions officer or registrar has sufficient experience with a given country, a given educational institution, and the language in which a document is issued to be able to verify authenticity on the basis of a photocopy of an original official document.

WHY DOES ONE NEED TO WORK WITH ORIGINAL CREDENTIALS?

Forged, altered, counterfeited, and other types of falsified documents may be used by persons seeking further education, professional licensure, or employment that requires proof of completion of a level of education that they do not have or that they do have but cannot document because of financial or political circumstances. For example, some institutions will not issue a grade report if a student owes money for unpaid tuition. Some institutions will not issue a grade report if a student has left the country illegally.

Falsified documents can originate in any country, but they are especially prevalent in countries where there has been economic, military, political, or social distress. In the 1990s, this included Afghanistan, Bangladesh, Cambodia, China, Cuba, El Salvador, Ghana, Haiti, Honduras, Iran, Iraq, Kuwait, Laos, Lebanon, Myanmar, Nicaragua, Nigeria, Pakistan, Romania, Vietnam, and the former republics of the USSR and of Yugoslavia.

Most falsified educational credentials are submitted in the form of photocopies. Because of the sophistication of modern photocopiers, one can do many things with an original document and then photocopy it carefully enough or often enough to eliminate most traces of the alterations. It is much more difficult to alter an original document without leaving signs. Be aware, however, that original-looking, official-looking educational credentials can be manufactured, and so can official-looking original stationery, envelopes, signatures, stamps, and seals. Admission officers and registrars who do not work regularly with foreign educational credentials are likely to miss the signs that might be found by careful inspection of a photocopy and careful comparison of it with documents submitted by earlier applicants.

WHAT ARE ACCEPTABLE SOURCES FOR EDUCATIONAL CREDENTIALS?

Generally speaking, the only acceptable source for an official educational credential is the educational authority that issued it. The credential should be mailed by that authority to the receiving institution in the United States via regular international mail. This is, of course, the procedure that is followed by secondary and tertiary academic institutions in the United States.

However, there are many exceptions to the general rule. In some countries, such as Bangladesh, India, Myanmar, Nepal, Pakistan, and Sri Lanka, many tertiary institutions do not maintain a permanent record of a student's academic performance. The only information retained by the institution is the name of the degree, the month and year in which it was awarded at a formal convocation, and the overall grade average.

In these countries, the only official grade report is the one given to the student at the end of each examination. Whenever the information contained in these grade reports is needed by a third party, the student is expected to use photocopies or handwritten or hand-typed duplicates whose authenticity has been confirmed by the equivalent of our notary public. In these cases, it is reasonable to accept an original official mark sheet (grade report) and degree submitted by an applicant.

In some countries, such as Afghanistan, Cambodia, China, Cuba, Iran, Iraq, Laos, Libya, North Korea, and Vietnam, political circumstances in the 1990s prevent or prohibit a university or governmental agency from issuing educational credentials for a person who has left the country without official government permission. In these cases, it is reasonable to accept an original official grade report or degree submitted by an applicant.

Note that whenever an institution has accepted an original educational credential from an applicant, it is *mandatory* that the original document not be altered by the receiving institution in any way: no date stamps, staples, pen or pencil notations, or folds may be added. In addition, the original documents must be reviewed as soon as possible following their receipt, and they must then be returned to the applicant in the safest way possible (e.g., via hand delivery or registered mail or courier service).

In many cases, applicants will not have any official original documents, either because they were not permitted to have original documents in their personal possession or because the originals were lost during their escape. In such cases, photocopies of original documents can be used if an admissions officer or registrar (or staff member of a private foreign educational credential evaluation service) is experienced in working with educational credentials from the country involved and has sufficiently complete reference materials to determine that the document involved has not been falsified. In many cases, such expertise does not exist in the United States.

HOW CAN ONE DETERMINE WHETHER AN EDUCATIONAL CREDENTIAL IS AUTHENTIC OR FRAUDULENT?

It should be noted that a stamp or affidavit affixed by a notary public (or gazetted official or similar person in other countries) is absolutely no guarantee that an educational credential is authentic. A notary public verifies only that a copy of a document is identical to another document with which it has been compared. Even when a notary public exercises those duties conscientiously (which is not always the case), the document from which a copy has been made could have been falsified.

When evaluating an educational credential in which suspicious clues have been found, one should make a photocopy of it on which to make notes in pencil. The master copy should always remain unmarked, so that a photocopy of it can be sent to one or more agencies for verification of authenticity.

A number of steps must be taken to determine whether or not an educational credential is authentic:

1. Resource materials must be checked to verify that the issuing institution exists, that it issues educational credentials in the style and format of the credential being evaluated, and that the content is consistent with the type of educational program completed.

2. If the issuing institution is a tertiary academic institution, resource materials must be checked to confirm that the issuing institution offers the degree program that the credentials represent. For example, a degree in physical therapy from a recognized university that has never offered a degree program in physical therapy is a counterfeit or altered document, even though the university is legitimately recognized, and even if the degree contains original signatures, seals, stamps, and ribbons.

3. One must then determine that the credential is appropriate for the level and scope of the education obtained. If the educational program was completed at a university, it would be very unusual for the credential to be issued by a governmental agency, since most universities throughout the world have sufficient autonomy to issue their own documentation. This is not an absolute, however. For example, university credentials from Iraq bear the names of both the university and the Ministry of Higher Education and Scientific Research.

   In most countries, credentials issued for secondary education differ from those issued for tertiary education. That is not always the case, however. For example, in the countries of the former Soviet Union, it is quite common to find the same pre-printed *Akademechekaya Spravka* (academic record) issued for technical secondary school programs as is issued for programs completed at tertiary institutions.

4. In most cases, it is reasonable to expect that foreign educational credentials will be as complete and as accurate as credentials submitted by graduates of educational institutions in the United States. However, the level of quality control that exists at U.S. institutions is not present in every country of the world. Thus, legitimate official and original educational credentials issued in English by institutions in a country where English is not the only official language may contain printing or typing errors, or they may appear to be sloppily prepared. The errors and the appearance should be taken as clues that a document might not be authentic, but they cannot be relied on as absolute proof.

   Admissions officers and registrars who work with foreign educational credentials should develop and maintain a comprehensive file of sample educational credentials, arranged alphabetically by country, institution, and program (e.g., Egypt, Alexandria University, Commerce). Educational credentials received from applicants should be compared with those in the file of samples. Sample educational credentials printed in resource materials can also be used for this purpose. Document formats change with great frequency, so it is important to make sure that samples are kept for a wide variety of dates.

The three most common ways in which an educational credential is altered are change of name, change of grade(s), and addition of subjects. Other items that are frequently altered are the name of a degree, the field of study, and the year of graduation. Clues to look for include the following:

1. The document should be the same as, or very similar to, other documents issued by the same institution or agency in the past. If there are drastic changes in format, style, or content, the document may have been fabricated by someone who is not familiar with legitimate documents.

2. The document should be filled out properly and completely. Omissions of significant information should be questioned.

3. All information that is specific to the student should be entered into the document in the same typeface or printer face or in the same handwriting, color of ink, and thickness of ink, including the student's name, birth date, age, place of birth, identification number, name(s) of parent(s), name of school, name of qualification received, and grades received. Variations in these entries indicate that some data may have been added or changed after the credential was issued. Similarly, all subjects that appear on a grade report should have been entered with the same typeface, printer face, or handwriting. Check to make sure that none of these entries are crooked in relation to other entries.

4. Erasures, strikeouts, line outs, whiteouts, and other additions to a document may indicate an unauthorized alteration. Sometimes corrections are made and initialed by the person who is preparing an educational credential. However, anyone can add initials to a document to make it appear that an alteration was legitimately made.

5. Absence of part of a solid line or dotted line under entries specific to the student may indicate that correction fluid or correction tape has been used to cover a previous entry.

6. Absence of an official institutional seal or a seal that differs in size, format, content, or placement from seals that one finds on sample documents from the same issuing institution should be questioned.

7. Original official educational credentials always contain the signature and title of one or more persons responsible for issuing them. The absence of such official signatures indicates a likely problem with the document.

8. In some countries, the size, weight, and/or the texture of the paper are not like paper used in the United States. For example, the standard U.S. size of paper (8½" × 11") would not be used in a country where the standard paper size is 8" × 10½" or 9" × 12". Russian documents are usually printed on paper that differs in size from standard photocopier, printer, and typing paper in the United States, and it usually has a shinier surface.

9. Nonstandard format or content, including more or fewer signatures or seals than are normally used, may be an indication of falsification.

10. Preprinted information that appears typeset when that information is usually computer-generated, or the reverse, may be grounds for suspicion.

11. Color photocopy reproduction of institutional stamps may signal an unauthorized document. One needs to become familiar with the shades of color that are usually used in each country.

12. The smell of the document may also be a clue. For example, diplomas from the countries of the former Soviet Union should have a distinctive beeswax scent.

13. Ordinarily, documents should be issued in the (or one of the) major official language(s) of the country. Since 1991, it has become increasingly common to see documents issued in the national language of countries of the former Soviet Union rather than Russian. Documents from these countries issued prior to 1991 might be written in Russian only or in both Russian and the language of the former republic. However, there are some exceptions to the language rule. Official original documents from the following countries should be issued in English: Afghanistan, Bahrain, Bangladesh, Botswana, Egypt, Ethiopia, India, Israel, Japan, Jordan, Kenya, Korea, Kuwait, Lesotho, Malawi, Malaysia, Nepal, Oman, Pakistan, Philippines, Qatar, Saudi Arabia, Singapore, Sri Lanka, Sudan, Swaziland, Taiwan, Tanzania, Thailand, Uganda, United Arab Emirates, Yemen, Zambia, and Zimbabwe.

14. On some preprinted documents, the date of printing is included on the document in coded form. The date of printing should be earlier than the date on which the document was issued. For example, a grade report from a university in the Philippines cannot be authentic if the grade report is said to have been issued in 1986 on a form that is dated 1991.

15. American-style course numbers, credits, and grades are used in countries that have been influenced by the United States, such as Japan, Korea, Philippines, and Taiwan, but they are not commonly used in the rest of the world. If a grade report from another country looks as if it was issued by a U.S. institution, it requires close scrutiny.

WHAT DOES ONE DO WHEN SUSPICIOUS CLUES HAVE BEEN FOUND?

When one has found clues that indicate that an educational credential has been altered or is not authentic in other ways (e.g., may be a counterfeit), one should suspend routine processing and seek verification of the document's authenticity. This is most appropriately done by sending a photocopy of the unmarked original to the issuing institution, with a cover letter that asks for assistance. For example:

Dear:

[Name of applicant] has applied for admission to [name of university]. Copies of the documents submitted to us are enclosed for your information. Please review the enclosures and the information in your records, and at your earliest convenience please respond to the following questions:

1. Do the enclosed documents accurately represent this student's educational achievement?

2. We have noted the following items that do not usually appear in educational credentials we receive from [name of issuing agency]:

   a. The name of the student appears in a typeface that differs from [other data].

   b. Part of the dotted line below the date of graduation is missing.

   c. The 9 in the grade for Organic Chemistry is not the same as the 9 in the date of the academic year.

Your kind assistance in this matter is greatly appreciated. Please quote reference number [   ] in your response.

Sincerely,

Enclosures: As noted.

Be sure to send all letters via international air mail or, if possible, international courier service.

Sometimes it will not be sufficient to write to only one source for verification. Some governmental agencies and academic institutions are very slow in responding. Others do not have budgets to cover overseas postage. Some are simply unresponsive.

Fortunately, there are other sources of information, such as ministries of education; cultural affairs officers at foreign embassies; consulates and United Nations missions in the United States; cultural affairs officers at U.S. embassies and consulates in major cities throughout the world; educational advisers at Fulbright commissions; and educational advisers at U.S. and foreign offices of agencies such as the African-American Institute, AMIDEAST, and the Institute for International Education.

Conscientious credential evaluators develop files containing addresses, telephone and fax numbers of such resource persons, and similar information on knowledgeable foreign educational credential evaluators in the United States who can provide names of contacts.

WHAT DOES ONE DO WHEN A DOCUMENT HAS BEEN VERIFIED AS INAUTHENTIC?

Each institution should have a clearly stated policy concerning the submission of educational credentials that are not authentic. This policy should be stated on the application for admission and in other printed materials that customarily accompany an application for admission. If your institution has no such policy, work with your legal counsel to develop one. When you do have a policy in place, apply it. The confirmation that you have received from the issuing institution or other appropriate authority is your legal protection. In applying the policy, take into consideration other divisions of your institution that have a need to know, such as the dean's office, graduate department, office of financial aid, and housing office.

Even if you receive confirmation that documents have been falsified, do not use this as a basis for accusing an applicant of being the person who actually committed the falsification. You may never have proof of the identity of the person who did so. Instead, your approach should be that you do have proof that the documents were falsified, the applicant was responsible for submitting authentic documentation to you, and the applicant knew, or should have known, that the documents were not authentic at the time that they were submitted.

What does one do when a document is suspicious, but it has not been verified as inauthentic?

If there are clues that indicate that an educational credential is not authentic, but you have not received verification from the issuing institution or other appropriate authority, act with caution. If at all possible, postpone a decision until verification is received.

It is entirely appropriate to require the applicant to make arrangements to have a new, official, original educational credential or set of educational credentials sent to you directly by the issuing institution, just as you would do if the issuing institution were located in the United States. Even in the case of countries where the original documents have been given to the applicant (e.g., India), it is reasonable to require the applicant to request the foreign university to send directly to you an affidavit confirming the name of the degree awarded and the date of conferral.

Universities and governmental agencies in other countries almost always use international mail. Be suspicious of educational credentials delivered to you by a courier service, sent via express mail, or postmarked in the United States.

WHAT IS AN APPROPRIATE USE OF ENGLISH TRANSLATIONS OF FOREIGN EDUCATIONAL CREDENTIALS?

English translations of educational credentials written in another language should be used as guides for working through the original document. However, they should never be considered equal to the original, and they should never be used in the absence of the original.

It is very important to determine whether or not a translation is complete and accurate. One cannot presume that that is the case, no matter who prepared the translation. Many translators try to be helpful, and in the process they interpret a foreign educational credential into U.S. educational terminology that they might not completely understand. Sometimes a translator understands the U.S.

terminology, but the terminology chosen does not match the level of equivalence a U.S. educator would assign to the document being translated.

Checking a translation does not need to be a cumbersome and time-consuming task. It is possible to spot-check key items in a translation against the original document, instead of making a word-for-word comparison. Spot checks can be made by persons who cannot read the foreign language but who have learned how to read numbers, dates, grades, and degree titles.

It may be awkward at first, but it is possible to familiarize oneself with the educational terminology commonly used in a foreign language and to become able to locate words in a foreign language dictionary. It is possible also to teach oneself the Greek and Cyrillic alphabets and to learn enough Arabic and Hebrew words and Chinese characters to be able to spot-check an English translation for accuracy. Several professional associations and private foreign educational credential evaluation services offer workshops and training programs in which these skills are taught. (See the resources section at the end of this chapter.)

A conscientious admissions officer or registrar should be able to identify numbers, dates, and grades in languages that do not use Arabic numerals. For example, familiarity with Persian numerals and the Persian calendar makes it possible to identify grades, courses, and enrollment dates on an Iranian transcript and to verify that these items have been translated correctly.

Beware of changes in content. Grades reported in numbers or words should not be translated as letters. Grades should appear in the same sequence in a translation as they appear in the original document.

Many times translation services owned and operated by émigrés interpret a document as they translate it, substituting the name of a U.S. degree for the foreign degree name. However, these words should be translated literally. For example, license should be translated as licentiate, not as master, and *Diplom Kandidata Nauk* should be translated as diploma of candidate of sciences, not as doctor of philosophy.

Statements concerning the U.S. equivalent of a foreign degree, such as "this document is generally accepted to be the equivalent of a master's degree in the United States" are inappropriate in an English translation. A complete, literal, word-for-word English translation of the degree should be required.

WHO CAN PREPARE AN ACCEPTABLE ENGLISH TRANSLATION?

An acceptable English translation can be prepared by any person or agency that prepares complete, literal, word-for-word translations based on the original official documents. In general, official translations prepared by authorities at a foreign school or governmental agency are the easiest to verify and more acceptable than those issued by a translator working in a nonofficial capacity.

Although official English translations prepared abroad may contain grammatical and syntactical errors in English, the official translators who prepare them are generally trained to prepare translations of official documents and forms. These translators are likely to be more familiar with the formats of official documents and with the technical terminology required to prepare an accurate translation than are commercial translators.

If the foreign educational credential evaluator has substantial proficiency in the foreign language and can catch errors in translation, then it could be acceptable to permit the applicant to prepare the English translation.

WHAT ARE THE BEST PROCEDURES FOR REVIEWING FOREIGN EDUCATIONAL CREDENTIALS?

Anyone who is charged with checking, verifying, approving, and maintaining documentation must work within a procedural framework that has some control and that ensures that the treatment of the documentation is consistent from day to day. It is important to establish a step-by-step process that does not allow for the exclusion of detail due to negligence or oversight. This can sometimes be assisted through the use of a document checklist.

A document checklist contains all or most of the documents that you need to complete your job. Documents that are unnecessary can be waived, and those that have been reviewed and approved can be checked off. This system has the advantage of allowing anyone reviewing an applicant's file to see at a glance what is missing and what is still needed. A document checklist will also ensure that all applicants receive the same documentary review treatment.

When complex documentation is involved, an inventory list of the documents should be included in the application file, whether or not you use a document checklist as part of the review process. When new documents are received to replace incomplete documents, they can be added to the inventory listing.

To determine that all documentation is in order, documents must be reviewed, and their authenticity verified. It is usually best to do this as each document is received. In this way, questionable documents can be sent back to the issuing institution for verification while you are waiting for the applicant to submit additional materials.

All data entries should be reviewed. If an applicant presents a diploma that represents completion of a four-year program of study, the accompanying grade report should indicate which subjects were studied over a four-year period of time. A grade report should not be considered complete if part of a degree program is missing; this frequently happens when an applicant has requested a grade report prior to completion of an academic program and then never bothers to get a supplement or replacement after graduation.

If you are reviewing a grade report for an applicant who has not completed an academic program, it is important to determine whether the part that was completed represents full-time or part-time achievement. To do so, you need to have on file a grade report for another person who was enrolled in the same program or a detailed syllabus (catalog, calendar, or study book) that describes the degree requirements.

Once you are satisfied that a document is authentic and complete, initial and date it with a pencil. Initialing removes any doubt as to whether a document has been reviewed. The following steps must then be taken in evaluating foreign educational credentials:

1. Determine whether or not the issuing organization is a regular part of the educational system of the country involved. If the issuing organization is a tertiary (postsecondary) educational institution, determine whether or not it is officially recognized as a degree-granting institution by educational authorities in that country. Publications of the organizations described in the Resources section at the end of this chapter can assist you with this process.

2. Determine whether or not the credentials submitted to you are authentic. See the preceding section entitled ''How can one determine whether an educational credential is authentic or fraudulent?''

3. Determine whether or not the program of study represented by the educational credentials is an academic program leading to an academic degree, diploma, or certificate or a nonacademic program of the type that would be deemed noncredit, continuing education, adult education, or in-service training in the United States.

   Universities in the United States that have regional academic accreditation offer individual courses and coordinated programs that are not covered by that accreditation, such as cake decorating, chain saw maintenance, conversational Polish, certificate of preparation for a realtor's examination, certified public accountant (CPA) examination review course, and certificate in English as a foreign language. If you would not grant academic credit for such courses and programs completed at a university in the United States, then you should not grant credit for a course or program of similar status completed at a tertiary institution in another country. Most language and culture courses offered in other countries for American students are, in fact, the equivalent of noncredit adult education courses in the United States.

4. Determine the number of years of full-time study or the equivalent in part-time study represented by the foreign educational credentials. The publications noted in the Resources section of this chapter can assist you.

   Using 30 to 32 semester hours of credit per year of full-time study as a guide (or 45 to 48 quarter hours), use the quantitative information contained in the educational credentials and in the resource publications to determine the U.S. credit equivalents. For example:

   a. Four equal subjects per year = 8 semester hours of credit per subject = 32 semester hours of credit.

   b. Twenty units per year = 1½ semester hours of credit per unit = 30 semester hours of credit.

   c. Thirty-four *creditos* per year = 1 semester hour of credit per *credito* = 34 semester hours of credit.

   d. Forty semester hours of credit per year = ¾ U.S. semester hours of credit per foreign semester hour of credit = 30 semester hours of credit.

   You will need to develop conversion factors, institution by institution, just as you develop conversion factors when determining credit values for transcripts from U.S. universities and colleges that use quarter credits, term credits, points, and other quantitative variants from semester hours of credit.

5. Determine the U.S. grade equivalent of each grade reported on the foreign educational credentials. The publications noted in the Resources section of this chapter can assist you.

When calculating an equivalent U.S. grade average on a 4.0 scale for grades reported in percentages or any other numerical basis on a foreign grading scale, convert each foreign grade to the U.S. A-to-F grading scale first, subject by subject, and then calculate the grade average. Attempts to convert mathematically grades originally issued on a 6-point, 20-point, 100-point, or any other numerical scale to the U.S. 4.0 scale, will distort the resulting grade average.

RESOURCES

Two professional associations and three private, nonprofit foreign educational credential evaluation services offer workshops, training sessions, conference presentations, and publications designed to assist admissions officers and registrars with the evaluation of foreign educational credentials.

The American Association of Collegiate Registrars and Admissions Officers (AACRAO) offers special sessions at its national conference in April each year. It previously published the *World Education Series*, of which many volumes are still in print. AACRAO cooperates with NAFSA in jointly operating Projects in International Education Research (PIER). Since 1966, publications of PIER and its predecessor organizations have supplemented the AACRAO World Education Series. AACRAO, One Dupont Circle NW, Suite 520, Washington, DC 20036; telephone 202–293–9161, fax 202–872–8857.

NAFSA: Association of International Educators was previously known as the National Association for Foreign Student Affairs. It offers special sessions at its national conference in May each year. NAFSA has a series of publications designed to assist with the evaluation of foreign educational credentials. Its *ADSEC Bibliography* is the best source of information for those who are trying to assemble or improve a library collection in this field. NAFSA cooperates with AACRAO in jointly operating Projects in International Education Research. NAFSA, 1875 Connecticut Avenue NW, Suite 1000, Washington, DC 20009–5728; telephone 202–462–4811, fax 202–667–3419, Internet inbox@nafsa.org.

Educational Credential Evaluators, Inc. (ECE) offers a series of Professional Development Seminars (PDS) to train new credential evaluators and to increase the knowledge base of experienced persons and Customized Training Programs (CTP) to train one or more staff members of a single institution. ECE also publishes *ECE Presents . . .* , a series of monographs on foreign educational systems. ECE, PO Box 92970, Milwaukee WI 53202–0970; telephone 414–289–3400, fax 414–289–3411, Internet eval@ece.org.

International Education Research Foundation, Inc. (IERF) has published a number of resources in this field. IERF, PO Box 66940, Los Angeles, CA 90066; telephone 310–390–6276, fax 310–397–7686, Internet ierf@cerf.net.

World Education Services, Inc. (WES) publishes *World Education News and Reviews* (WENR), a quarterly newsletter of information on foreign educational systems, and conducts workshops to provide information to credential evaluators. WES, PO Box 745, New York, NY 10113–0745; telephone 212–966–6311, fax 212–966–6395.

9

SPEEDE/ExPRESS: Electronic Data Interchange (EDI) in Education: A Nontechnical Approach

Donald J. Wermers

Recent literature challenges schools, colleges, and universities to improve their many routine business processes by creatively, vigorously, and tenaciously increasing the use of current and emerging electronic tools in routine daily work (Evert, 1990; Jones, 1990; Lonabocker, 1990). "The real beginnings of using this technology in higher education during the 1960s (keypunch cards, sorters, etc.) evolved into real progress in the 1970s as data were entered and accessed directly online with staffed terminals. Real breakthroughs occurred in the 1980s with [t]ouch-[t]one telephone/voice response applications, distributed processing, fax, etc." (Wermers, Patterson, and Scott, 1992, p. 276). Past successes in implementing these technologies will continue to motivate higher education to apply emerging technologies to routine administrative processes through the 1990s and beyond.

Business, industry, and finance usually are first to apply new electronic technology tools to routine business processes—with education following. Electronic data interchange (EDI) is the most recent example of such technological progress. Emmelhainz (1990, p. xiii) reports "that EDI is fast becoming the standard way of exchanging business documents, not only in this country but also in the rest of the world. EDI provides a faster, more accurate, less costly method of communication than do traditional methods of business communications such as mail, telephone, and personal delivery. However, EDI is doing more than just changing how businesses communicate; it is changing the way businesses operate."

EDI is having a major impact in the business world. Similar impacts are emerging in education, as demonstrated by a few EDI pioneers such as Arizona State University and Maricopa Community College, Brigham Young University, and Ricks College, all of public education in Florida, the University of Maryland system, and several schools and colleges in Texas. Each day more and more institutions are becoming users of EDI. Increasingly, school districts, state departments of education, other education agencies, and their software vendors are also pursuing EDI implementation.

The purpose of this chapter is to introduce and provide an understanding of the EDI concept and describe how EDI may be used for some of the routine processes in admissions and registrar offices. This chapter also describes the role of the SPEEDE (Standardization of Postsecondary Education Electronic Data Exchange) Committee and the ExPRESS (Exchange of Permanent Records Electronically for Students and Schools) Task Force in developing EDI standards and promoting the use of EDI in education.

The reader might view this chapter as "EDI and SPEEDE/ExPRESS 101." It offers a basic foundation of knowledge about EDI by defining it, examining its key concepts, and providing examples of how and why it is a tool that can improve many routine processes in education. The process of sending and receiving transcripts is illustrated as one example of EDI use in education. The chapter is divided into three sections. The first describes EDI; the second addresses the role of SPEEDE/ExPRESS in EDI standards development; and the third section focuses on the future of EDI in education.

WHAT IS EDI?

"One study has concluded that 70 percent of a company's computer input is generated from 70 percent of its trading partner's computer output. Think about this!" (Cannon, 1993, p. 13).

Imagine the efficiencies that could be realized if a significant percentage of the data received from external senders could be entered into your computer without paper and without redundant human activity. EDI is a tool that has the potential to enable business, government, and education to use electronic technology to exchange data more efficiently. EDI is one of at least three different forms of electronic communication, two of which are already familiar. The first, electronic mail (e-mail), is the person-to-person communication of unstructured (free format) messages between individuals. It is the electronic replacement for telephone or letter communication. The second, person-to-computer communication, occurs when an individual at a terminal enters data to, or accesses data from, a mainframe. Neither of these two types of electronic communication is EDI because neither possesses the characteristics reflected in the following examples of EDI definitions:

- The direct computer-to-computer exchange of standard business forms (Akerman, 1985).

- The interorganizational exchange of business documentation in structured, machine-processable form (Emmelhainz, 1990).

Figure 9.1
Electronic Data Interchange (EDI)

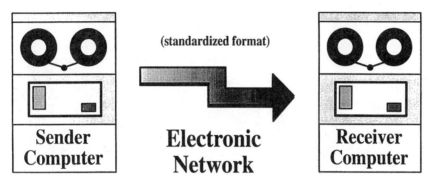

- The transfer of structured data, by agreed message standards, from one computer system to another, by electronic means (Parfett, 1992).

- The computer-to-computer communication of data from common industry or education documents using standard data formats (Stewart, 1992).

- The computer-to-computer exchange of business information using a standardized data format (Neary, 1993).

These are but examples of various definitions that convey the same meaning, that is, transmitting data elements directly from the sender's computer to the receiver's computer over an electronic network in a standardized format (Figure 9.1). This transmission occurs without paper, human interpretation, or redundant rekeying of data.

Figure 9.2 demonstrates the key concept behind EDI by contrasting EDI with the traditional method of transmitting a purchase order between a buyer and a seller. The upper part of the illustration shows the traditional method (printing data on paper, manual processing, mailing, receiving in paper format, manual processing, human interpretation, redundant data entry) and is recognized by all who work with paper transmission of computer data. With EDI, data previously entered into the buyer's computer are extracted and transmitted electronically to the seller's computer, where the data are entered electronically without rekeying.

Of the various definitions, Cannon's (1993, p. 2) definition and his explanation of its various phrases provide the clearest picture of EDI: "EDI is defined as the electronic transmission of standard business documents in a predefined format from one company's business computer application to its trading partners' business computer application."

This definition contains five key word phrases: (1) electronic transmission, (2) standard business documents, (3) predefined format, (4) business application, and (5) trading partner. The nuances of these five phrases must be understood to comprehend fully the meaning of EDI.

Figure 9.2
EDI versus Traditional Methods

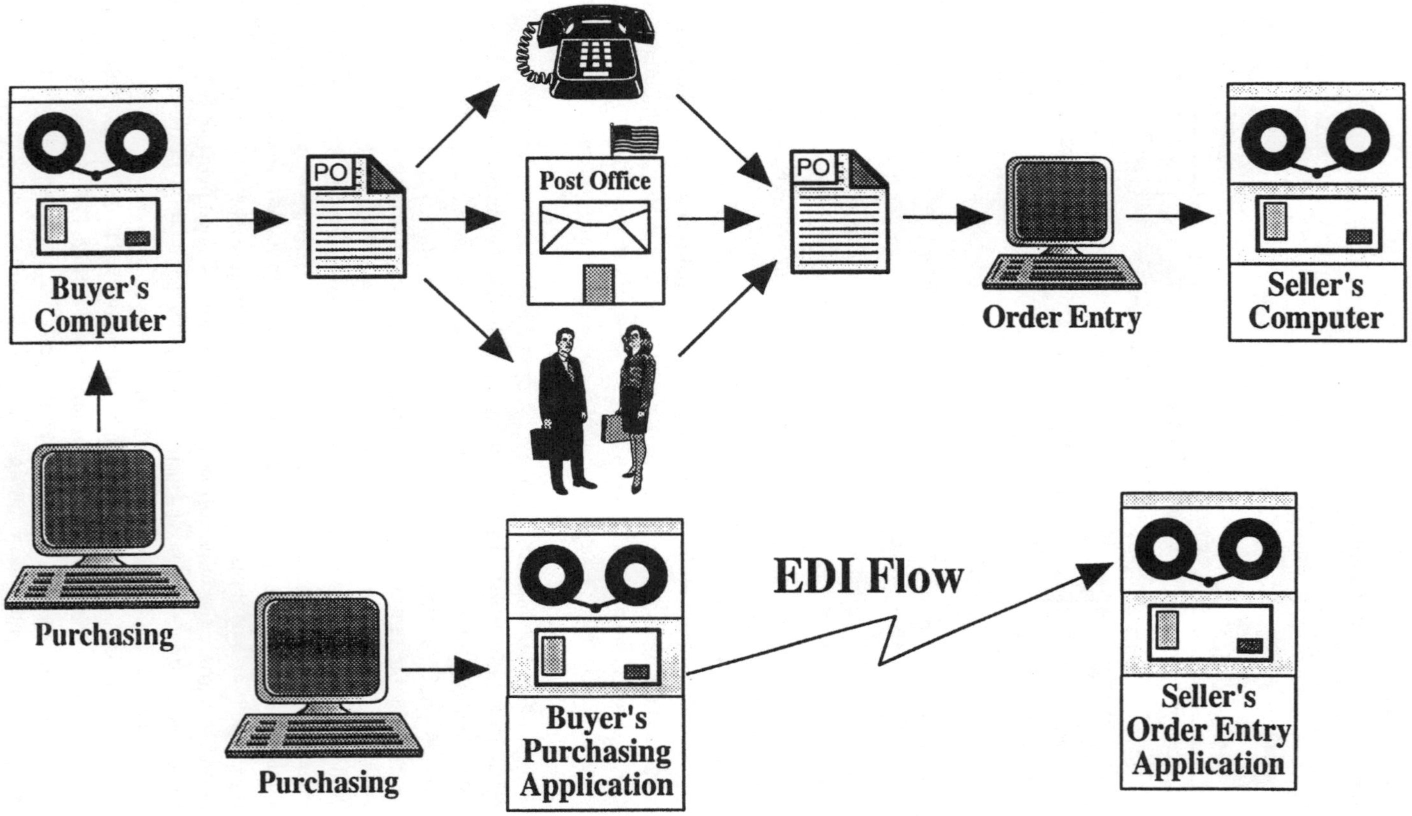

Since one of the primary purposes of EDI is to speed the communication of information, *electronic transmission* is central to the EDI concept. Actually, transcripts and other documents can be transmitted rapidly with a variety of express delivery options, but at a relatively high cost, or by facsimile transmission (fax), that is, the transmission of a digitized document image over telephone channels. But both express mail and fax delivery mechanisms start and end with a paper document, and data received on paper in a nonstructured format require interpretation and rekeying by the receiver (Emmelhainz, 1990). EDI eliminates paper and all labor-intensive activity associated with the handling of paper.

Standard business documents refer to those documents that are transmitted in a "routine business transaction" and include purchase orders, invoices, shipping manifests, and other similar documents specific to an industry. In a pre-EDI business environment, these documents are transmitted in a paper format, whereas with EDI, they are transmitted electronically. Following are just a few of the routine business transactions specific to the education "industry" that are candidates for EDI applications:

- Academic transcripts
- Financial aid transcripts
- Enrollment verifications
- Applications for admission, financial aid, housing
- Course descriptions
- Purchase orders, requisitions, and invoices
- Payments and other transfers of funds

Cannon's third key phrase is *predefined format*. Before electronically transmitting a document, EDI requires that it be converted to a predefined (or standard) format so it can be understood by both the sender's computer and the receiver's computer.

Figure 9.3 illustrates this concept with a simple example of communication between two people of different languages. A German citizen wishes to convey a message to a French person. Neither can speak the other's language. However, both are conversant in English. Thus, they can communicate using the English "standard." The message in German is converted to English and transmitted in English. The message is received in English and translated to French. The process required for two computers to communicate is similar to language interpretation. The standard format required for EDI communication is the "language" that both the sender and the receiver can understand. Such standards permit the sender's computer and the receiver's computer to interact directly without human interpretation. Establishing and maintaining standards are critical in the EDI environment and are one major responsibility of the SPEEDE Committee and ExPRESS Task Force. Standards and the role of SPEEDE and ExPRESS in their development are addressed later in this chapter.

Figure 9.3
Concept of Standards

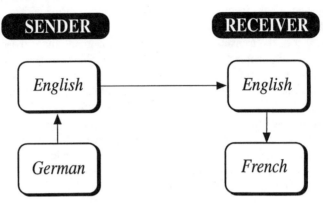

Cannon's fourth key phrase, *business application*, specifies much more than the phrase "computer-to-computer," a phrase used in many definitions of EDI. Emmelhainz (1990) refers to "computer-to-computer" as "door-to-door," where data are transmitted electronically, but the receiver prints out the data upon receipt, interprets them, and rekeys the data into the appropriate business application system (Figure 9.4). Door-to-door loses two major EDI benefits: the elimination of human interpretation and the elimination of redundant keying of data. For EDI to provide maximum benefits, the term "computer-to-computer" must be replaced by "business application-to-business application."

Application-to-application, the truest form of EDI, means that "data are moved electronically, without additional human interpretation or rekeying, between the sender's application program (such as a purchasing system) and the receiver's application program (such as order entry). When EDI is fully integrated with application programs, not only do data flow electronically between trading partners without the need for rekeying, data also flow electronically between internal applications of each of the trading partners" (Emmelhainz, 1990, p. 5). Not only is the document received electronically, but the data elements are coded directly into the receiver's system without rekeying, and the data are in the appropriate format for internal processing by the receiver (see Figure 9.2). However, even door-to-door EDI offers significant benefits and may be an excellent initial reason for an institution to get started with EDI.

The fifth key phrase, *trading partners*, simply refers to those to whom data will be sent and those from whom data will be received. In education, EDI trading partners are primarily other schools and colleges, professional (e.g., law, medical) school admissions services, and teacher certification divisions of state departments of education. As EDI becomes the "way of doing transcript business," trading partners will include private industry, especially those larger organizations that recruit large numbers of college graduates.

Figure 9.4
Receiver's Processes with Door-to-Door EDI

Paper

Now that the EDI definition and its key phrases are understood, document characteristics and institution characteristics that lend themselves to the use of this tool must be identified. First, Emmelhainz (1990) suggests that any document produced in a standard form potentially can be transmitted electronically. Emmelhainz further suggests that if any one or more of the following institution characteristics are present, EDI should be pursued:

- Large volume of repetitive standard actions
- Organization operates on a very "tight" margin
- Organization operates in a time-sensitive environment
- Organization has received requests for EDI transmission from trading partners

The preceding document and institution characteristics clearly point to the use of EDI for a number of procedures in education, the sending and receiving of transcripts being one obvious candidate.

EDI FOR TRANSCRIPTS

Figure 9.5 compares the traditional process of transmitting academic transcript data in the current on-line environment with EDI.

The objective is to move demographic and academic student data from the sending institution's computer to the receiver's computer. Part A of Figure 9.5 shows how this is done in the current environment. The sender's computer "talks" to a printer, which produces a paper transcript. The sender now completes the laborious and costly routine of authenticating, folding, inserting, addressing, and posting the paper transcript. The postal service then transports the transcript to the receiver, where another laborious, manual process is undertaken: opening the envelope, removing and unfolding the transcript, filing, and so on.

Figure 9.5
Traditional Methods versus EDI for Transcripts

A. Traditional Process

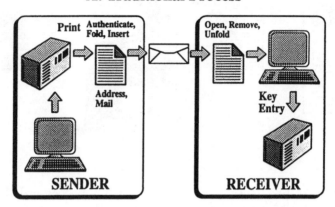

B. EDI Process

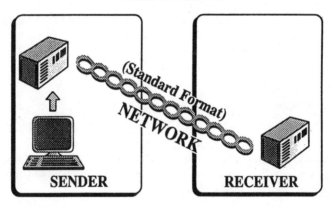

Paper transcripts are received in various formats, which complicates the required human interpretation before the receiver redundantly keys the data to the computer file. Note also that data elements are as accurate as they ever will be at the time they are produced by the sender. Subsequent human interpretation and redundant keying of the data by the receiver subject the data to error. Obviously, the traditional process of transmitting transcript data from one institution's computer to another is highly inefficient, insecure, and prone to error. In contrast, the EDI process, as illustrated in Part B of Figure 9.5, allows the data entered in the registrar's computer system at the sending institution to be entered electronically in the receiving institution's computer system without manual and paper processing and without rekeying.

Remember the quote from the beginning of this section: 70 percent of one company's computer input is generated from 70 percent of its trading partner's computer output. Maybe it isn't 70/70; maybe it's 50/50 or 20/40—or even 10/10. An exact accounting isn't necessary; it's immediately obvious from Figure 9.5 that substantial benefits can be achieved by developing EDI applications in the education environment. As listed by Cannon (1993) and Emmelhainz (1990), these benefits include the reduction of human interpretation and rekeying, reduction in transaction time, improved responsiveness to students and receivers of transcripts, administrative cost savings, and improved efficiencies.

EDI STANDARDS AND SPEEDE/ExPRESS

As previously noted, EDI requires a predefined format or standard that precisely defines the elements of the electronic message. The standard permits both the sender's computer and the receiver's to understand each other without additional human intervention. Data must be in coded format. The receiver's computer must be told, in advance, what data to expect and in what format. The data must then be transmitted in that specific manner in order to be read and understood by the receiving computer. "EDI standards provide the structure required for computers to be able to read, understand, and process business documentation" (Emmelhainz, 1990, p. 63). Well-designed EDI standards for education, therefore, are crucial, and their development is one critical area of involvement for SPEEDE and ExPRESS.

SPEEDE is a standing committee of the American Association of Collegiate Registrars and Admissions Officers (AACRAO). The ExPRESS Task Force functions under the umbrella of the Council of Chief State School Officers (CCSSO). Funding to support the activities of SPEEDE and ExPRESS is provided through a contract with the National Center for Education Statistics (NCES). The primary responsibility of both SPEEDE and ExPRESS, acting separately and together, is to develop and maintain EDI standards for education.

Although SPEEDE and ExPRESS function under the umbrellas of educational organizations, they develop and maintain EDI standards within the structure of the American National Standards Institute (ANSI). It is not essential for the reader to understand fully the organizational structure of ANSI or the long and detailed process for developing EDI standards. However, since well-developed and constantly maintained standards are critical for EDI to be a successful tool, schools and colleges (as well as other potential trading partners) that are in the process of developing EDI transactions or contemplating such development must have the confidence that the standards have resulted from a recognized, tested, and accepted process. These standards must be expected to survive the test of high-volume usage over a long period of time. The following brief introduction to the organizations and processes within which EDI standards are developed (summarized from Data Interchange Standards Association, 1994) should provide the reader with that confidence.

ANSI was founded in 1918 as the coordinator for national standards in the United States. This voluntary standards system consists of a large number of standards developers (including professional societies, trade associations, government, and, now, education) that write and maintain one or more national standards. Thousands of individuals, companies, labor organizations, consumer groups, industrial organizations, government agencies, and educational institutions voluntarily contribute their knowledge, talent, and effort to standards development. As a result of these efforts, for example, a consumer can buy a light bulb at the local hardware store with confidence that it will fit the socket upon returning home. Similar standards enable a fire-fighting unit to arrive at a fire site certain that their hoses will connect to hydrants and to other fire-fighting equipment, even if the site is in a different city.

ANSI provides an open forum for all concerned interests to identify standards needs, plan to meet those needs, and agree on standards. ANSI itself does not develop standards, but ANSI approval of a standard indicates that the principles of openness and due process have been followed in the approval procedures and that consensus has been achieved among those affected directly and materially by the standard.

In 1979, ANSI chartered a new committee, known as the Accredited Standards Committee (ASC) X12—Electronic Data Interchange—to develop uniform standards for electronic interchange of business transactions. The operations of ASC X12 are governed by its organization and procedures manual, which provides a system of orderly administration and incorporates the procedures required by ANSI. The work of ASC X12 is conducted primarily by a series of subcommittees and task groups whose major function is the development and maintenance of EDI standards. Their recommendations are presented to ASC X12 for ratification.

ANSI ASC X12 is the standards organization within which the SPEEDE Committee and the ExPRESS Task Force function. ANSI ASC X12 and its processes thus assure the education community that EDI standards available for use in education have been developed in a proven standards-development process.

Where do SPEEDE and ExPRESS fit in the ANSI organization? Figure 9.6 illustrates that SPEEDE and ExPRESS are the initial members of Subcommittee A (Education Administration) of ASC X12, one of the standing committees of ANSI. ASC X12 approved Subcommittee A in 1995 as one of its twelve standing subcommittees. Others in the education administration arena are in the process of becoming Subcommittee A members.

ASC X12 Subcommittees are the following:

A   Education Administration
C   Communications and Controls
E   Product Data

Figure 9.6
SPEEDE/ExPRESS in EDI

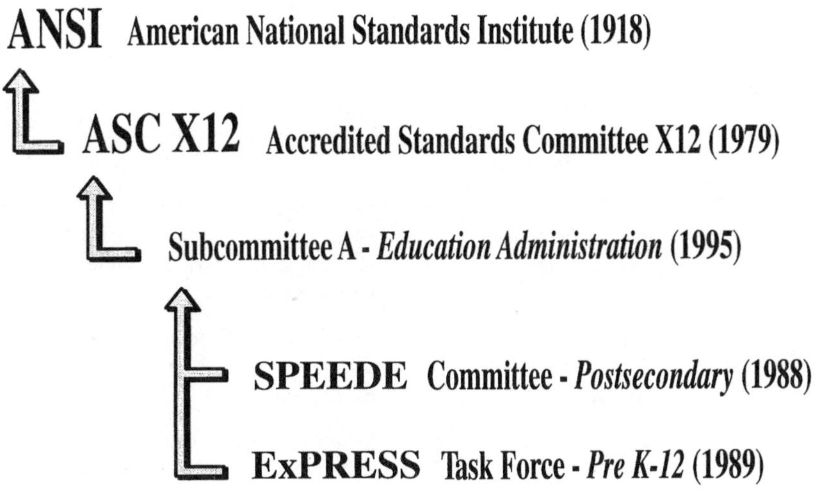

ANSI American National Standards Institute (1918)

ASC X12 Accredited Standards Committee X12 (1979)

Subcommittee A - *Education Administration* (1995)

SPEEDE Committee - *Postsecondary* (1988)

ExPRESS Task Force - *Pre K-12* (1989)

F   Finance

G   Government

H   Materials Management

I   Transportation

J   Technical Assessment

K   Purchasing

L   Industry Standards Transition

M   Distribution and Warehousing

N   Insurance

In summary, SPEEDE and ExPRESS work through ANSI ASC X12 procedures (1) to obtain consensus among all other industries involved in EDI to have
education standards accepted and approved as national standards and (2) to have
modifications to previously approved standards accepted and approved.

In EDI terminology, a standard that has been approved or recognized for
development is known as a transaction set. Table 9.1 lists those SPEEDE/
ExPRESS standards that have been assigned a transaction set number. The first
transaction set, the student educational record (TS 130), was approved as a draft
standard for trial use in February 1992. Three others—TS 131, TS 146, and TS
147—were approved in October 1992. The complete, specific details of these
four transaction sets are available in *A Guide to the Implementation of the
SPEEDE/ExPRESS Electronic Transcript* (SPEEDE/ExPRESS, 1994). Three additional transaction sets—TS 188, TS 189, and TS 193—have been recognized
by ASC X12 for development by SPEEDE/ExPRESS.

Table 9.1

SPEEDE/ExPRESS Transaction Sets Approved and Recognized by ASC X12 for Development (as of November 1994)

TS Number	Name	Description
Approved		
130	Student Educational Record (Transcript)	Communicates from registrar to receiver a student's academic record.
131	Student Educational Record (Transcript) Acknowledgment	Communicates from receiver of student's academic record to sending registrar an acknowledgment that the record was received.
146	Request for Student Educational Record (Transcript)	Communicates from one institution to another a request for a student's educational record.
147	Response to Request for Student Educational Record (Transcript)	Communicates back to the requesting institution that the request was received, but the receiving institution is unable to respond immediately with a student transcript (CCSSO, AACRAO, and NCES, 1993).

TS Number	Name	Description
Recognized by ASC X12 for Development		
188	Request/Response for Educational Course Inventory	Communicates from one institution to another a request for one, more, or all course descriptions and communicates the response back to the requesting institution.
189	Application for Admission to Educational Institutions	Communicates from sender to an admissions office a prospective student's application for admission.
193	Financial Aid Transcript	Communicates from financial aid office to receiver a student's financial aid history.

In addition, ASC X12 subcommittee F (Finance) has developed a number of transaction sets to support student loan activity. One, TS 190 (Enrollment Verification), was developed for use by postsecondary institutions to transmit enrollment verification data in EDI. TS 190 was selected as the pilot EDI implementation by a consortium of three North Carolina universities: the University of North Carolina at Wilmington, North Carolina State University, and the University of North Carolina at Chapel Hill. This transaction set, together with the emergence of the National Student Loan Clearinghouse, is expected to yield major efficiencies in the reporting of student loan enrollment verifications.

CONCLUSION: WHERE IS EDI IN EDUCATION HEADED?

Before consulting the crystal ball to predict where EDI might be headed in education, it is essential to explore further the question of why institutions would want to develop EDI applications. Another glance at Figure 9.5 provides some intuitive justification. As previously noted, EDI improves security, accuracy of data, speed in transmission, and service to students while at the same time reducing costs. The combination of these benefits should provide very strong motivation for educators to develop EDI capability.

It is easy to justify EDI development. The difficulty lies in moving from justification to implementation. Let us therefore examine the current status of EDI development in education and speculate upon where it may be headed.

AACRAO reported that as of March 1995, 604 institutions, organizations, and school districts in 39 states and four Canadian provinces were involved at some level of exchanging student records electronically, with involvement ranging from "planning discussions in progress" to "in production." By way of comparison, the January 1994 "SPEEDE/ExPRESS Activity List" had reported only 327 such institutions and organizations in 33 states and four provinces (Bainbridge, 1994). In slightly more than one year, then, the number of schools and colleges pursuing EDI had increased by 277 (85 percent), and the number of states increased by six (18 percent). In addition, the number of EDI professional presentations on the agendas at state, regional, and national conferences is increasing. The number of state and regional groups conducting EDI and SPEEDE/ExPRESS workshops is also on the rise. These workshops are in addition to the AACRAO workshop presented annually since 1990.

These data suggest that EDI development in education is headed in the right direction. Not only are developments continuing, but the pace is increasing as well. This reflects the early EDI experience in business and industry, namely, a slow start with rapid growth following.

In the midst of all of these positive signs, however, are two potential roadblocks that continue to impede EDI progress. One is the need for a *critical mass* of participants to realize a return on investment in developing EDI (Wermers, Patterson, and Scott, 1992). EDI is an electronic development of a type different from campus independent innovations. Unlike such developments as automated registration and automated degree summaries, EDI can be valuable and cost-effective only if other campuses have EDI capability. This is necessary to assure a volume of exchange that will make it financially feasible to implement. In this sense, EDI is no different from telephone or fax installations, that is, if you have the only one, with whom will you be communicating?

Like telephones and fax, the more EDI installations in existence, the greater

Figure 9.7
Critical Mass

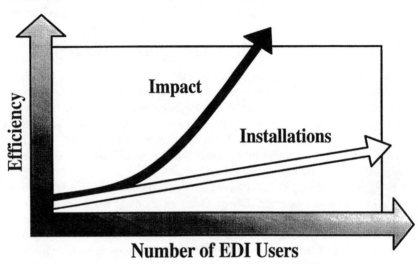

their utility and the more efficient transcript exchanges become. As illustrated in Figure 9.7, a linear increase in EDI installations results in an exponential increase in EDI impact. For example, if two Wisconsin campuses exchange transcripts electronically, some efficiencies, albeit small, will result. If all thirteen university campuses exchange via EDI, the efficiencies increase greatly. If all of the Wisconsin school districts begin sending transcripts electronically, the impact becomes enormous. However, one problem with the critical mass concept is that one may be tempted to wait until many already have EDI capability before investing in its development.

A different approach might be to identify those *critical few* to which a large number of transcripts are sent or from which the bulk of transcripts are received. These are the campuses/school districts to approach first as potential trading partners with which to work in developing EDI capability. As shown in Figure 9.8, just a few other campuses with the capability of sending/receiving transcripts electronically—if they are the right few—can result in major efficiencies without waiting for the critical mass to evolve. Thus, these "right few" can actually become the critical mass for each other. For some, a critical mass may be only one other institution (e.g., Arizona State University and Maricopa Community College; Brigham Young University and Ricks College); for others, it may be a few institutions (e.g., the Austin, Texas, school district and four universities); for large universities, the critical mass may be as few as two professional school admissions services, such as the Law School Admissions Services (LSAS) and the American Medical College Application Service (AMCAS).

Another example of the critical few concept can be illustrated by the Uni-

Figure 9.8
Critical Few

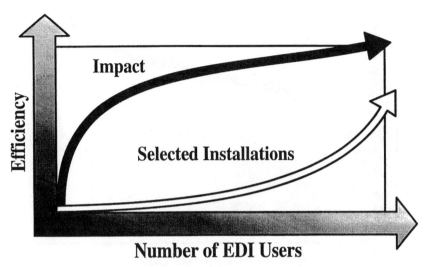

versity of Wisconsin–Madison graduate school. The graduate school has an enrollment of 10,000 students representing every state and most other nations. Initially, it was believed that EDI would need to be in place worldwide for it to be of major benefit in the admission process. A cursory glance at the volume of transcripts received from different institutions quickly dispelled that notion. Although students apply for admission from institutions worldwide, over 30 percent of the transcripts are received from the thirteen baccalaureate degree-granting campuses in the University of Wisconsin system. The "Big Ten" institutions contribute another 10 percent of all transcripts received. After identifying the next ten major feeder universities, it was calculated that over 50 percent of all transcripts received by the graduate school come from 33 institutions (see Figure 9.9). Almost all of these 33 institutions are either exchanging transcripts electronically now or in the process of developing EDI capability. In this example, thirteen sister campuses within the same university system actually provide the critical few. With each increment of a few other groups of institutions, efficiency can be increased exponentially.

Since the ultimate value of EDI capabilities depends on its development on many fronts, it is essential for each campus to identify its major trading partners (critical few) and move EDI from the idea stage to implementation. As the number of pockets of critical few developments increases, the critical mass will emerge rapidly.

The second potential roadblock is familiar to all. Inherent with each proposal for a new computer application is a degree of difficulty in having the proposal accepted by the decision makers on campus (Wermers, Patterson, and Scott,

Figure 9.9
University of Wisconsin–Madison Graduate School

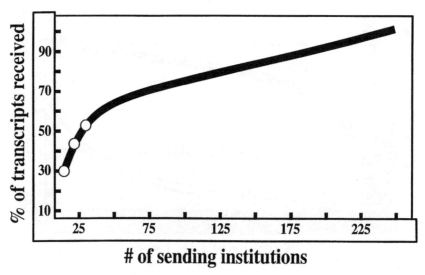

# of sending institutions

1992). Figure 9.10 suggests that two major factors contribute to that degree of difficulty: (1) the number of people/offices involved in (or affected by) the proposed implementation and (2) the financial resources required. As increases occur in one or both of these factors, the level of difficulty in implementing a new project increases. Figure 9.10 plots four electronic technology enhancements on a scale of difficulty on these two factors. The development and installation of an automated registration system rank high on both people involved and costs, as does automated degree summary development. Installation of a laser image system in a registrar's office would rank high on financial resources required but low on people/office involvement since it can be a project internal to one or a few offices.

Fortunately, EDI ranks low on both factors. First, developing electronic transcript exchange capability involves only three offices: the sending office (registrar), the receiving offices (admissions offices), and the information technology office. Second, costs to develop (purchase of EDI software; in-house mapping and programming) are substantially less than for the other three developments illustrated. More specific information on costs, as well as additional information on all aspects of EDI (i.e., technical requirements, costs, standards, institutions currently in production, steps to get started, etc.), is available from the AACRAO EDI coordinator, the AACRAO SPEEDE Committee, the NCES ExPRESS Task Force, and presentations at regional and national AACRAO meetings and at the various EDI and SPEEDE/ExPRESS regional and national workshops.

In conclusion, EDI is another conceptually exciting enhancement for registrars and admissions professionals. Although the term ''paperless office'' may be

Figure 9.10
EDI-Sell/Install Factors

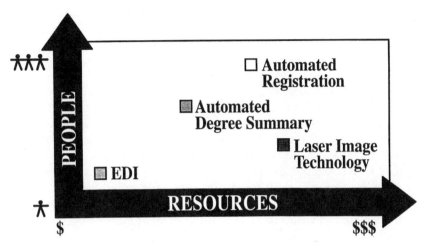

heard less and less, we see great progress in the use of electronic technologies that at least reduce our reliance on paper. This progress is evident with each implementation of a new electronic tool such as Touch-Tone telephone/voice response technology, student direct terminal access to both general institutional information and the student's own record data, automated degree summaries, laser image technology, and so on. Similarly, EDI as a tool to transmit academic records and other data provides many benefits over the current paper environment. However, the greatest benefit of EDI implementation occurs when it is integrated and bridged with other student service software to provide a complete service package.

Follow closely the scenario of a student transferring from one institution to another in the electronic world of doing business and imagine what each new step means for the student and for the offices involved: the student accesses the electronic admission application from the institution to which she is applying and keys her application onto the computer. Then, she directs the computer at her current institution to transmit her transcript. The transcript is sent and received electronically in the SPEEDE/ExPRESS standard. After the acknowledgment of receipt is sent, the transcript data are entered directly on the receiving institution's data system, without rekeying, and linked to the application data. The course data are processed on-line with the institution's automated transfer course evaluation system, at which time course equivalencies are assigned. The results of the transfer evaluation are then electronically passed through the automated degree progress summary system.

Now the student can access her records at the receiving institution by Touch-Tone telephone or personal computer (PC) and monitor the status of her application, the results of transfer evaluations, and requirements remaining for the degree. Of course, these same electronic tools will also permit her to apply and monitor the status of her applications for financial aid and housing. Although some human monitoring may be a part of the actual processes at each institution, theoretically and conceptually, the entire process—from the student's submission of an application for admission and request for transcript through inquiry about the result of a degree summary—can be done without human intervention or rekeying. That is exciting!

As this scenario demonstrates, we are continuing to acquire new tools in our electronic toolbox to better provide our many services to students. EDI is just one of these tools, but a very important one. The beauty of EDI is that all of the four basic ingredients necessary to develop electronic exchange of data are in place: most campuses have automated student data systems; the transaction sets have been developed and approved; vendor software products are available; and electronic networks are there for transmission. To develop EDI capability requires only that the sender and receiver work with the technical support staff in putting these ingredients together to work for all of us.

REFERENCES

Akerman, G. 1985. *Introduction to Electronic Data Interchange: A Primer.* Rockville, MD: GE Information Services.

Bainbridge, L. 1994. "SPEEDE/ExPRESS Activity List." Washington, DC: American Association of Collegiate Registrars and Admissions Officers.

Cannon, E. 1993. *EDI Guide: A Step by Step Approach.* New York: Van Nostrand Reinhold.

CCSSO, AACRAO, and NCES. 1993. *SPEEDE/ExPRESS: An Electronic System for Exchanging Student Records.* Washington, DC: National Center for Education Statistics.

Data Interchange Standards Association. 1994. *1994 DISA Information Manual.* Alexandria, VA.

Emmelhainz, M.A. 1990. *Electronic Data Interchange: A Total Management Guide.* New York: Van Nostrand Reinhold.

Evert, H. 1990. A day in the registrar's office circa 2003. *College and University* 65: 171–175.

Jones, B. 1990. Imagine . . . for admissions officers and registrars. *College and University* 65: 235–241.

Lonabocker, L. 1990. Security in the age of distributed processing. *College and University* 65: 203–212.

Neary, M. 1993. *Introduction to EDI and the SPEEDE/ExPRESS Implementation Guide.* Washington, DC: Committee on the Standardization of Postsecondary Education Electronic Data Interchange (SPEEDE), American Association of Collegiate Registrars and Admission Officers, and the Task Force on the Exchange of Permanent Records Electronically for Students and Schools (ExPRESS), National Center for Educational Statistics and the Council of Chief State School Offices. October.

Parfett, M. 1992. *What Is EDI? A Guide to Electronic Data, Interchange.* 2d ed. Oxford, England: NCC Blackwell.

SPEEDE/ExPRESS. 1994. *A Guide to the Implementation of the SPEEDE/ExPRESS Electronic Transcript.* Washington, DC: Committee on the Standardization of Postsecondary Education Electronic Data Exchange (SPEEDE), American Association of Collegiate Registrars and Admissions Officers, and the Task Force on the Exchange of Permanent Records Electronically for Students and Schools (ExPRESS), National Center for Educational Statistics and the Council of Chief State School Officers. May.

SPEEDE/ExPRESS Workshop. Conducted at AACRAO SPEEDE/ExPRESS Workshop, Simon Fraser University, Harbour Centre, Vancouver, British Columbia, Canada.

Stewart, J. 1992. The electronic exchange of student transcripts using the national ANSI ASC X12 Standard Format. South Campus, Miami-Dade Community College.

Wermers, D.J., Patterson, L.M., and Scott, T.J. 1992. SPEEDE simplified: The user perspective. *CUMREC Conference Proceedings*, 276–289.

10

Student Access
Record-Keeping Systems

Louise Lonabocker

INTRODUCTION

Ask students what frustrates them most about their college or university, and you're likely to hear, "long lines," "bureaucracy," or "being sent from office to office." In an effort to address these complaints, many campuses have begun learning about, and implementing, Total Quality Management (TQM) concepts. TQM strategies have enabled these institutions to engage in systemic thinking about the constant improvement of all processes that deliver value to customers and to organize work around the needs and preferences of those customers instead of within traditional departments. Walls are disappearing, and students, staff, and faculty are working together to design and deliver services in convenient, appropriate ways (Marchese, 1993). For example, the registrar's office may join forces with the student accounts office, the information technology department, and a group of students to design systems for course registration on Touch-Tone telephones or computer terminals, with account reconciliation via the entry of a credit card number.

Reengineering is another term used when basic assumptions about the way things are done are reexamined. The goal is to go beyond the automation of an existing process to design systems that fit the needs of the customer. Reengineering encourages designers to use technology to do things that are not already being done, to recognize a powerful solution, and then to seek the problems it might solve. The aim should be to cross boundaries between offices, increase efficiency, eliminate duplication of effort, locate decision points where the work is performed, and make use of appropriate technologies (Penrod and Dolence, 1991).

One outcome of the successful employment of progressive analysis and management models such as these has been a dramatic shift in the way many institutions now view their student information and record-keeping systems. Many institutions, for instance, now believe that within proper security restrictions, students should have open access to their records. This includes inquiry access to their records and also update access where appropriate. Update access should reside with the person or people providing the initial data or making decisions that result in the need to update a record. There should be no rekeying of data or approval by anyone who does not add value to the process. Distributing access and update functions to students has a number of advantages, such as timeliness and accuracy of information; reduction of forms, printing, and storage; and elimination or redeployment of data entry staff (Carson, 1987). Examples of transactions appropriately performed by students themselves include course registrations, degree audit requests, transcript requests, and address changes.

When reengineering or designing distributed systems for student access, the most successful and innovative institutions have wisely selected interfaces that are appealing and intuitive to students: telephones, computers, and automated teller machines. Examples of systems in place at several colleges and universities are described in this chapter. Many other institutions have, of course, implemented similar systems.

TOUCH-TONE AND VOICE RESPONSE TECHNOLOGY

Admissions and records personnel at Brigham Young University (BYU) and Georgia State University pioneered the integration of Touch-Tone telephone/ voice response technology with a registration system. BYU developed its system as an efficient and inexpensive way for students to register and introduced it in 1984. The university wanted a registration system that was convenient and simple, gave students immediate feedback, and provided up-to-the-minute information for departmental chairpersons and registration administrators. The immediate feedback gave students complete control over the course selection process and enabled them to select the teacher, time, and place for each course.

Students at Brigham Young register for classes by interacting directly with the microprocessor, Perception Technology's VOCOM. The VOCOM unit answers the telephone, interprets the tones, and sends messages to the host computer. The telephone keypad functions like a computer keyboard/terminal. Registration can be initialized or changed for any student. Students access the system by entering the telephone number given in the registration materials. After gaining access to the system, they use the numeric action code plus the five-digit class index code for each course. The system confirms the action and states the department name and course number. The VOCOM makes it possible to give voice responses for an existing on-line system that previously gave only visual responses. Linking the registration and VOCOM systems and programming took approximately 90 days of work by one programmer.

These pioneers had little to go on. Scripts had to be developed. No one knew how long an average transaction might last or how many calls a student would make. Today, thanks to advances in voice response scripting tools and host communication software, this technology is within reach of institutions that previously did not have the technical wherewithal to implement it.

Students using the system are usually provided with instructions and a worksheet for accessing the system. Students begin by keying in a personal access number (normally, their identification number or Social Security number) and their date of birth or personal identification number (PIN) for verification of eligibility to register. Students enter course requests using course index numbers; the system then informs them either that they are registered for the courses or that the courses are closed, canceled, or in conflict with other courses.

Special permission for closed or restricted courses can be handled in one of several ways. First, these exceptions can be processed manually, as was done in the past. Second, students can be given special, randomly generated one-time-use codes, which are distributed to departments prior to registration. The student enters the code, and the system verifies that the code is valid for the particular class requested. Finally, departments can enter permissions on a course authorization screen. A course and section-specific schedule code is entered along with the student's identification number. The approval is thus captured at the source, where it belongs, and students can complete their registration without additional intervention.

Institutions that wish to ensure that students have seen an adviser prior to registration may distribute via the adviser a registration access code, which the student enters when logging on. Some institutions issue new PINs each semester, again distributed through the adviser.

Voice response systems are usually preceded by campuswide publicity to students, staff, and faculty via letters and flyers, posters, buttons, videos, training sessions, and articles in campus newspapers. Some schools involve students in contests to design logos or to name the system. While registration usually has been the first application of Touch-Tone/voice response technology at most institutions, some have developed other applications using this technology. These include final grade dissemination; notification of missing items in admissions or financial aid; ticket sales for athletic events; and selection of a student insurance, meal, or parking plan. Students at some institutions can also use Touch-Tone/voice response systems to check course availability, sign up for a course wait list, review account balances, request an admission application, or charge tuition and fees to a credit card.

Credit card payments can be interactive, with the system used to verify the transaction with the credit card-processing center while the student is on the line. Payment is thus immediate, with funds deposited directly to the institution's account.

Today over 300 colleges and universities use Touch-Tone/voice response technology for registration. Institutions planning to develop similar systems will benefit from the American Association of Collegiate Registrars and Admissions Officers (AACRAO) publication *Touch-Tone Telephone/Voice Response Registration: A Guide to Successful Implementation* (Bell, 1993). The guide includes information about costs and benefits, preparing a proposal request, selecting a hardware vendor, developing and recording a script, selecting a voice, designing a registration work sheet, training staff, introducing and promoting the system, and preparing a video.

Voice response technology is ideal for students transacting business from work or home or even while on vacation. But there are several other proven ways to distribute access to student information. Several of these are now described.

AUTOMATED TELLER MACHINES

The automated teller machine (ATM) concept has gained widespread acceptance in the delivery of financial services. This type of equipment, without its cash-dispensing unit, can be equally useful for transaction automation. At Boston College, broad and open access to university databases—within security restrictions—is an accepted strategy. Boston College therefore developed a public access record-keeping system called U-VIEW, which allows students to access their own academic, biographic, account, and financial aid information. This system was inspired by a similar development at Indiana State University.

The first U-VIEW device was installed in August 1988. The U-VIEW system first made use of IBM terminals and later added consumer transaction terminals manufactured by Diebold. (Consumer transaction terminals look like ATMs without a cash-dispensing unit.) The first such device was installed in February 1989 outside the registrar's office. A magnetic strip on each student's ID card is encoded with the individual's ID number. This number identifies the student to the security system, permitting access to his or her own records. The ID card, which is also bar-coded with the student's identification number, serves as a passport with universal usage across campus for building access, check cashing, library privileges, and dining services.

The menu-driven U-VIEW system allows students to select transactions that display a wide array of academic and financial records, including the student's class schedule and grade information; address(es) and phone number(s); and status information about library, financial aid, or other appropriate accounts. Students can also use the system to request a degree audit report, to check on their registration appointment time or final exam schedule, or to obtain appropriate information about their academic adviser.

The machines can be restricted to visual displays and print transactions or used for transaction processing like voting in student elections, room selection, fee options, ticket requests, registration, and drop/add.

Consumer transaction terminals are durable and have many attractive features. These include character graphics to simplify instruction; function keys for faster transaction selection; and an 80-column, high-speed printer. Students must log off to recapture their ID card. The machines have the ability to retain lost, stolen, or invalid ID cards. They provide access to an array of information previously available only through a specific office and are reliable, requiring only normal maintenance like checking the paper supply and retrieving captured ID cards. The system has been well accepted by students, who use it routinely to access information.

These transaction terminals ensure greater confidentiality, because to access their records, students must insert a valid ID card, which serves as an authenticator, and their PIN. There is no "middle person" relaying the information. Students can query the machine often without feeling intimidated. To maximize the number of transactions processed, the system always displays a popular "item of the day" as the first item on the first menu. For example, at the end of the semester, "print grade report" is the item of the day (see Figure 10.1). Transaction terminals are busiest at the beginning of the semester, during registration, and after grade processing.

Students appreciate the print option, although there seems to be less concern about having a piece of paper than when distributed systems were first introduced. The printout is open-ended and is ejected after each print request. To protect student privacy, neither the screens nor the output contains the student's name or identification number.

Offering U-VIEW transactions on the ATMs was not a complicated process, because the information to be displayed resided on the mainframe. The technical support programmer assigned to the project spent a few weeks designing the menus and displays. Transmitting the data between the mainframe and the ATM was more of a challenge, requiring over a month of this person's time.

Hofstra University adopted a somewhat different approach, installing touch-screen student information kiosks available 24 hours a day at locations throughout the campus. The kiosks provide general information about the university to students, staff, and guests. General information about the university, such as a faculty/staff directory, the course schedule, and information about campus events, can be obtained at the kiosks. Students also have access to personal information, including their academic and financial records.

Yet another type of system is in place at Florida State University. Its Seminole ACCESS card uses magnetic strip technology to allow students to access financial and academic information on self-inquiry terminals, check out equipment in the recreation complex, control access to student job postings, use statewide ATM machines, and process debit transactions at merchant locations in the college community.

ATMs, voice response, and computer-based systems are complementary. ATMs quickly and easily display a limited set of functions, and the devices conveniently serve a resident population. Voice response technology, on the other hand, is ideal for part-time or commuter students who want to transact business from work or home or for resident students when they are away on

Figure 10.1
U-View: Logon and Menu Displays

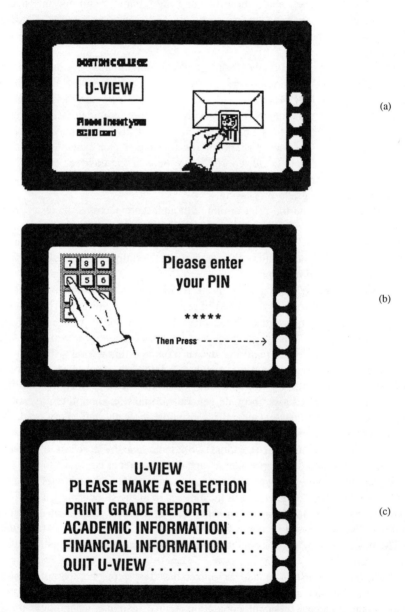

(a)

(b)

(c)

Figures (a) and (b) illustrate the logon procedure; Figure (c) shows the U-View menu.

Figure 10.2
Display Student's Customized Schedule of Courses

COURSE	L P A	TITLE	HRS	ASG	MAX	
MATH 4216A2	X X X	INTRO TO STATISTICS	3	19	35	PERMIT REQD
MWF10		DELIU				
MATH 4221A	X X X	PROBABILITY W/APPLS I	3	20	35	*OK TO ADD*
MWF10		CARLEN				
MATH 4260A	X X X	INTRO TO MATH STATISTICS	3	13	35	TIME CONFL
MWF1		TONG				
MATH 4263A	X X X	MATH STATISTICS II	3	22	35	CAN'T RETAKE
MWF9		TONG				
MATH 4266A	X X X	NONPARAMETRIC STATISTICS	3	7	35	CLASS RESTR
MWF11		SPRUILL				
MATH 4305A1	X X X	FINITE DIM VECTOR SPACES	3	29	35	MAJOR RESTR
MWF12		HEIL				

---Enter L to continue listing

vacation. Terminals or microcomputers provide students with an opportunity to conduct more involved transaction processing, such as searching the schedule of classes and constructing an entire course schedule.

COMPUTER-BASED SYSTEMS

While Brigham Young University and Georgia State University were refining their Touch-Tone/voice response systems, other schools were investigating alternative ways to allow student access to information stored on the host computer. Georgia Institute of Technology recognized that computer terminals provide a visual display not available on a telephone set and allow more involved transaction processing, like changing addresses, constructing a complex schedule with labs, or viewing the master schedule. Furthermore, its technical students were computer-literate, there were several student terminal clusters and a campus network already in place, and no additional hardware was needed to develop the system.

Georgia Tech introduced its menu-driven Student Access System in 1985. Students can log on to the system through the campus network; the state's university system computer network, called Peachnet; or the Internet. Once on the system, students can perform a wide array of functions. Registration transactions include the ability to check registration time and registration holds; view a customized master schedule of courses, including the maximum and actual size of each class (see Figure 10.2); participate in a registration practice session; and register for classes or drop/add. Course descriptions can be viewed, and the course schedule can be displayed in a variety of formats including a matrix or

Figure 10.3
Display Student's Schedule with Textbook Requirements

```
Enter command? db


Textbook information - current as of:  3/01/91 at      9:26:37


     1.    ECON4330A          REGIONAL ECONOMICS              3 P/F TTH1:30-3
            No textbook information available - Check at bookstore
     2.    HIST1001P          U.S. HISTORY TO 1865            3 L/G MWF1-2
            REQ MORGAN         PURITAN DILEMMA
            REQ SILVERMANAMERICAN HISTORY BEFORE 1877
            REQ OATES          ABRAHAM LINCOLN
            REQ DOUGLASS       NARRATIVE OF THE LIFE OF FREDERICK DOUGLASS
            REQ CUNLIFFE       GEORGE WASHINGTON:  MAN AND MONUMENT
     3.    MGT 4195D          INTEGRATED MGT PROBLEMS         3 L/G TTH9:30-11
            REQ BYARS          STRATEGIC MANAGEMENT

Time left:    5:56
```

weekly schedule or a version that lists the textbooks required for each class (see Figure 10.3). When students complete registration, the program displays the total fees for the quarter and allows the student to request a printed copy of the schedule and fee assessment. Academic departments have access to the system to clear holds and grant permission for closed and restricted courses.

The full range of student record transactions is available, including the ability to change addresses and telephone numbers, withhold the disclosure of directory information, display grades, request an official transcript, or view a transfer course equivalency table. Financial aid information is available, and students can use the system to complete a financial aid application or apply for on-campus housing. The system also allows students to vote in student government elections, complete various surveys, or leave a comment. This latter feature enables students to identify bugs, suggest improvements, or express their satisfaction with the system.

To log on to the system, students enter their nine-digit student identification number and a private security code. The first time a student logs on, the birth date is used as the security code. The system immediately prompts for a new code to be used for all future accesses and will not allow the new code to be the same as the birth date. Security provided by the operating system ensures that persons logged on can execute only the appropriate programs. Extensive logging is performed, which provides an audit trail of all database changes and statistics on system usage.

Terminal-based systems have been developed at many colleges and universities. Registration and drop/add are available on most of these systems. Access to other types of information varies from school to school.

Marquette University developed a menu-driven student access system called Window to complement its voice response registration system. Students use Window to review the master schedule for course availability for current and future semesters, to update addresses, and to withhold the release of directory information.

Using the Academic Information Management (AIM) system at Brigham Young University, students can register up to three semesters in advance, access the master course file, and request a list of classes taught by a specific instructor. When a course is closed, student requests for that course are logged by the system, and the name, class, and major of those students are given to the academic department teaching the course. If the department adds seats or sections, these students are contacted.

Students at Clemson University can use their Student Information Services (SIS) system to display general information, such as academic calendars and examination schedules, or personal information, such as transcripts or degree progress reports. One popular feature of the system is the class roll selection, which allows students to see a list of all students enrolled in each of their classes. For more information about these students, the campus directory is available on the system and can be used to retrieve student telephone numbers and electronic mail addresses.

The Clemson system also includes displays tailored for applicants to graduate programs at Clemson and for graduate students. Students applying for graduate programs can review the status of their graduate school application, including the receipt of forms and test scores. Enrolled graduate students have access to a display showing their advisory committee, the receipt of their curriculum and graduation forms, and the results of their comprehensive examinations.

ADAPTIVE TECHNOLOGY

Information technology can also be used to alter tasks to allow disabled students to function independently without relying on students or staff to accommodate their needs. At the Massachusetts Institute of Technology (MIT), an Access Technology for Information and Computing (ATIC) lab serves students with a variety of disabilities and injuries. Students may have disabilities that include physical, visual, hearing, neurological, or learning difficulties or injuries such as repetitive strain injuries, broken hands, or dislocated shoulders that affect their ability to access information on computers. Technologies used to accommodate persons with disabilities include voice recognition, enlarged font, voice synthesis/screen reading, braille embossing, alternative keyboards, word prediction, and head-pointing devices.

Public computing facilities should be accessible to students with mobility impairments, but these students will be able to access the system even more easily if it is available from a home computer. Students in wheelchairs can search the library catalog or use electronic mail to contact professors. Students with visual impairments can use microcomputers equipped with speech synthesizers and on-screen magnifiers. Textbooks can be scanned, then read to the student by the computer (Biderman, 1993).

THE INTERNET

The Internet is a worldwide communication link between educational institutions, businesses, and government agencies that offers informational services to students, including library catalogs, campus directories, job postings, documents on a vast range of subjects, schedules, weather reports, computer programs, electronic discussion groups, and bulletin boards.

The World Wide Web adds an intuitive interface to the Internet and has revolutionized the way information is accessed, presented, and searched. Many universities are now developing intranets, which are private networks inside an organization.

At Boston College all resident students have a data connection to the campus network and to the Internet. Students thus have access to the range of information and services available on the Internet, and to the campus network, which features an interactive catalog that simplifies browsing among program descriptions, course descriptions, department home pages, faculty research interests, course syllabi, and the student access system used for registration and information access. Other features allow students to calculate a cumulative average, find staff and student directory information, and link to other sites either within the university or on the Internet.

ELECTRONIC FORMS

Forms are ubiquitous. Some are simple, like an address change, and require no approval. Others, like course withdrawal, may require the approval of the instructor and the student's academic dean. Still others require action by the form recipient, such as assignment to a dormitory room. Finally, some, like a financial aid application, require a way to track the progress and status of the form throughout a lengthy process. Electronic forms can improve accuracy, timeliness, and routing. The information is captured at the source, each field can be edited as the data are entered, the form is transmitted to the recipient or approver, who can act on it immediately, and notification can be transmitted back to the originator or to other parties on campus.

At the Georgia Institute of Technology, the Student Access System allows students to complete electronically forms such as a financial aid application, a request for a room assignment change, or a transcript request. The completed transcript request results in faster processing because the student enters the data on-line. At Clemson University, students can sign up for placement interviews or request a housing room assignment.

At Boston College, students can declare or adjust a major electronically. If department approval is required, the transaction instructs the student to go to the academic department. After the student has discussed the major with the individual responsible for approving majors, that person approves the electronic change-of-major form, the student's major is changed on the student file, and notification is sent to the student's dean, who may then change the student's adviser.

FUTURE DEVELOPMENTS

The systems described in this chapter are only the beginning of what students will soon be able to accomplish. Statewide networks and links with feeder schools can be developed allowing students to complete admission or financial aid applications, check the status of their applications, send a transcript, view a transfer course equivalency table, or obtain a credit evaluation and degree audit. Using electronic data interchange (EDI), students will be able to apply, enroll, register, and pay from their desktop.

Expert advising systems can be designed that will prepare a graduation path with optimum sequencing of courses. Courses that are offered biannually could be scheduled in advance, and students could relax knowing that courses leading toward graduation will be completed on schedule.

Universal messaging allows messages originating in one medium to be automatically translated into another so that users get their messages no matter how they access their mailboxes. A grade change processed in the Registrar's Office could generate an electronic message to the student that could be delivered via text-to-speech synthesis when the student checks voice mail.

Chip card technology, which turns a student ID card into a computer, can be used to store and update information each time the card is used. The chip card can be used to track usage of facilities, control security system access, monitor the frequency of check cashing, record test and class attendance, or house a current transcript or degree audit.

CONCLUSION

The rapid evolution of information technology is changing the way students conduct research, communicate with faculty, and interact with administrative offices. The very definition of a computer has changed in recent years. Intimidating room-sized boxes have become user-friendly portable companions. Some industry pundits believe that in the future, the only distinctions among computers will be size and connectivity (Lewis, 1993). Whether it is the worldwide Internet, a national data superhighway, a desktop supercomputer, a pocket-sized personal computer, or a smart television, things will continue to change.

The challenge for higher education in the 1990s and beyond is to unleash the creativity of its students, instructors, and administrators through new services and features made possible by information technology. It will be essential to rethink the essence of our business in order to improve the quantity, consistency, and availability of the services that institutions of higher education provide. From inquiry to registration, from advisement through extracurricular life to graduation, the content and delivery of the collegiate experience are being re-defined every day. Reengineering for continuous improvement is one way of envisioning an institutional response to this challenge.

REFERENCES

Bell, Melanie Moore. 1993. *Touch-tone Telephone/Voice Response Registration: A Guide to Successful Implementation*. Washington, DC: American Association of Collegiate Registrars and Admissions Officers.

Biderman, Beverly. 1993. Putting information technology to work for persons with a disability. *CAUSE/EFFECT* 16(2) (Summer): 21–27.

Carson, Eugene. 1987. Distributed access to administrative systems. *CAUSE/EFFECT* 10(5) (September): 6–12.

Holcombe, John. 1990. The Student Access System: Georgia Tech's do-it-yourself project. *AACRAO Conference Proceedings*. Washington, DC: American Association of Collegiate Registrars and Admissions Officers.

Kramer, Gary L., and Rasband, H. Garth. 1993. Providing students critical academic planning assistance using academic Information Management (AIM): A remote access program. *CUMREC Conference Proceedings*. San Antonio, TX, May.

Lewis, Peter H. 1993. A glimpse into the future as seen by chairman Gates. *New York Times*, December 12.

Lonabocker, Louise. 1993. U-VIEW Plus for the MacIntosh: Registration using a graphical user interface. *AACRAO Conference Proceedings*. Washington, DC: American Association of Collegiate Registrars and Admissions Officers.

———. 1989. U-VIEW: A student public access recordkeeping system. *College & University* 64(4) (Summer): 349–355.

Marchese, Ted. 1993. TQM: A time for ideas. *Change Magazine* 25(3) (May/June): 10–13.

Norwood, Bill R. 1993. Evolution of smart card technology: Impact on higher education information systems. *CUMREC Conference Proceedings*. San Antonio, TX, May.

Penrod, J.I., and Dolence, M.G. 1991. Concepts for reengineering higher education. *CAUSE/EFFECT* 14(2) (Summer): 10–17.

Ridenour, David. 1988. Allowing students read-access to their own computer records. *CAUSE/EFFECT* 11(2) (March): 12–16.

Taveras, Luis, Swann, Marie, Craig, Kenneth, Hawkins, J. Michael, and Ingoglia, Eugene. 1993. Hofstra University's student information kiosk. *CAUSE/EFFECT* 16(1) (Spring): 23–32.

11

Electronic Imaging: A Tool for Document Management

Helen L. Perkins

INTRODUCTION

> It is no secret that in today's corporate, government, and business world, well-managed organization-wide information is a powerful strategic, economic, and competitive weapon. However, in most organizations today, much of that information is scattered through many offices, is contained in a mix of paper and computer media, is largely disorganized and under used, is frequently almost impossible to find, and is often not readily available when it is needed in decisionmaking. (Langemo, 1993, p. 3)

Ring a bell? Even records professionals who do not want to openly admit that documents are "frequently almost impossible to find" would probably agree that student information is "scattered through many offices," is housed in a mix of "paper and computer media" (not to mention microforms), is somewhat disorganized, and often is "not readily available when . . . needed."

While the onset of computer-based information systems has brought student records into the age of technology, it has provided only a beginning. It has given professionals a taste of electronic document management and a distaste for paper documents and has taught them, if nothing else, that they no longer have to be dependent on paper. Processes that for years were performed on paper are now much more efficiently handled by the computer, from admission decision making, to awarding financial aid, to posting of final grades and degrees. Student services throughout the nation are being streamlined so that students receive more accurate and timely information.

Most student services offices are familiar with, and use, microfilm media, and almost all have on-line computer systems for managing student data. However, on-line systems do not reduce the paper load that significantly. Offices still have reams of reports, applications and application support data, and other student information, such as drop/add forms, withdrawal forms, and course waivers and substitutions, to name a few. While many in the student services professions use microforms for archiving old, infrequently used documents, that is often their only application.

A technology similar to, but more versatile and sophisticated than, microfilm is electronic imaging. This technology, like microforms, quite simply takes a paper document, makes an image of it, stores the image, and reproduces it for later use. With electronic imaging the process of filming is replaced by scanning, film is replaced by an optical disk, and the special equipment needed to retrieve the microform is replaced by a computer and laser printer. The preference for electronic imaging over micrographics is twofold. First, its similarity to, and ability to integrate with, computer systems make electronic imaging compatible in offices already heavily dependent on computerized systems for the management of information. Second, electronic imaging is far more than a storage solution; it is, in fact, lauded by many to be the answer to efficient, comprehensive document management—the new work flow solution.

Given its potential and the attention it is receiving in the business world, it seems appropriate to examine the technology and determine how it can best be used in the student services profession. The remainder of this chapter describes in some detail the hardware and software components of a system, various systems and how they apply to different situations, current and future applications in the profession, benefits of such a system in the profession, issues surrounding the technology, and finally some advice from current users in admissions, records, and financial aid offices.

HARDWARE REQUIREMENTS

Electronic imaging systems have been referred to as "automated filing cabinets" that allow simultaneous, on-demand retrieval by one or more persons. In principle, any piece of paper in an office can be scanned, stored, and identified by a systematic on-line database. When needed, the information can then be printed on a laser printer or viewed on a computer monitor(s) by any number of persons. Systems range in size and cost from very simple, one-station, single-user units to large networked or mainframe systems that serve as department-wide or institution-wide solutions.

The hardware for an electronic imaging system generally consists of the following components: a personal computer, high-resolution monitor, scanner, disk drive, printer, fax, and magnetic tape backup. A network system would also include a jukebox, several servers—generally one high-powered one—and several to many PC work stations.

The personal computer can be either an IBM compatible or Macintosh. The power and memory requirements depend largely on the application. This piece is often already in place in an office but, if not, can be part of the purchased system or a separate purchase. The network system requires a rather powerful client server to hold the software, another less powerful one for the jukebox, and yet another for the scanner. However, the server for the scanner can double as a work station.

Since the primary purpose of the monitor is to display the image of the scanned document, it is desirable to have a high-resolution device with a screen large enough to view an entire document (sometimes legal size or larger) and at the same time a window containing the database, a message, or other information stored on the magnetic drive. The monitor often includes such features as roam, scaling, zoom, and rotation, all of which are useful when viewing very old documents and documents of different sizes and shapes.

The scanner, the most critical component of the system, is the device that converts the paper document into the digital imagery that the computer understands. Good scanners can handle various sizes and weights of paper and can be programmed to convert them to a uniform size for printing. They usually scan from 200 to 600 dots per inch, with 300 being an acceptable standard. There are low-end, midrange, and high-end scanners, varying in speed from less than one second per page to several minutes per page. The speed required will, of course, depend on the volume of pages to be scanned.

There are two types of scanners: flatbed and rotary. The flatbed operates just like a flatbed copier, scanning one side of a page at a time, with either a manual or automatic feed or both. The rotary scanner, used for high-speed production, operates much like some micrographic equipment, with the document pressed against a drum that rotates the document past the scanning array.

The scanner scans the image, digitizes it, and stores it on either an optical disk, compact disk (CD), or a PC or mainframe hard drive. For highly confidential information that is being protected against copying, WORM (Write Once, Read Many) disks are necessary. Optical WORM disks are available in either 5.25-, 12-, or 14-inch formats. For disks that contain information that can be altered, rewritable disks are acceptable. They are usually 3.5- or 5.25-inch. In the past a large mainframe or minicomputer system with a high volume of information to store used the larger-capacity 12- or 14-inch disks, while a microcomputer-based system with a smaller amount of information would use the 5.25-inch disk. However, the expanded capacity of the smaller 5.25-inch disk is fast making the others obsolete.

The storage capacity of the disks varies and changes constantly. Whatever is written about storage capacity one day is obsolete the next. In 1990 the capacity of the 5.25 optical disk was 940K; currently it is over 2 gigabytes (GB). The more common CD holds 640K; however, that is also changing rapidly. A new disk, the Digital Versatile Disk (DVD), soon to be released for data, will hold far more than today's CD. The video version of the DVD appeared in 1997 with promise of the digital version in late 1997. The new DVD by Maxell Corporation of America is advertised to have a single side capacity of 3.9 GB and the DVD-RAM, a rewritable version, will have a capacity of 2.6 GB on a single side with 5.2 GB on a double side.

It is hard to predict the number of disks needed to hold documents because the answer depends largely on the amount of information in a particular document. A dense document requires more space than one with few words and a generous amount of white space. For example, at one institution, eleven filing cabinets of transcripts filled both sides of five 5.25 disks and one side of a sixth (the disks' capacity was 940K). One disk (both sides) held approximately 14,000 transcripts or two full filing cabinets of transcripts packed tight, not in folders.

The optical disk is "played" or read on an optical disk drive, while the CD is read on an ordinary CD drive available for almost any computer. In the case of optical, there are usually at least two disk drives per system, one to hold the disk that has the information to be retrieved and one for disk backup. Often systems have more than one user and, therefore, require some sort of mechanism that will retrieve the particular disk that is needed at the moment. One method is to use large numbers of disk drives, one for each disk. This is acceptable for systems that have all of their information on five to ten disks. However, the most common method of retrieving disks from an unattended location is with a device called appropriately a "jukebox." Optical disks are stored in the jukebox, and when a particular disk is needed, an electronic arm retrieves it and puts it in the disk drive. CD jukeboxes are available, as are rotating packs that operate like the CD packs in CD audio players.

Besides being viewed, scanned images are often printed or faxed to another location. The printer can be any printer used in connection with a computer system. Usually a laser printer, it can be low- to high-end, as long as it can print the number of dots per inch (dpi) required for good quality (at least 300 dpi). It quite often doubles as a printer for the mainframe, network, or other applications on the PC that runs the imaging system. The FAX board allows the image to be faxed without its ever becoming a piece of paper again. A magnetic tape drive should be used to back up the system regularly. It might also be used to transfer information to another user.

SOFTWARE REQUIREMENTS

Essential to the operation of all this hardware is, of course, appropriate software, and there are any number of choices for the purchaser, including packages for all configurations of hardware: stand-alone PC, stand-alone Macintosh, networked PC and Mac, mainframes, and minicomputers. Some software is proprietary, that is, sold only as a part of a complete system, including the hardware. Some software may be purchased "off the shelf," that is, ready to work with hardware that can be provided by the purchaser or a system integrator who will put the package together. Some "frills" or add-ons may be different, but, by and large (although vendors would probably disagree), the systems all perform the basic tasks adequately.

The basic software includes the operating system, the application software, and the database management software. Some more sophisticated systems might include database integration software, forms processing software, or workflow/document management software.

The operating system controls the processing. The types most commonly available include DOS, Windows, Macintosh, OS/2, and UNIX. The selection of the operating system, of course, depends on the computer and the applications software.

The applications software supports the specific document-processing applications, such as scanning, printing, viewing, and so on. The applications software is the programming that actually causes the image to be read, digitized, and imprinted on a disk or magnetic drive. Information on the piece of paper must be converted to something a computer can understand, and the software manages this by changing the characters and white space on the document to bit-mapped images. (William B. Green has a detailed description of this process in his book, *Introduction to Electronic Document Management Systems*, 1993.) The applications software also allows the image to be retrieved for viewing, printing, or faxing and supports other features such as the ability to manipulate the on-screen image, search for words, zoom on hard-to-read data, rotate images to the side or upside down, and/or place from one to nine images on the screen at once.

In some systems one workstation houses all of the applications software and performs all of the tasks, while other systems may have separate workstations for functions such as scanning, printing, retrieving, and indexing. The purchaser may request application software to meet specific needs. For example, one institution wanted all of its transcripts to print on standard 8.5" × 11" paper, even though many different sizes and shapes were scanned. Some companies suggested reducing all of the transcripts on a copier prior to scanning, but the institution persisted, and finally several companies developed modifications to meet this requirement.

Integral to the application software is the database software that indexes the images. Generally, the fields on the database (index) are designated by the user in conjunction with the system vendor, so it is the responsibility of the user to define clearly the data elements necessary for retrieval and any possible reporting needs. The index for student transcripts, for example, would typically contain the student's last name (with several occurrences), first name, middle initial or name, Social Security number or personal identification number, degree, and date of degree. Some might include the birthday to narrow the definition, while others interested in expanding reporting options might select the major and/or minor.

The database can be integrated with other existing student databases and can be created by downloading information from the mainframe to the database. There are several options on the market which help eliminate the time-consuming task of entering data into the database. Optical Character Recognition

(OCR), Intelligent Character Recognition (ICR), and Optical Mark Recognition (OMR) can be incorporated into an admissions application, for example, where information is lifted from the application and automatically inserted into the student information system database. Bar codes are another method of avoiding data entry. The University of Southern California sends to all applicants a set of bar code labels which must be attached to all documents supporting the application process. When the documents are scanned, they are automatically attached to the student's already-created index. The University of Southern California uses bar codes. Each student is assigned a bar code and sent a page with bar code labels. Any document supporting the application, such as transcript, letters of reference, test scores, and so on, must have one of the labels attached. When the documents arrive, no indexing is necessary because the bar code refers the document to the student's already created electronic folder.

There is generally a separate database file for each application, for example, one for transcripts and another for grade rosters. It is important that the user be able to create, independent of the vendor, any future database files, since the vendor usually charges a large fee for an analyst's time to create new applications. While some of the earlier systems were protective of their database programs, most systems today have programs that are accessible and user-friendly, thereby giving the user the flexibility of adding future applications. These are enhanced by the user-friendly graphical user interfaces such as those employed by OS/2, Windows, and Macintosh. There is no reason that creating an index should be any more complicated than creating a file for labels in Word Perfect, for example. Therefore, buyers should be extremely cautious of any software that requires the presence of a systems analyst for the creation of a new application.

Networked systems obviously need software to run the network, and all of the major software packages, such as Novell and Apple Talk, are being used for this purpose. In some single-station systems, the various components are networked together, while in others there is simply an interface program in the computer. Usually, systems that run on networks also require some administrative software for the management of the files and the security of the documents. Complex jukebox systems attached to the network will usually require special software. Also, the network server will require an operating system of its own, which must be compatible with the existing network and also be familiar to computer services personnel. Network issues are complex and require the advice and examination of someone from the computer services area.

While all software systems perform the same basic tasks, most have features that distinguish them in some way from the others. Some vendors boast that nine images can be seen on a screen at one time. Others point to their rotation feature, or zoom. Some systems have software that can scan and convert microfilm directly from the film to optical disks. Other systems might offer sophisticated peripheral software for forms processing, database integration, workflow applications, or free-form text search. Any and all applications are good. However, the more complicated the system, the more expensive the initial outlay and maintenance, and the more difficult the implementation.

CHOOSING THE RIGHT SYSTEM

Many configurations of electronic imaging hardware and software are available, and today's purchaser can require that the system meet specific needs and standards. The systems can be either stand-alone, networked, or housed on a mainframe or minicomputer. The proprietary systems are generally dedicated to the exclusive use of document imaging applications, although some of them offer the flexibility of adding other PC applications such as word processing and spreadsheets. When only one person is using the system, the simplest stand-alone system may be adequate. Only one computer is needed, and the scanner, printer, and disk drives all run from it. One person sits at the computer and scans, views, prints, and indexes. This system is popular in smaller institutions that use it for specific purposes such as archiving. The University of Montevallo in Alabama, for instance, uses a single-station unit with two major applications: archiving transcripts and grade rosters.

When a system is decentralized and used by more than one person, PCs and/ or Macintoshes can be networked, or a mainframe or minicomputer can process the applications and store the disks. In networked versions one computer, or the client server, generally serves the scanner, one houses the application software, another serves the jukebox, and several serve as viewing/printing stations. Sonoma State University in northern California has a Macintosh networked system in admissions and records on Macintosh models. The core consists of three Macintoshes: one functions as a directory server, another functions as the optical server, and the third is the scanning station that can also serve as a retrieval station. The latter is connected to a flatbed scanner, and the directory server is attached to a jukebox that holds fifty 5.25-inch WORM cartridges. This is a prototype of a simple network system. A department or enterprise-side system would have more servers, more scanning stations or one very large scanning station, and many more work/viewing stations.

The mainframe and minicomputer versions—sometimes referred to as centralized or host-based systems—support all components with as many viewing stations as there are terminals. The mainframe versions generally use large disks, a jukebox, and many terminal servers for retrieval of information. Both the mainframe and networked systems often support applications other than electronic imaging. Often the mainframe student information systems are integrated with the imaging systems to create a seamless work flow environment.

Systems are packaged by vendors in several different ways. The proprietary system comes with all components in place. The computer, scanner, disk drives, and printer all bear the name of the vendor, even though they are usually manufactured by another company. Usually, a proprietary system does not allow use of any existing equipment. This type of system was very popular in the early stages of the technology, when most purchasers were so unfamiliar with the hardware and software that they were unable to understand how existing equipment could be used in such a system. This type of system is still popular with users who need a complete system and maintenance agreement on all hardware and software, that is, users who do not have much internal support. Another reason a system might be proprietary is that it uses technology specific to it. One of the most affordable systems of this sort is the Can-O-File by Cannon, which is in use at several institutions, including the University of Houston–Clear Lake, Northern Arizona University, Clinton Community College (Iowa), Dixie College (Utah), and Jackson State University (Mississippi).

The most popular systems today, however, are "open" ones that are able to use existing hardware or that allow the purchaser to make a separate hardware purchase that can result in savings. The vendor is primarily interested in selling the software that runs the system and hopes to supply some of the hardware and a healthy maintenance contract. Northeast Louisiana University purchased a software package that included some hardware. However, on its own it purchased four IBM PCs, which are connected by an IBM token ring network. One computer serves as the database server; a second, similar model serves as the optical server, which drives an NKK jukebox—part of the software purchase—with other PCs serving as scan/index/retrieve stations. Some institutions, like Troy State University in Montgomery, have started with a one-station MIMS 3000 expandable system, which they hope to eventually use as part of a network plan. This is a popular approach at institutions which have enough money for a beginning, with plans for more funds in the future. In this scenario, an open-architecture system is imperative.

Open architecture systems also use software that easily integrates with other software and allows third-party software to run against the system. For example, to run a report from an imaging system, a user could select to employ a familiar reporting program rather than one already configured into the system. Or, if large documents are scanned into the system, a complex text search program can be attached. Open architecture systems also have the capability of automatically moving documents out of the imaging software and into another application, like a word-processing program.

It is possible to apply a do-it-yourself approach to assembling a system; however, there are companies—brokers or integrators—that will put the components together to a buyer's specifications. It is important that the purchaser make sure that the company has been in the imaging business for some time, is reputable, and is likely to be in business in the future. At request for proposal time, a company profile should be requested.

When selecting a system, it is important to consider the following. Systems with open architecture are generally better investments than proprietary systems because they give the user the flexibility to use existing hardware and to expand in the future if needed. Since most of the data handled in student services offices is confidential, the system must have various levels of security. WORM disks must be used for documents that do not allow for any changes, such as transcripts. Training, service, and support are all related issues, and any lack of them by a vendor should signal the purchaser to "back off." The vendor's reputation is critical. Some software companies, integration companies, and even some proprietary companies have gone out of business after barely having begun. Buyers should concentrate on companies with long years of experience in imaging or a related field.

CURRENT APPLICATIONS

The uses of electronic imaging in admissions, records, and financial aid offices are limitless. That is, they are limited only by money, imagination, and an innovative spirit. While this author originally thought the "paperless office" would be a reality by the end of the 1990s, unfortunately, this now seems a bit overzealous. However, even though the technology has not lived up to its first "press," it has made a significant difference in some institutions of higher learning across the nation, and it will continue to do so with the addition of forms processing, workflow, and document management tools.

Clearly, one of the greatest potential uses of the system was first perceived to be the archiving of transcripts. Many institutions that did not have their transcripts backed up on any type of microform were attracted to the new technology as an easier way to create a backup. Moreover, those institutions that were already using microforms saw electronic imaging technology as a more streamlined alternative. The practice is generally to archive transcripts of records prior to those on an on-line system. For example, one institution in Alabama archived its approximately 75,000 transcripts (front and back) in six months, using one full-time employee and one half-time employee. It took one person approximately two and one-half days to archive one full filing drawer when that person did nothing but scan and index.

One reason registrars like the system is that it looks like the student information systems they are currently using. One institution in northern California, for instance, has its optical system integrated with its student information system, and it is transparent to the user whether he or she is requesting a transcript from the imaging system or from the on-line system. The user simply requests a transcript, and the integrator discerns which system to use. Programs can be written so that the transcripts all come from the printer in one size, even though several different sizes may have been scanned in.

Another popular use in the records office is electronic storage of grade rosters. Even though the grades are permanently stored on most student information systems, most registrars want to keep a copy of the original grade roster in the event questions arise in the future. An imaged version serves as a replica, which includes the instructor's signature. After scanning, the paper roster can be disposed of.

The University of Houston–Clear Lake Records Office uses its system to meet the office goal of purging the records of students who have not attended the university for five years. Personally identifiable documents are shredded after storing on an optical disk system only those documents determined to have some usefulness to the university for a specified period of time. Such documents include grade rosters, statistical reports, and transcripts of students inactive for over ten years.

Some registrars scan in transfer transcripts, drop/add forms, withdrawals, course substitutions or waivers, and any other information related to the student's enrollment. According to one records official, a typical student's file contains 20 pieces of paper, but this paper is often scattered in several filing systems in an office. By using an electronic imaging system, these paper documents can be scanned onto an optical disk or other acceptable media, "attached" to the student's file in the database, and noted in the index. This information subsequently can be gathered together by means of a system called "foldering," which creates for each student a "folder" containing an electronic duplication of all the paper transactions accumulated by a student throughout his or her career. This is very useful at graduation audit time, when the information can either be printed out for the graduation auditor, transferred to a disk, or put on the magnetic drive to be used on a network.

Electronic imaging systems are also extremely popular in large admissions offices, where considerable space is needed to temporarily store admission information needed for the admissions decision process. Typically, paper documents such as applications, transcripts, letters of reference, test scores, and any other supporting documents are stored in student folders, which counselors must check out in order to participate in the admissions decision process.

Such was the case at the University of Southern California when this institution decided to purchase its first imaging system, which enabled admissions counselors to pull up their lists of applicants for review and access all of their records electronically. Counselors no longer had to check out folders, and several could be working on the same student record simultaneously. Southern Cal also had a FAX Gateway, which automatically scanned faxed applications, the first of which was received in the fall of 1993. This technology, which might be new to many institutions today, soon became obsolete at Southern Cal, and personnel there began looking for a more streamlined system, which was installed in 1996. Among the new technologies employed is the use of barcodes assigned to each student upon receipt of application.

Although admissions offices do not have the same long-term storage problems as records offices, valuable space can be regained by eliminating the need to create a paper folder for each applicant. Above all, a more streamlined and efficient approach to handling admissions data can be developed which gives immediate access to personnel who may be answering the telephone or walk-in inquiries. Further, by taking advantage of the newer and more advanced OCR, ICR, and OMR systems, admissions personnel can cease the tedious task of entering demographic data on applicants.

Financial aid offices appear to be among the hardest hit when it comes to paper. The financial aid office at the University of Texas began addressing this problem in 1989 and installed an electronic imaging system in August 1990. According to personnel in that office, the system paid for itself the first year in the decrease in student help needed to manage the paper. Like many other financial aid offices, the University of Texas personnel decided that rather than recapturing the past, they would concentrate on the future. Thus, they began to enter only the current—1990–91 and 1991–92—files. They hope to eventually place a Macintosh computer on the desk of each of their 60 full-time employees in order to make access to the system even more convenient in the future.

After initial projects such as archiving transcripts, grade rosters, financial aid records, and admission support information, some offices have expanded into scanning documents such as systemwide regulations. For instance, in 1992 at Sonoma State University, all of the systemwide regulations were scanned, indexed, and linked to a free-form text-searching system. The dean of admissions and records describes one great benefit of this application: "Ironically, our adding these documents proved to be a brilliant stroke because when we were audited by our system-wide auditors, we had all of the documents that they were looking for in MARS [Sonoma's system]. We simply put them at a retrieval station, gave [the auditors] five minutes of instruction, and turned them loose. They were able to find in seconds the documents that would have taken hours to find in our old environment" (Frank Tansey, 1994).

The Sonoma University catalog is also on the system, along with other policies that relate to a student's career. According to the vendor of this system, the free-form feature allows "multi-word, proximity, wild-card, logical, complex, and nested searches," with an additional feature "which allows a search on any word resembling the target word. The feature integrates easily with the document imaging system allowing the user to view the actual page of the document containing the searched word(s)."

Document *management* is the key to effective use of an electronic imaging system. No matter what the application, when an office has determined that it cannot contain the paper any longer nor bear the burden this accumulation of paper places on its clientele by contributing to poor service, that office needs to begin concentrating on managing the documents rather than being managed by them. Such was the case at Northeast Louisiana University. With 425,000 total pages to be archived, a total of 140 file drawers of documents, and an excess of 200 retrievals daily for these records, it was obvious that something had to be done in the records office at that institution. They were out of space and bogged down with making approximately 4,000 to 5,000 document copies each month, to say nothing of retrieving and replacing the documents in a paper-filing system. After extensive study, a committee appointed by the president recommended an optical filing system.

More and more offices are facing similar problems and seeking solutions, not only because of the space that can be saved but, perhaps more important, because information can be retrieved and disseminated more efficiently and quickly to one or more destinations simultaneously. This can greatly improve service to students in an age when total quality management and continuous quality improvement are foremost on the minds of most administrators.

BENEFITS OF ELECTRONIC IMAGING SYSTEMS

If the uses are limitless, then so are the potential benefits of the electronic imaging system. Certainly, the fact that it rids offices of much paper is among the greatest benefits. Electronic imaging frees up valuable space by dispensing with the need for large-volume filing systems. Electronic document storage also aids in the protection of our environment by not creating duplicate copies of paper with more paper, which not only uses more trees but creates a future disposal problem. JoAnn Constantini, in an article in the *Records Management Quarterly* (1994), states the following on the subject:

At last we hear people concerned about things being environmentally sound or talk of reuse of materials to eliminate mindless waste. Thus, the idea of continuing to fill warehouses with paper documents which eventually are shipped off to landfills is preposterous! The consistent increases in paper prices have begun to erode our love affair with paper. Companies are now indicating a preference to invest in integrated systems rather than to support the continuing increased costs of paper and the subsequent costs of its movement, storage, and destruction. (p. 28)

Most student services offices need space, but the soaring cost of building has made it difficult, if not impossible, for some institutions to avoid overcrowding. Clearly, eliminating the storage necessary for the large amounts of paper required in admissions, records, and financial aid offices would go a long way toward creating much-needed space. Sonoma State University was faced with a serious space problem when it increased enrollment and applications by 50 percent over a five-year period. After putting documents from nine lateral file cabinets on optical disks, valuable space was regained.

Many support electronic imaging systems because of the easy and quick retrieval features. Certainly, it is easier and quicker to pop up an image on the screen (and print or fax it if necessary) than it is to locate a document in often overcrowded filing cabinets. Moreover, this retrieval advantage enables professionals to provide faster service to their clients—students, faculty, advisers, and administrators.

A third major advantage is the potential of shared data, with multiple users able to access the same data simultaneously from different locations. Graduate school offices, for instance, can easily access data on undergraduate applicants from their same institutions; admissions counselors can share applicant data among themselves and with the financial aid office, academic advisers, records office personnel, and others. Northern State University in South Dakota took a campus-wide approach and initiated an ambitious plan to link advisers throughout the campus to a new student information system and electronic imaging system. This approach allowed advisers not only to see online data on the SIS system, but supporting documentation on the electronic imaging system. A system such as this virtually eliminates the need for adviser folders.

Fourth, the advantages of the document itself cannot be overlooked. The print quality is excellent, and it can be reproduced on any type of paper. The viewed document can be manipulated to zoom, rotate, scroll, or display several pages at once. The database has the capability of housing messages, such as "holds" on transcripts. The document is more secure, particularly if it is stored on WORM optical disks, as the scanned image cannot be erased or tampered with.

Most systems have built-in fax capabilities, and as SPEEDE/ExPRESS becomes the norm for transmission of transcript data, linkages will most likely be developed to facilitate the optical storage of images transmitted through that medium.

Last, but certainly not least, is the beneficial effect an electronic imaging system can have on the office staff. In most offices current records are computerized, and many staff members sit at colorful, easy-to-use computers accessing data. Unfortunately, there are still those who have to go into dirty vault areas and retrieve worn, often dirty paper documents and reproduce them on a copier. Nobody likes to do it, especially when a document has been misfiled. On an electronic imaging system, documents are never lost, and no one spends days searching for that one person whose name is "Smith" but whose record is filed under "Jones."

ISSUES RELATED TO ELECTRONIC IMAGING

Given all these obvious benefits, why is electronic imaging still so rarely found in student services offices across the nation? Only a few years ago, electronic imaging was lauded as the revolutionary technology that would carry admissions, records, and financial aid offices into the twenty-first century *without paper*, and yet today many still remain skeptical. The reasons are varied and center around five major issues: cost, archivability, stability/portability, standardization, and legality.

In a profession often strapped for money, electronic imaging is an expense administrators may find hard to justify. The first electronic imaging systems were extremely costly, and the mere figures frightened away potential users. Recently, however, several new developments have made systems more affordable. The technology has become more accessible and more competitive so that, for instance, a turn-key system for a small application can now be purchased for around $12,000. The advent of systems that use off-the-shelf software, allowing buyers to either purchase their own equipment or use existing equipment, has also resulted in significantly decreased costs. One vendor advertises a product, which includes an 8-meg 486SX PC with monitor, scanner, laser printer, image processing board, OCR software, and WORM drive, for the "reasonable price" of $15,000. That is indeed reasonable when five years ago similar systems were selling for $45,000 to $55,000. Costs for larger systems, however, can soar into the millions for organization-wide systems, with medium-size centralized systems starting at around $80,000, including software and hardware.

Lease or lease-purchase options are now available on most systems, thereby giving the purchaser an alternative to a large onetime outlay of money. Additional costs to the user often include a maintenance agreement (usually about 15 percent of the purchase price per year) and the cost of optical disk or CDs, which vary in price according to the size, material, and type.

Archivability is a big issue with registrars, particularly when they use the medium for storing and retrieving transcripts. As of this writing, there is still no definitive answer as to the life expectancy of the optical disk itself. Claims range from 10 to 100 years (the latter by Sony, manufacturers of a dual-alloy disk). However, the technology is so new that these claims are based on accelerated aging tests conducted by the manufacturers and not scientific agencies. The variety of recording materials, methods, and equipment also makes it difficult to compare the manufacturers' studies. Registrars are naturally hesitant about archiving transcripts on a medium that does not have a proven life span. However, this ought not be an insurmountable problem: since the disks are affordable, it is not unreasonable to transfer the imaged documents to new disks 10 years after the manufactured date. Hopefully, the industry will develop standard life expectancies by the time it is necessary to transfer again, that is, in approximately 20 years.

A more critical problem to most is the stability or life expectancy of the hardware, not only because hardware wears out but because newer and better equipment is manufactured every year. Most assume that the optical disk will outlive the hardware; therefore, the question of portability becomes crucial in the purchase of a system. One solution is to purchase equipment the user understands, that can be easily upgraded or replaced, and that will handle the software and optical media. This problem might be minimized by using CDs since CDs are typically read on standardized drives. It is also important to select equipment and manufacturers that have a history of offering backward compatibility for at least one generation of the product line so that the user has the opportunity to upgrade. This problem is not unlike the evolution of word-processing programs. Reliable manufacturers typically offer backward compatibility to a previous version, being careful to ensure that users can make an easy transition to newer and better technology. Hopefully, the same consideration will come from the electronic imaging industry.

Standardization has been another big issue since the inception of electronic imaging. Users have been concerned that there are no standard disk size, no standard disk medium, no standard disk drive, no standard configuration of software, no standard language: no standards, period! The disk drive for one system probably will not play back a disk from another, and the computer-based index may or may not integrate with a second system if one becomes obsolete, or the manufacturer goes out of business. In the past, adding a second system or moving a current system to a new one could be virtually impossible since nothing on the systems matched. However, most viable products today are on open architecture systems that are generally portable and compatible. Some offices, previously using a proprietary system, are moving to the more open architecture systems, thus creating a system that is compatible with existing hardware and software. The vendor of such a system has the ability to convert the old optical disks to the new format, thus eliminating much of the problem of standardization. Systems which use CDs have a more stable environment because the CDs and disk drives are governed by an international standard which makes them compatible. In other words, generally any CD can be played in any CD drive. However, this does not mean that the index and its linkage to the image will be preserved, only that the images can be viewed from one CD drive to another. The database software determines how the index is tied to the image. Some outsource companies today are simply scanning old records to CDs and supplying an alphabetical listing of the contents of each disk. The viewer has only to search for the name on the appropriate disk. Some institutions are considering using this type of technology for long-term back-up storage only.

There is also the question of interfacing with other archiving technologies. Great strides have been made by companies that support micrographics and optical disks to integrate the two systems, and lately the technology has expanded so that microforms can be scanned without first having to produce them on paper.

Perhaps the largest issue is legality. Documents from admissions, records, and financial aid offices are often subpoenaed, and the admissibility of an optical image in court remains unclear to many. Briefly, there are three questions to consider: (1) is this the best evidence? (2) has the document been maintained in the regular course of business; that is, do you usually produce documents from this system? and (3) is the document authentic?

The rule of best evidence requires that an institution provide the best evidence available, and, if a transcript is requested, for example, the best evidence is the best legal copy of that document that can be produced. For years documents have been photocopied from the original paper or from some microform or printed directly from a computer and forwarded to the courts, so the question of admissibility of an optically stored document seems almost ludicrous to this writer and has been referred to as "whimsical" by another (Constantini, 1994, p. 27).

Second, the document must be produced for the courts just as it usually is in the regular course of a workday. Therefore, if all transcripts from a given period are produced from optical disk, the ones for the courts may be also.

Finally, the document must be authentic, which, of course, is not a new issue. The document coming from the electronic imaging system is as authentic as the document previously scanned into it. Therefore, the question of authenticity is raised on the front end of the transaction, not the final output. Robert F. Williams, one of America's leading authorities on the issue of legality of documents, says that no one "is about to mount a serious challenge" to the legality of documents produced from an electronic imaging system (Langemo, 1993, p. 8).

While the concerns and issues previously described are legitimate, there has perhaps been an overreaction among records officials in higher education. Since institutions of higher education are typically conservative and must always be accountable to the public, caution is perhaps natural. However, the need for better document management makes it imperative that our profession take a serious look at electronic imaging as a viable option and cease the debate over the issues. If student services professionals had dragged their feet over computerization and its lack of standardization and legality, students might still be registering on legal-size notepads and receiving typed grade reports. If microfilm and microfiche had not been accepted, some institutions might still have rooms and even buildings full of paper documents.

WORDS OF ADVICE

Some persons from institutions that have already purchased imaging systems offer the following advice when making a consideration for your institution.

1. Make sure your office has a plan for the retention and disposal of records. Such a plan provides the guidelines for long-term archiving and short-term record storage, defines who needs access to files and how often, and points the way to the type of system needed. The University of Houston–Clear Lake performed an extensive study of its records retention and disposal plan prior to initiating a search for its system. (A copy of the plan can be found in Perkins, *Electronic Imaging in Admissions, Records and Financial Aid Offices*, 1996.)

2. Analyze the uses of the system, including possible future expansion. Talk with offices that might one day want to network with your system to make sure you select a system with enough expansion capability. When the records office at the University of Kansas requested approval to purchase new microfilming equipment, personnel reviewing the request determined that there might be a better solution, especially when they concluded that they needed more than just a system in the records office. In fact, they decided that they wanted capabilities for retrieval stations in each of their major offices (records, admissions, financial aid, and the placement center).

3. Study the issues. Books and articles are readily available in any library or through interlibrary loan. Attend seminars, if possible. Do not be discouraged if your quest takes a long time.

4. Develop a detailed proposal, making it specific enough that you get what you want. Ask other institutions for their specifications. Discuss the plan with the administration. Talk with a variety of vendors, requiring them to demonstrate not only their product but also how it can meet your specific needs. If possible, visit locations using the equipment.

5. Finally, make your choice and begin work on a thrilling project that will literally change the face of your office.

Constantini (1994) affirms that "traditional records management is virtually dying!" According to her, "the fact that we have made our way, where we have managed billions of documents without the benefit of automation, is impressive, at best, but no longer acceptable" (p. 27). The profession has, in a way, answered Constantini's challenge with sophisticated on-line computer systems that perform many of the admissions, financial aid, and records offices functions. However, there are still new ground to be broken and mountains of paper to be conquered. Coupled with forms processing, workflow, and document management, electronic document imaging may play a very significant role in meeting these challenges.

The industry's claim that information is just a keystroke away is inviting to the student services profession both for the relief it gives the office staff and the more efficient service it provides to our clientele. Faxes and PCs, once the objects of much speculation and suspension, are today universally accepted means of data management. By the time you read this, perhaps electronic imaging will be too!

REFERENCES

Constantini, Jo Ann. 1994. Survival skills for information professionals in the decade of turbulence. *Records Management Quarterly* 28(1): 26–30.

Green, William B. 1993. *Introduction to Electronic Document Management Systems.* New York: Harcourt Brace Jovanovich.

Langemo, Mark. 1993. A rationale for and the fundamentals of electronic imaging systems. *Records Management Quarterly* 27(3) (July): 10.

Perkins, Helen L. 1996. *Electronic Imaging in Admissions, Records and Financial Aid Offices.* Washington, DC: American Association of Collegiate Resistrars and Admissions Officers.

Pomplun, J. 1996. Document imaging as an advising tool. Presentation given at CUMREC Conference, Nashville, TN.

12

Training in Automated Systems

Laura M. Patterson

TRAINING AS A CORPORATE PRIORITY

The infusion of technology into the instruction, research, and administrative processes in American higher education has occurred gradually over the past 30 years. Universities and colleges have invested heavily in technology, making it a fundamental part of the infrastructure. Since technology is so basic to the university's existence, the rapid pace at which technology changes has created significant management challenges for administrators, faculty, and executive officers. These complex management issues, coupled with the forces external to the university for higher levels of fiscal accountability and a more responsive learning environment, demand that institutions plan strategically in the development and deployment of their information and technology resources. In order to realign our institutions to ensure a return on the huge investments being made in information systems, the strategic response must recognize and address the human response to the merging of technology into the jobs and processes of the institution. Training in information technology must be part of an institution's strategy for the future.

A first and obvious reason training in automation must become a priority for universities involves the need to keep staff current in the systems, technologies, and tools employed in the organization. The integration of technology into existing jobs and the creation of new jobs to manage information and technology represent major changes in student services and records management. Universities invest heavily in computerized systems for communication, data management, research support, instructional technology, and administrative support. Consequently, employees in a wide range of jobs and at all levels of the organization are faced with the need to learn to use computer hardware and software.

Systematic training available at the appropriate time and level is important for preparing new employees to meet performance expectations and to become productive as quickly as possible. Continuous, systematic training also is necessary to enable experienced staff to overcome job obsolescence and to prepare them to meet future job requirements (Gist, Rosen, and Schwoerer, 1988).

A second reason training in information technology systems is essential to the future of organizations is that it is both an effective and necessary response to external forces that often decrease budgets while simultaneously increasing demand for the services. Doing more with less and doing it better are expected during times of decreasing budgets, downsizing, and organizational restructuring. Fast, elegant systems are essential to our competitive, demanding environment. Staff must be well trained in the systems they are using in order to exploit the capabilities of technology to deliver the immediate, complete service that our clients expect to receive and that we wish to deliver. Moreover, as the delivery of instruction changes to incorporate distance education, just-in-time learning, and other new modes and methods, the delivery of administrative services also must change. The delivery of service already has become linked to the institution's technology infrastructure and will become even more so in the future. Thus, the university's workforce must be skilled at working within a rapidly evolving information technology environment.

Few university administrators would disagree that the exploitation of the information technology infrastructure and the automation of administrative processes are critical for the model of service delivery of the future. Yet, the impact of technology and automated processes on staff development and training often receives little attention. Training is one of the most critical steps in the implementation of new technology, but it often receives the least planning, attention, and financial support. It is a thankless and painstaking task and often pales beside the glamour of the high-tech bells and whistles of the system being implemented. However, without an effective and appropriate training component, even the most sophisticated information system is destined for failure. The success of a systems implementation effort is often directly tied to the effectiveness, flexibility, and creativity of the supporting education and training programs. But far too often this aspect of systems implementation is ignored, and the university acceptance and use of the system directly suffer. Lack of acceptance and use of a system is expensive and wasteful, almost always results in lost productivity, and may represent a lost opportunity for advancing the institution's strategic goals.

During the era of centralized, mainframe computing few employees actually had access to automated information systems. Systems often were difficult to use and required special skills. Access to systems required the user to be in a specific physical location accessing a terminal restricted to a particular function. The users of information systems in universities were typically in two groups: researchers and administrators. Researchers were the first computer users on campuses, and they utilized information systems for storing and analyzing data.

As administrative systems became automated, trained experts in service offices such as admissions, the registrar, and the bursar were considered the users of the institution's information systems. These users typically received training from system developers at the time a system was implemented. After that, new employees in these departments were trained by the other user experts in the office. The experts typically used the system for conducting the university's business processes, but they usually relied on paper output to complete their business requirements or to provide data or information to other administrators who requested it.

The proliferation of microcomputers, high-speed networks, and personal productivity tools on the desktop has significantly expanded the potential-user community in our institutions. The computing environment has changed, and many industries have shifted to new ways of doing business that put control in the hands of the customer. The explosive growth of the number of users on the Internet, coupled with the availability of intuitive communication software, is likewise changing the delivery of both instruction and academic support services in higher education. At many colleges and universities students have been given direct, electronic access to data and services for many administrative processes such as applying for admission, registering for classes, receiving grades, maintaining demographic information, and accessing publications. This widespread use of microcomputers and the expanded data communication capabilities have created a different type of user at our institutions, namely, one who expects to employ a variety of media and systems to obtain services or complete job duties. This new class of user expects fast, professional support for the software and systems being used.

Automated, institution-wide systems and enterprise-wide data stores are fast becoming an integral part of the resources needed in the delivery of service and the execution of job duties at all levels and facets of our institutions. As students' expectations for immediate service increase, and pressure from the public for increased accountability continues to mount, executive officers, managers, student support personnel, faculty, and clerical staff all expect to receive immediate access to systems and data at their desktops as part of their suite of personal productivity tools. This greatly expanded base of clients using automated systems and requiring immediate access to data has created a new level of demand for training and support that many institutions are struggling to meet. The new community of users needs and expects a level of support that heretofore has not been required. Adequate user training and support will have a profound effect on the futures of our institutions and on the quality of instruction and service we provide. But how, especially in times of shrinking resources, can institutions support the level and variety of training that broadly distributed access to data resources and information systems requires? The answer is that we absolutely must adopt a strategy that recognizes that data and information systems are valuable institutional resources. Furthermore, like other key institutional resources such as physical facilities and libraries, our information resources must be managed, and easy access must be facilitated. Education and training in institution-wide student systems and enterprise-wide data are critical to the future of our organizations.

THE NEED FOR A PARADIGM SHIFT

In the past, training and support for automated systems typically were the responsibility of the information technology (IT) departments on our campuses. IT staff trained the relatively few direct users of the system. Often, the users who needed to be trained typically had themselves been involved in the design and development of a system, so the training required at the time of implementation was minimal. Institutions have only recently been faced with the challenge of training large numbers of users outside the administrative service providers like the registrar's and admissions offices. Now, however, we must provide for the training of faculty, advisers, staff, and, most important, students.

To plan for institution-wide support of systems and data, institutions need to first develop an institutional data management policy that clearly identifies roles and responsibilities for access and training. The training that needs to occur must address not only the use of the tools for accessing systems and information but the interpretation of the data, the privacy laws and other regulations governing their use, and the acceptable practice standards of their institutions. This requires a new model of training in which the technology experts and the user experts team together to provide the breadth of instruction necessary to support the information infrastructure of our institutions today. As the user community expands with information and technology accessible by virtually everyone, the roles and responsibilities of the administrative service providers in our institutions continue to change. We are moving away from the role of records keepers and admissions officers to a role of data managers and access facilitators. We are the liaisons between the technical developers and a new community of end users. Consequently, the training demand extends beyond staff within our office to every potential user of distributed systems across our organizations. Our training strategy must include not only the training of staff within our organizations but the cost-effective, ongoing training of systems users across the entire institution.

Organizations concerned about technology and user training have many training strategies and models from which to choose. However, despite the influx of technology into higher education, a review of the literature reveals surprisingly little research on comprehensive training strategies or models for a distributed computing environment. Moreover, little research has been conducted to assess the effectiveness of various training methods in successful systems implementation.

TRAINING FACTORS

The training strategy proposed in this chapter employs a combination of practices from tested training methodologies and instructional design principles. It

Table 12.1
Reactions to Computers by Expectancy Type

Psychological Reaction	Efficacy	Outcome	Reinforcement
Fear	Low	Low	Low
Apprehension	N/A	N/A	N/A
Opposition	N/A	N/A	Low

also offers solutions for addressing a number of issues related to the effect that trainee characteristics have on training outcomes. The ideal training model for a broadly distributed computing environment must be specific to automated systems, yet general enough to accommodate both the variety of systems used by organizations and the wide range of previous experiences that trainees will present.

Experience suggests and research supports the hypothesis that trainee characteristics have significant impact in the training of adults in acquiring computer skills. Thus, organizations concerned with enterprise-wide training in systems and data must address the effect of individual differences related to computer usage and training. Three key individual difference variables that need to be taken into consideration in the development and delivery of training are trainee attitude, locus of control, and demographic factors such as age and gender.

Trainee Attitude. Experienced trainers of adults using computer-based information systems report that the trainee's attitude toward computers and toward change in general seems to influence significantly the ease with which he or she learns the new technology. It is a commonly held belief that "computer phobia" is widespread in the general public, but there is little research to document this notion.

Meier (1985) proposes a social learning model for providing insight into individual differences in attitudes toward computers. He proposes three new terms, computer "opposition," "apprehension," and "fear" instead of the more commonly used clinical terms "resistance," "phobia," and "anxiety." Meier's hypothesis is that computer opposition, apprehension, and fear differ in the degree to which trainees possess low efficacy, outcome, and reinforcement expectations (see Table 12.1).

In Meier's model, persons who possess computer fear probably present the greatest training challenge. They believe that the consequences of working with the computer will be negative and that they do not know how to control these consequences. They also lack a belief in their personal capacity to perform. Trainers report that some people seem to go to great effort to avoid training in new systems. According to Meier's social learning model, these individuals probably possess computer fear.

Computer-apprehensive persons are keenly aware of their inability to predict what actions are necessary to control forthcoming outcomes in the systems they are being trained to use. According to the table, these people may have the self-perceived competence, but until they are trained and are able to have some control over the outcomes, their concerns will influence their attitude toward computers and the systems in which they are being trained more than their self-perceived competence does. In implementing new systems, the present author has observed that some people vacillate between support and opposition, often appearing supportive in public but then expressing opposition to the system during training. It is possible that these people accept the new system but are apprehensive about their ability to control the outcomes until they are trained and become experienced users.

The third group of computer-aversive persons in Meier's model are those opposed to computers. The persons who are opposed to computers will avoid training at all costs, not because they lack the competence or have low self-efficacy expectations but because they disagree with the use of computers in general or with the system being implemented specifically. In the author's own experience (in new systems implementation), computer-aversive persons have provided significant challenges in training but have also provided the greatest training rewards when, after training, their opposition changed to support. As these individuals become more experienced with computers, their opposition becomes more specific; for example, a dean who eventually accepted and indeed began to promote computer-assisted advising (after a significant effort on the part of the author to demonstrate the capabilities and benefits of the system) continued to refuse to consider the use of electronic mail and electronic con-ferencing as tools for instruction.

The present author could find very little in the literature to document the existence of "computer phobia," yet experienced trainers report that individuals' reactions to computers and systems do seem to have an effect on training in new systems.

Locus of Control. The issue of outcome expectations in Meier's model refers to the connection a person believes to exist between his or her behavior and an event. Locus of control is a related construct that has been investigated exten-sively in psychology literature. Locus of control research examines whether individuals see the outcomes of their efforts as being attributable to their own behavior (internal locus of control) or to factors beyond their personal control (external locus of control). Studies have shown that persons with an internal locus of control tend to cope and perform better under stressful conditions than do persons with an external locus of control. According to Hawk (1989), since the prospect of using a computer creates stress for many people, the locus of control variable may contribute to differences in how they react to computer systems.

Coovert and Goldstein (1980) found that individuals with internal locus of control were more likely to view computers as beneficial tools than were persons with an external locus of control. However, Hawk (1989) found that Coovert and Goldstein's results regarding locus of control did not generalize to information systems used at work. That is, while locus of control may influence individuals' attitudes toward computers initially during training, after users became proficient, it did not appear to affect attitude toward information systems used at work. Hawk also reported that differences in the attitudes of external-control and internal-control users emerge if user involvement in the system development is taken into account. With high levels of involvement, little difference exists between the computer attitudes of internals and externals. However, when users are not highly involved in systems development, the attitude of external-control users is substantially less positive than that of internal-control users. Hawk's findings suggest that locus of control alone is not as important in determining user attitude as is the interaction of locus of control and user involvement in the development and design of the system.

The present author believes that high user involvement plays an important role for novice computer users by repeatedly exposing and educating them in a system prior to implementation and training and thereby affecting their attitude toward it. The research of Coovert, Salas, and Ramakrishna (1992) supports this notion. They found that attitude toward computers plays a large role for individuals with little computer experience. As one's attitude toward computers becomes more positive, interacting with a computer is viewed more positively, and an individual is more likely to indicate a willingness to interact with a computer in the future.

Noe and Schmitt (1986) report that trainees' perceptions that there is a choice regarding participation in the training influences motivation to learn and subsequent learning. One of the challenges in training staff in computer systems is that typically the workers have little or no choice about whether or not a system will be implemented. The implementation of a specific type of technology or new system is usually a decision made by upper management, implemented by middle management, but affecting the front-line worker most directly. This worker rarely has input regarding the selection of hardware or software, especially of large, enterprise-wide systems. If Noe and Schmitt's study can be generalized to training in computer information systems, the results give additional support to the importance of user involvement in software selection or in systems design and development. They also support the importance of educating workers about a system before training in the system occurs.

Demographic Factors. Thus far, the author has examined the trainee characteristics of attitude and locus of control in training adults in computer skills. The final trainee characteristic discussed is demographic factors.

Many age-related stereotypes exist in the workplace, probably none more than in the area of technology. Job-related stereotypes regarding age and technology depict older employees as being more difficult to train in technology, fearful of computers, resistant to change, less receptive to new ideas, and less capable of learning when compared with younger employees. However, Waldman and Avolio's (1986) meta-analysis of age differences in job performance indicated that when objective criteria were used, performance actually increased with age.

But, as Gist, Rosen, and Schwoerer (1988) point out, the studies in the meta-analysis dealt with job performance. Very little data relevant to age-related differences in training performance exist.

Gist and her colleagues looked at the influence of training method and trainee age on the acquisition of computer skills. They found that age had a significant main effect on performance. Older trainees displayed significantly lower performance in computer software training than younger trainees did. The authors caution that we must separate cohort effects from age effects before drawing conclusions about age differences in performance. "Cohort effects derive from common experiences shared by individuals born at the same time. In the present experiment, cohort effects with respect to familiarity with computer hardware and software are possible" (p. 263). To control for the possibility of a cohort effect, the authors attempted to assess trainees' past computer experience and familiarity. Even when previous computer experience was held constant, age effects were still present. Although more research is needed to replicate the age effects of the Gist et al. study and to pinpoint the source of learning difficulty for older trainees, these findings strongly suggest that age of trainees is a characteristic that must be taken into account in the design of training.

Gender is another demographic factor that could influence trainee attitude and performance in training in the acquisition of computer skills, due, in part, to commonly held stereotypes. Traditionally, computers are considered a "male" domain. For example, Dambrot and colleagues (1985) reported that students who planned to major in computer science tended to be male and to have a more positive attitude toward computers than females did. In studying children from kindergarten through college, Wilder and colleagues reported that boys liked computers and video games more than girls did at every level. They also reported that females viewed themselves as less comfortable and less skillful at computers than did males (Wilder, Mackie, and Cooper, 1985). In a study of gender differences in attitudes toward computers, Temple and Lips (1989) found that among university students both gender groups reported similar levels of enjoyment and interest in computers. However, the females reported less confidence and comfort with computers than their male counterparts did. These findings suggest that in designing a training curriculum and plan for the wide range of users in a distributed computing environment, trainers may need to take into consideration the effect of gender of trainees and attitude toward self-efficacy in computer skills.

DEFINING AND IMPLEMENTING A WHOLE PRODUCT APPROACH TO TRAINING

The community of systems users in higher education has expanded to encompass almost everyone with an association to the institution, including the occasional user as well as the staff member responsible for university business processes. This expanded user base, coupled with the information from research on the impact individual characteristics have on the success of training and computer skills, requires us to adopt a "whole product" approach to training. Clearly, a wide variety of techniques and strategies must be employed to achieve a successful, comprehensive training program for automated systems in today's environment. The following three-step approach is recommended.

1. *Analyze the Training Need.* To meet the information and technology training needs of the wide range of users in our current and future organizations, it is necessary that we employ a broad definition of training. This definition includes both training and education. The training model should include training for both those who need "exposure" to a system and those who truly need to develop expertise. The training for the occasional user will be very different from the training for the person expected to become the expert system or service provider. Different techniques and strategies will be considered and developed for each of these, as there is no "one size fits all."

In developing the training program, it is important to evaluate the consistency of the goals of the organization and the potential impact of the automated system. Consider, as an example, the implementation of a computerized degree progress checking system. Within the last decade, many institutions have implemented degree progress checking systems with the primary purpose of improving the delivery of academic advising. In the implementation of computer-assisted advising, an institution must determine if the basic premise of the goal "improving advising" is to improve the quality of the advising sessions between advisers and students or to increase the number of advisees an adviser is able to service. If the institution is attempting to increase adviser/student contact, the emphasis of the training will be for advisers in functions such as using the degree audit report as an advising tool, learning to recognize warning signals in student performance or inadvisable sequences in course selections, using the audit to move into discussions of career exploration, and so on. Advisers may even become the distribution point for the audit, thus forcing student/adviser contact. If, however, in this era of doing more with less, the goal of the automated degree progress checking system is to increase the efficiency of advisers so that an advising staff can serve more students, the emphasis of training would be with the students themselves. The goal of this training would be to empower the students to make their own decisions regarding course selections to satisfy degree requirements and, perhaps, see an adviser only at certain points during the student's career. The point is that training in the system must be consistent with both the organization's goals and the objectives of the trainee's job. Otherwise, goal conflict will occur. Many organizations have experienced conflict at the time a new automated system is implemented because the system's goals were not consistent with the organization's goals. Unfortunately, the conflict often is not apparent until training occurs.

In addition to analyzing the goals of the organization and the goals of the system, the development of a training program in automated systems must include an analysis of the jobs of the workers who will use the system to determine their training needs. In this proposed training model, determining training need encompasses (1) a definition of the elements of effective performance using the new system and (2) identification of the job components that will benefit from training. Automating major administrative student systems, for example, recruitment and admissions systems, registration, and student records systems, almost always is accompanied by extensive job redesign. Careful up-front analysis of processes of job design and subsequent training needs is necessary for training to be effective.

2. *Design the Instruction.* The content of the training obviously will depend on the type of system. Content may include information technology tools, system navigation, data definition and interpretation, organization policy and procedures, and user responsibilities. Initial rollout of a new system to an entire organization may require different training content than ongoing training and orientation in existing systems for new staff. The training model needs to include "future-oriented" training in new functionality being added to existing systems, or new features of future releases of software broadly used on campus.

The development of technology-based learning has had a significant impact on the design of instruction and training systems. Interestingly, research indicates that while the design of instruction is critical to learning outcomes, the system for delivery of well-designed instruction has little or no effect on learning outcome (Clark and Solomon, 1986). These research findings suggest that a contingency model based on learner characteristics should address the design of the training for adults in computer-based information systems; the method of training delivery is inconsequential.

In contrast, Gist, Rosen, and Schwoerer (1988) found a significant effect for method of delivery of identical training content. The authors hypothesized that modeling would be a more effective method of training older trainees in computer software, while a computer-based tutorial would be more effective for younger trainees. Surprisingly, their results showed no interaction between age and training approach but did show a significant performance effect for type of training for both groups. For both groups, modeling was more effective than a computer-based tutorial.

The research cited on the effects of attitude, locus of control, and demographic factors on training in acquisition of computer skills strongly suggests that employing strategies that include consideration of these trainee characteristics is worthwhile. A contingency-based approach to training might be appropriate. A contingency model would suggest that one training design is more effective than another when training adults in technology in the workplace. Such a model suggests that organizations should assess trainee characteristics to determine the most appropriate training method for the training need at hand.

The different characteristics of the trainees (i.e., previous computing experience, age) require different strategies for effective training outcomes to occur. Thus, it is important to offer a wide range of education and training methods and media, including, but not limited to, classroom work, computer-based tutorials, videos, presentations, on-line and written documentation, newsletters, and so on. In addition, "hot line" and "help desk" support should be considered a part of the ongoing training program. The training needs to be available at the time a staff member needs it, not at the time it is convenient for the training organization to offer it. In many cases, to reduce anxiety and achieve maximum training outcome, it often is important for the training and support to be available to the trainee in his or her environment rather than in a training center.

3. *Evaluate Training Effectiveness.* Ongoing, regular evaluation of training effectiveness is necessary to maintain a robust, dynamic training environment. Evaluation and feedback at the time of training and at regular intervals beyond are necessary. In addition, productivity measures before and after training should be employed in order to determine the effectiveness of systems training on work processes. Training in automated systems in an ongoing process and feedback on effectiveness need to be incorporated in the continuous improvement of the training program.

CONCLUSION

Education, training, and support are essential to the information-age community. Those who can effectively use our institutions' information resources, whether as customer or service provider, will be successful. Those who cannot will not fully participate. Hence, the implementation of flexible, robust, accessible training and support in information technology and automated systems is critical to the future of our organizations.

REFERENCES

Bandura, A. 1982. Self-efficacy mechanism in human agency. *American Psychologist* 37(2): 122–147.

Bracker, J.S., and Pearson, J.N. 1986. Worker obsolescence: The H.R. dilemma of the 80's. *Personnel Administrator* 31: 109–116.

Clark, R.E., and Solomon, G. 1986. Media in teaching. In M.C. Wittrock, ed., *Handbook of Research on Teaching*, 3d ed. New York: Macmillan.

Coovert, M.D., and Goldstein, M. 1980. Locus of control as a predictor of users' attitude toward computers. *Psychological Reports* 47: 1167–1173.

Coovert, M.D., Salas, E., and Ramakrishna, K. 1992. The role of individual and system characteristics in computerized training systems. *Computers in Human Behavior* 8: 335–352.

Dambrot, F., Watkins-Malek, M., Silling, S., Marshall, R., and Garver, J. 1985. Correlates of sex differences in attitudes toward and involvement with computers. *Journal of Vocational Behavior* 27: 71–86.

Gist, M., and Mitchell, T. 1992. Self-efficacy: A theoretical analysis of its determinants and malleability. *Academy of Management Review* 17: 183–211.

Gist, M., Rosen, B., and Schwoerer, C. 1988. The influence of training method and trainee age on the acquisition of computer skills. *Personnel Psychology* 41: 255–265.

Goldstein, I. 1980. Training in work organizations. *Annual Review of Psychology* 31: 327–372.

Hawk, S. 1989. Locus of control and computer attitude: The effect of user involvement. *Computers in Human Behavior* 5: 199–206.

Meier, S.T. 1985. Computer aversion. *Computers in Human Behavior* 1: 171–179.

Noe, R.A., and Schmitt, N. 1986. The influence of trainee attitudes on training effectiveness: Test of a model. *Personnel Psychology* 39: 497–523.

Swanson, R.A., and Gradous, D. 1986. *Performance at Work: A Systematic Program for Analyzing Work Behavior.* New York: John Wiley and Sons.

Temple, L., and Lips, H.M. 1989. Gender differences and similarities in attitudes toward computers. *Computers in Human Behavior* 5: 215–226.

Waldman, D.A., and Avolio, B. 1986. A meta-analysis of age differences in job performance. *Journal of Applied Psychology* 71: 33–38.

Wilder, G., Mackie, D., and Cooper, J. 1985. Gender and computers: Two surveys of computer-related attitudes. *Sex Roles* 13(3/4): 215–228.

13

Disaster Preparedness and Recovery in a Records Management Environment

Virginia K. Johns and Elaine Wheeler

CASE STUDY: UNIVERSITY OF CALIFORNIA, SANTA BARBARA, REGISTRAR'S OFFICE FIRE, FEBRUARY 26, 1991

As was so often the case, I worked a little late on Tuesday, February 26, 1991. I remember spending some time going through all of the items on my desk, completing those things that could be resolved quickly and adding other, more time-consuming tasks to my already long "to-do" list. I locked up and left my office satisfied that I had established priorities for the remainder of the week, that our newly installed Registration by Telephone (RBT) system was working like a charm, and that my desk looked more orderly than it had in weeks.

The only thing unusual about the day was that the campus had received bomb threats, which were accompanied by messages protesting the involvement of the United States in the Persian Gulf War. The threats seemed so ridiculous. Who would consider using bombs to advocate the dissolution of a war? Any real threat against the campus community seemed unlikely. There were dozens of production tasks to keep us busy in the Registrar's Office, and when we weren't being forced to evacuate (as had happened on a few occasions the previous week), we kept our noses to the grindstone and pressed on to ensure that students were being served more efficiently than ever before.

After dinner, I settled into my evening with a little television, some reading, and a couple of phone conversations with friends. Just as I was preparing for bed, I received a phone call from a student who worked as a reporter for the campus newspaper. He asked if I knew that RBT was not working. I replied that I was unaware of any problems but would check it out right away. I made a few test calls, which resulted in the normal function and response of the system, and satisfied myself that the "malfunction" was either student error or something that had self-corrected. I made a mental note to review with a systems analyst all of the transaction logs first thing in the morning to determine if there were any problems not readily discernible from the testing I could perform on my own. I turned off the light and fell asleep.

At approximately 12:30 A.M., my phone rang again. My boss was calling to say that the Office of the Registrar in Cheadle Hall was on fire. The origin of the fire was centered in my division of the office. Could I please come to assist with damage assessment? Few calls can elicit the kind of classic stress response generated by that brief conversation. I assured my supervisor that I was on the way.

During the six to eight months preceding this phone call, I had been working with three colleagues from other institutions on a presentation for the April meeting of the American Association of Collegiate Registrars and Admissions Officers (AACRAO). The name of our session was "Disaster Preparedness and Recovery. Are You Ready?" You can imagine how that title echoed in my mind as I dressed, wondering if I was ready. I layered on old sweats, pulled on good socks and sturdy shoes, grabbed a few snacks from the kitchen and headed out to my car. I was standing in the lobby of Cheadle Hall before 1:00 A.M.

By then the fire, which had started at approximately 11:20 P.M., had been extinguished. However, hot spots (particularly above the drop-ceiling) continued to erupt into flames, and the firefighters were working to prevent further damage to the office. As I walked through the charred remains of our newly remodeled office, my mind began to catalog the damage. Seven of my twelve staff no longer had so much as a pencil to return to in the morning. Heavy smoke had invaded and damaged every inch of the office and much of the five-story building in which we were housed. Every staff member would share in the trauma that was to come. Brand-new terminals, scanning equipment, telephones, typewriters, printers, and furniture were covered with oily soot generated by the petroleum products used in the manufacture of the carpeting and furniture that had burned in the flames. Intense heat had caused doors to buckle and windows to break. Electrical power was out. Water and debris extended well beyond where the fire had been contained. My mind raced with the realization of how much there would be to do before service could be restored.

In collaboration with the campus and county fire marshals, I inspected debris and helped to reconstruct the scene. I identified where equipment had been placed when I locked the office the previous evening. I listened as they conferred about the point of ignition and possible causes of the fire. I drew sketches of desk and cabinet configurations. We talked about how much paper was stored in the vicinity and whether the printers were turned off or on. We discussed the contents of the cabinets, and I assured them there had been no chemicals stored in the area. As the experts continued their methodical probe, I couldn't help but ponder the fact that the "paper" they referred to was really my team's "work in progress." They were going to have to expend significant effort to reconstruct the scene from their perspectives.

The initial assessment regarding the origin of the fire indicated an accidental ignition emanating from faulty wiring. With this vague assurance that nothing could have been done by our staff to prevent this fire, I tried to see the damage from a recovery point of view. I began to feel thankful that the newly erected fire wall had held fast and prevented the destruction of our permanent record cards (PRCs). The 250,000 PRCs were still locked snugly in their fire-resistant cabinets on the other side of the wall. I was grateful that my own staff didn't yet know that their personal territory in the office had been so viciously violated. What I didn't know was that every single one of those documents, before they could again be handled to produce transcripts, would need to be cleaned by gloved hands using special rubber sponges. It would be weeks before staff in that seemingly untouched part of the office would be able to resume their work in progress.

IN THE DARK OF NIGHT

In the predawn hours that followed the fire, I reevaluated the priorities I had established just the night before. The office certainly would not be usable, but work in progress would need to be collected, and operations would need to be initiated in some other location. Emergency phone lines would have to be established so that we would not lose contact with the students who still needed transcripts, registration assistance, enrollment verifications, and so on.

Contact was established with supervisors from the departments of Communications Services and Information Systems and Computing to initiate the movement of telephone and computer lines to temporary locations. Facilities Management staff had already started to clean away dangerous debris and clean up the Cheadle Hall lobby. Administrative and Business Services personnel started to assemble in the building to assess potential liability and necessary insurance claim actions. Vice chancellors conferred to identify possible locations for our operation and make the necessary resources available. Little by little, the campus emergency plan came to life as the night turned to day.

BY THE LIGHT OF DAY

As dawn broke, I pulled from my wallet the carefully compiled and reduced photocopy of our office emergency phone list and began to call all of the staff to prepare them for the devastation that awaited their arrival. I advised each person to come in old, comfortable clothing and shoes. It seemed likely that we would each have the opportunity to go into our own work areas, identify priority work in progress, remove necessary materials, relocate to temporary quarters, and commence work assignments. Within an hour, those plans were dashed.

In the morning, new evidence came to light that suggested that the fire had been the work of an arsonist. By now, the administrative team, composed of the registrar, associate registrar, and the three assistant registrars, had assembled on-site. The campus police were called, and the office was declared a "crime scene." This simple declaration meant that we could not disturb the scene in any way, and only the police would be admitted into the office. Work in progress would simply have to wait. At almost the same time, specialists from the Environmental Health and Safety Office pronounced Cheadle Hall a "sick building" and requested the removal of all personnel. Consequently, Administrative and Business Services contracted with a disaster recovery service provider, and we quickly formulated a plan to intercept all staff members and redirect them to a nearby employee lunchroom.

While we met with staff to discuss ever-changing information, answer questions, soothe worries, and formulate a course of action, Food Services personnel provided us with hot coffee and breakfast rolls. We began to divide the office into four task-specific teams.

The first team was composed of those employees whose work areas had been destroyed. They were asked to make two lists; the first contained a description of all physical items known to be in their area at the close of business the previous day, while the second identified all work in progress and action items that could be recalled. Although the human memory is not always perfect, the listings proved to be useful in the following days and weeks as we reconstructed what turned out to be minor losses of original documentation and haggled with insurance adjusters over replacement of supplies and equipment.

The second team included those employees who could best represent the office by providing in-person information at the entrance to Cheadle Hall. This team also took responsibility for making and placing temporary signs on and around the office so that individuals seeking service would be redirected easily to the temporary information booth.

A third team took responsibility for documenting telephone scripts so that consistent and accurate information would be available to anyone who called the office. Communication Services provided the assistance necessary to group phone lines in the pattern we requested. Many of the telephone lines were routed to a central voice mail recording that provided a brief statement about the fire and the status of records. Callers were advised that operations were expected to return to normal within a few days and told that if their call could wait, their patience would be appreciated. Callers with urgent requests requiring immediate attention were advised to call a specific number. An unaffected campus department provided office space so that this team could answer all of these urgent incoming calls.

The fourth team was established to formulate a plan for moving and safeguarding the transcript records. Their previous discussions about disaster preparedness guided their thinking and strengthened their resolve to ensure that every single record (a quarter of a million PRCs and thousands of other documents) would be accounted for during the cleanup and relocation phases of the recovery process. (The PRCs could have been reconstructed from microfilm records stored off-site and computer files, but because the fire occurred before we had completed our data conversion, this would have taken many months.)

In the midst of these initial recovery activities, we were once again forced to evacuate because of a bomb threat. As we stood together in the predesignated assembly area wondering if things could be any worse, the southern California skies opened. A sudden rainstorm pushed us to seek shelter under a building overhang, and those who moved too slowly were quickly drenched.

The new threat passed (no bomb was found during this particular scare, although three pipe bombs and two incendiary devices were located during other scares in the same week), and we were allowed to return temporarily to our meeting room. Once the work teams had initiated their assigned tasks, the registrar and associate registrar focused on the physical losses and worked toward securing facilities and equipment. Assistant registrars remained free to troubleshoot and keep the information flowing between the task-specific teams, the registrar, and the campus emergency response team. Daily meetings became standard procedure. These meetings provided an opportunity to ask and answer questions, soothe stressed nerves, brainstorm solutions to new problems, and assign tasks.

THE AFTERMATH

Even though our office emergency plan was as yet incomplete, the process of working on the plan had provided a solid base from which to operate as we formulated responses to ever-changing problems. The earlier discussions, collection of information, added safety features, and training helped guide our actions in those critical hours immediately following the disaster and in the months of recovery that followed.

The first three weeks of recovery were facilitated through the assistance of a professional disaster recovery firm. Their expertise, coupled with our heightened awareness of critical needs and recovery processes, enabled us to work together to quickly set work schedules, arrange appropriate security, and solve problems. By the time they left, we were back in business from another location and well on our way to restoring our records.

LESSONS LEARNED

Most of the planning we had done in the office centered around the notion that we were most vulnerable to earthquakes. We had taught our staff (1) to "duck, cover, and hold" during an earthquake, (2) proper procedures for evacuation and reassembly for check-in, (3) chain-of-command information protocol related to the campus emergency plan, and (4) all about personal safety issues. We encouraged staff to get involved in the planning process by inviting an expert to address the topic of safety during one of our regular staff meetings.

Staff were then asked to evaluate their own workstation for hazards. The entire office was then assessed by experts from the campus Environmental Health and Safety Office, with results of the assessment shared during a subsequent staff meeting. Corrective actions to remove hazards and improve conditions were initiated immediately. A greater awareness and sense of personal ownership of the condition of the office, protective measures for the security of records, and the safety of office personnel emerged throughout the office.

BLUEPRINT FOR DEVELOPING A PLAN

How does all of this relate to preparing your own disaster plan? The effects of a disaster are simply new problem sets to be solved. Disaster planning should be conceptualized like any other major undertaking in a records office, such as implementing Touch-Tone registration, devising a degree audit system, or responding to new federal regulations pertaining to financial aid. The scope of the project, problem, and desired outcomes must be defined adequately. Tasks and responsibilities must be delegated to specific individuals who have both the skill and the authority to take action. Reasonable, measurable, and attainable goals and deadlines need to be set. A competent coordinator needs to keep the planners on task and the project moving forward on time. Simply put, successful planning of any kind includes determining tasks, milestones, and measures of success; delegating work assignments; and taking action. The same ingredients are necessary to develop a good disaster plan. At a minimum, you can improve your recovery procedures by undertaking activities that are usually cited as good management strategies: (1) encourage effective team building, (2) develop solid procedures and cross-train employees, (3) improve communication and information flow, and (4) identify backup systems and alternate sites for production.

Developing a records management program is a good business practice. Whether the records in your office are paper or electronic, it is important to have a records inventory, a documented filing system, retention schedules, archiving procedures, and a systematic purge process. An active records management program, namely, one that is not only designed but actually used, plays a key role in disaster preparedness and recovery. The records inventory will identify what needs to be recovered; written documentation of what and how many records are under your control will provide an excellent framework for reconstruction; archiving procedures will provide backup copies so that recovery is possible; and retention schedules and related purge processes will control the size of your vital records so that timely recovery is practical.

Technology can be a useful tool in any records management program. Consider using microfilm, microfiche, imaging, tape backups, electronic vaulting, or database mirroring as primary and secondary storage media. Be sure to review and update (or develop) your records management program in coordination with the development of your disaster plan.

The rest of this chapter will guide you through the steps necessary to develop a disaster plan tailored to your unique environment. Worksheets are included to simplify this task. Our hope is to make the process less time-consuming by providing a conceptual framework. This is an interactive chapter; your participation is necessary to bring this information to life as a usable plan for the protection of your records.

Think about it for a moment: you probably purchased insurance for your car, your house, and your possessions. Somewhere in the hierarchy of your organization someone purchased insurance for the office equipment and computing facilities. Insurance for your records can be purchased only with time and brainpower. Methodically completing each of the worksheets and utilizing the information will ultimately produce a plan that gives you "records insurance." You will consider it a small price to pay if ever you are unfortunate enough to need it. If that is not enough motivation, take a minute or two to think about how different parts of the plan can serve multiple purposes. Documenting procedures can facilitate your staff development, training, and cross-training efforts. Purge processes can assist in cutting costs. The plan you develop can serve as documentation for a current system in preparation for automating records. This planning process will help you and all of your colleagues to think aggressively about the resolution of problems.

If at any time during the formulation of the plan you become stymied, there is probably a weakness in the general procedure. Stop struggling with the plan and go back to the source to clarify the procedure and make modifications, if necessary. The authors have found this to be a useful exercise that has on occasion pointed the way to significant improvement or cost savings in day-to-day operations.

A blueprint and set of worksheets to assist in the planning process are included at the end of this chapter. Make copies of the blueprint and worksheets and have them at your side as you read through the following narrative. You may find it helpful to the development of your plan to make notes on the work sheets about the specifics of your office and records environment.

GETTING STARTED

Each plan must have a coordinator who will manage the planning process and be held accountable for its completion in a timely manner. Much of the plan activity will involve coordinating with, and collecting information from, knowledgeable "others." Essential proficiencies for the coordinator include excellent oral and written communication skills, the ability to resolve complex problems and to synthesize and organize information, a high level of motivation, and persistence. The plan coordinator may find it useful to delegate portions of the checklist and enlist the aid of one or more persons to assist with the data collection. Some offices will find it useful to appoint co-coordinators. However, it is recommended that designation of authority and responsibility be clearly defined if more than one person is assigned to this task.

The plan coordinator is not necessarily the person responsible for coordinating the overall disaster response. The completed plan will identify responsible authorities for various aspects of preparedness and recovery. The plan coordinator is responsible for ensuring that a plan is developed. Check to see if your campus has developed an emergency operations plan. You may be able to build upon an existing campus plan. Enlist the aid of professionals such as environmental health and safety directors, campus police, administrative and business services personnel, and the campus fire marshal. Document all available resources on Worksheet 1.

FACILITIES MANAGEMENT AND PERSONNEL SAFETY

Take some time to think about where you are geographically located and what types of emergencies you are most likely to experience. It is important to identify the types of emergencies and resulting damages most likely to occur so that you can tailor your plan accordingly.

Your plan does not need to exhaust all of the possibilities or provide a scenario for every contingency. Construct a solid plan that covers the basics for the disasters most likely to occur, involve all staff in the process, and then rely on good managers who can analyze the specific situation, determine how to proceed, and activate the plan when needed. Advance planning for even one type of disaster will better prepare you for any disaster.

Keep in mind that disasters are not always a result of acts of nature. Some can be avoided with routine safety checks. Use Worksheet 2 to identify preventive measures that might be effective in reducing risk of injury to personnel or damage to facilities, records, and equipment (e.g., securing equipment to prevent movement during earthquakes, shielding records to prevent fire or water damage, etc.).

Develop a checklist for each type of expected emergency that outlines the immediate actions to be taken, evacuation procedures, and follow-up responses. Map out alternate evacuation routes and identify a group congregation site. A sample checklist is included as Worksheet 3.

Use Worksheets 4–6 to collect and maintain information essential to personnel safety: (1) staff training in emergency procedures (operation of fire extinguishers; cardiopulmonary resuscitation, or CPR; first aid); (2) emergency medical information; and (3) up-to-date emergency services contacts.

Construct an office emergency kit containing items such as first aid supplies, tools, flashlight and batteries, radio and batteries, emergency medical forms for staff, emergency contacts, clipboards with checklists, pen or pencil, and so on. Be sure to replace batteries and replenish supplies on an annual basis. Additional information about emergency kits is readily available through your local chapter of the American Red Cross.

TECHNICAL PROFILE

Offices involved with records management in the 1990s typically have a significant reliance on technology. Computers and associated peripheral devices are depended on to carry out the daily business operations. The trend is toward less paper, with electronic media used to store official university documents and data and to facilitate university procedures. The technological infrastructure is therefore an important consideration when developing a plan for disaster preparedness and recovery. Coordinate with those support organizations and personnel who are integral to your records management functions and enlist their participation in the development of your technical profile. Use Worksheets 7–11 for building your technical profile.

The profile will include an inventory of equipment, data, and applications. Identify parties responsible for recovery in each of the inventoried areas along with their plans for recovery. If particular equipment, data, or applications are considered more vital than others and may need to be recovered first, this should be indicated in the profile. However, as we have previously mentioned, recovery plans must be flexible. One of the first steps in the recovery phase is to analyze the status of each application system. Items on the ''vital'' list might change depending on the time of the year, the part of the processing cycle for each system, and the extent of the damage.

The profile will be helpful during the recovery phase should some of your technical infrastructure be destroyed or inaccessible. The equipment inventory will be useful not only for replacing individual pieces of equipment but also in stating the requirements (space, power, etc.) for alternative facilities should you need to relocate your equipment. Once the profile is complete, work with the campus personnel who are responsible for insurance and related contracts. Identify appropriate vendors and sources who could assist with recovery through the provision of a ''hot site'' or who specialize in restoration and cleanup. Consult the section on additional resources at the end of this chapter for more information.

RECORDS INVENTORY

As noted earlier in this chapter, a records management program can play a key role in disaster preparedness and the ability to recover vital records. Computerized records will have been inventoried as part of your technical profile. Critical documents and files not covered by this profile (paper, microfiche, microfilm) should also be inventoried, using Worksheet 12.

Define critical functions performed by staff in your office. Design procedures that will allow you to perform these functions during the recovery phase while your technical infrastructure and records are being restored. It may be necessary to use manual procedures on an interim basis. However, keep in mind that laptops or borrowed computers can be a good way to accomplish a variety of tasks. Off-site storage of a set of backup discs that contain templates for critical forms and processing outlines can save lots of time in an emergency.

ON THE ROAD TO RECOVERY

Creative application of technical tools can enable you to continue providing some level of service while the technical infrastructure is being restored after an emergency. Voice response systems can be used as bulletin boards to inform the campus community of revised schedules, relocated services, and alternate procedures. Telephones and electronic communication can be substituted for in-person contact and allow staff to work from remote locations, possibly even from home. Spreadsheets on stand-alone workstations can be used to capture data normally input into computer applications, thus facilitating a speedy return to normal operations. Word processors, graphics, and presentation tools can be used for making signs or announcements, redirecting traffic, and so on.

KEEPING IT ALIVE

In order to have a highly effective plan when you need it, the information must be up-to-date, and personnel need to be familiar with its contents. Schedule a safety review at least once a year to devote time to this project. Invite ownership of the plan by including all office personnel in the review and update process.

In the 1994 Northridge, California, earthquake, which occurred while the authors were preparing the draft of this manuscript, California State University, Northridge, suffered extensive damage resulting in the loss of all of its classroom facilities. Would the plan you are formulating assist you with prompt recovery of your schedule of classes and room assignment activities? If the building collapsed that houses all of your transcripts, financial aid documents, or admissions records, could you reconstruct the files? Could you do it quickly? How would you do it? Where would you start? *Think about it for a moment.* . . . Now get moving!

APPENDIX 13.1: BLUEPRINT FOR PREPARING A PLAN

Blueprint for Preparing a Plan	Worksheet
Getting Started	
Identify a Plan Coordinator and Planning Resources	1
Facilities Management	2
Identify possible types of emergencies	
Identify probable types of damage	
Identify prevention measures	
Personnel Safety	
Develop emergency checklists	3
Select evacuation routes and congregation site[1]	
Provide training	4
Collect emergency medical information	5
Construct emergency kit[2]	
Identify emergency contacts	6
Technology Profile	
Identify a Technical Recovery Coordinator	7
Establish Technology Recovery Team	
Prepare Technical Profile	
Inventory equipment	8
Inventory data	9
Inventory applications	10
Develop Provisions for Recovery	11
Records Inventory	12

1.   Insert a campus map and a detailed description or map of specific evacuation routes and congregation sites.
2.   The American Red Cross has several suggested items for inclusion in your kit. Contact your local chapter for information.

MAKE SURE TO KEEP COPIES OF ALL YOUR COMPLETED WORKSHEETS IN SEVERAL LOCATIONS, INCLUDING ONE AT LEAST 50 MILES FROM YOUR OFFICE. TRADE WORKSHEETS WITH A COLLEAGUE AT ANOTHER INSTITUTION.

Worksheet 1. Planning Personnel and Resources				
Contact Title	Contact Name	Phone Number	Notes	Referrals to Other Resources
Plan Coordinator				
Env. Health & Safety				
Campus Police				
Admin. & Bus. Serv.				
Fire Marshal				
Facilities				

Worksheet 2. Facilities Management - Prevention Measures

Type of Emergency	Type of Damage	Prevention Measures
e.g.,		
Earthquake	Breakage, Personal Injury	Lock down devices for equipment, protective film for windows to prevent shattering, fasten cabinets and bookcases to wall, etc.

Worksheet 3
Sample Checklist

Earthquake

Immediate Action

if indoors, get under a table or desk, or brace yourself in a safe doorway (such as an archway where a door cannot slam shut and hurt you); stay away from windows; do not attempt to restrain falling objects

if outdoors, move to an open area away from the overhead hazards such as power lines, trees or falling brick

Evacuation

after the shaking stops: check for trapped persons or personal injuries and administer first aid as appropriate (administer after evacuation if possible)

evacuate and congregate on the campus green by the Library, securing equipment and offices and collecting personal belongings only if it is safe to take the time to do so; if you were in another campus location at the time of the disturbance, try and make your way back to the congregation area

the staff member closest to the location of the Emergency Response Kit should collect the kit on the way out and post the sign "Emergency Kit Removed"; each manager should check to see that the kit has been collected, if it is safe to do so

Follow-up

turn over Emergency Response Kit to a manager present in the congregation area

managers take roll call for their team and try to account for missing staff (managers present will also take roll for any team whose manager is not present at the congregation area); one manager is assigned to be the contact with emergency personnel, including notification of staff not accounted for

managers present at the congregation area assess the situation and determine further actions
- send staff home
- return to secure offices, then go home
- return to office
- relocate to another part of campus
- in case of a major disaster, follow further instructions in the campus Emergengy Operations plan and/or activate department Disaster Recovery Plan
- other

look out for possible secondary effects such as hazardous materials spills or tsunamis

Worksheet 4. Emergency Preparedness Training				
Employee	CPR	First Aid	Fire Extinguisher	Other

WORKSHEET 5
EMPLOYEE EMERGENCY INFORMATION FORM

It is the department's responsibility to keep information on file which will allow us to arrange for proper medical treatment and inform your next of kin should an emergency arise. Personnel has suggested that the following information be collected and kept current on each employee with the understanding that it is confidential and will be used only if there is an emergency.

Employee:_____

Next of Kin or Emergency Contact:

Name: _____

Address:_____

Telephone: (home) _____ (work)_____

Relationship:_____

Physician:

Name: _____

Address:_____

Telephone:_____

Home:

Address:_____

Telephone:_____

Medications or special medical conditions:

Optional - but strongly encouraged that you supply this information; list those things that would be important to emergency personnel (i.e., allergies, medications required, etc.)

_____

_____

_____

_____

_____

Worksheet 6. Emergency Contacts				
Contact	daytime	other times		
Fire				
Police				
Medical				
Environmental Health and Safety				
Facilities Management				
Department Managers	work	home		

Worksheet 7. Technical Profile - Recovery Team

	name	work phone	home phone

Technical Recovery Coordinator:
Alternate:
Identifies other members of recovery team; assures that each team member develops a preparedness and recovery plan; responsible for overall coordination of the technology recovery.

Communications Coordinator:
Alternate:
Responsible for restoration of network and phone services and related equipment.

Operations and Facility Coordinator:
Alternate:
Responsible for restoration of cpu, dasd and tape equipment and replacement facilities, if required.

Data and Applications Coordinator:
Alternate:
Responsible for restoration of databases, files and programs and instituting appropriate security.

Terminal and Workstation Coordinator:
Alternate:
Responsible for working with Communications Coordinator to implement and test user-operated equipment, including workstations, terminals, printers, scanners.

Administrative Support Coordinator:
Alternate:
Records decisions made by Technology Recovery Team; works with Personnel Services to assure compliance with relevant policies and procedures (altered work schedules, temporary work furloughs, etc.); tracks requisitions for equipment and services; assists Technical Recovery Coordinator in tracking financial resources and commitments.

Worksheet 8. Technical Profile - Equipment									
Device	Serial Number	Size	Power Req	Weight	Quantity	Vendor Contact	Insurance Coverage	Notes	
Central Processing Units									
Disk Controllers									
Disk Drives									
Tape Controllers									
Tape Drives									
Printers									
Terminals									
Terminal Controllers									
Workstations									
Fax Machines									
Voice Response Units									
Modems									
Communications Equip									
Scanners									
Phones									
Typewriters									
Other									

Worksheet 9. Technical Profile - Data

System Description	Data Required	Primary Storage	Location	Backup Storage	Backup Schedule	Location
e.g.,						
Final Grades	Adabas Database	3380 DASD	North Hall CC	AM2300-2400 tapes	nightly	off-site vault

Worksheet 10. Technical Profile - Applications

System Description	Data Required	Software Required	Functional Contact	Technical Contact	Vital Ranking
e.g., Registration	Adabas Database	Adabas	Joe Asst. Registrar	Susan Programmer	urgent
		Natural			
		Complete			
		MVS			
		PLI			

Worksheet 11. Develop Provisions for Recovery

Contact Title	Contact Name	Phone Number	Notes	Referrals to Other Resources
Insurance Company				
Hot-site				
Equipment Leasing				
Clean-up Crews				
Restoration Specialists				
Facilities Options				

Worksheet 12. Records Inventory—Critical Documents and Files							
Records	Volume	Primary Storage	Location	Backup Storage	Backup Schedule	Location

ADDITIONAL RESOURCES

Agencies

FEMA (Federal Emergency Management Agency), Post Office Box 70274, Washington, DC 20024

American Red Cross (Consult your telephone directory for local chapter)

Disaster Recovery Service Providers

Blackmon-Mooring-Steamatic Catastrophe, Inc. was the company that provided valuable assistance to the 1991 disaster recovery effort at the University of California, Santa Barbara. Consult your local telephone directory and your campus business office to identify service providers in your area.

Electronic Mail Lists

Disaster Recovery: drp-l@marist.bitnet

Registrar: regist-l@listproc.gsu.edu

College and University Automation: info@cause.colorado.edu and cumrec-l@listserv.nodak.edu

REFERENCES

Davis, Glenn. 1992. *Disaster Recovery Plan for North Hall Computing Facility.* University of California, Santa Barbara. July.

Fortson-Jones, Judith. 1983. How to develop a disaster plan for books and records repositories. *History News* (May): 30–31.

Greenwood, Frank. 1990. A competitive suggestion. *Information Executive* 3(2): 63.

Moad, Jeff. 1990. Disaster proof your data. *Datamation* (November 1): 87–93.

Pflieger, Fran, ed. 1992. *Emergency Preparedness.* Alexandria, VA: Association of Higher Education Facilities Officers.

Rohde, Renate, and Haskett, Jim. 1990. Disaster recovery planning for academic computing centers. *Communications of the ACM* 33(6) (June): 652–657.

Wheeler, Elaine, Gunter, T. Luther, and Pietrzyk, Catherine. 1989. Disaster preparedness . . . and Recovery. Are You Ready? *AACRAO Conference Papers*, 77th Annual Meeting, April 1991. Washington, DC: American Association of Collegiate Registrars and Admissions Officers.

14

Technology Brings Change to the Registrar's Office

Wayne E. Becraft

There is nothing wrong in change if it is in the right direction. To improve
is to change, so to be perfect is to have changed often.

Winston Churchill

Change has been a constant in registrars' offices at colleges and universities for
over four decades. We anticipate that change will continue to occur and that as
more and more technological advances are implemented, the rate of change will
continue to accelerate for the foreseeable future. What do we foresee for the
future?

Use of the national information infrastructure, the nation's information highway, will continue to expand until universal access is achieved. Schools and
colleges will routinely make access to the information highway available to all
students, faculty, and staff. Families will have access to the information highway
from their homes.

There will be a merging of the current communications technologies. Telephone, television, and computer will merge into the information highway so that
voice, video, and data can be transmitted simultaneously over fiberoptic cable
or over the airwaves. This will soon enable us to access voice, images, and data
at any time from any source.

College catalogs will no longer be printed but instead will be made available
electronically. Furthermore, these electronic catalogs will no longer be the static
documents of the past but will include sound and live-action video in addition
to text and still images. Students will be able to literally "tour" campuses,
campus facilities, programs, and courses by accessing the electronic catalog.
Virtual reality will make the tours three-dimensional and truly participatory by
permitting you to be "inside" the images you are seeing.

Students will be able to select options from a visual or audio menu. Select the "campus tour" option, and the computer will simulate for you a tour of campus facilities. Select the "residence hall" option, and you will be led on a tour of a dormitory building and room by a resident of the dorm who will describe on-campus life for you.

Select the "department" option, and you will be presented with a list of academic departments and programs of study from which to choose. Select one of the departments to receive an introduction by the department chairman followed by a list of courses that constitute that program. Select the course and section of your choice, and the instructor will describe the class for you and give a brief sample lecture. If you decide you want to register for a course, simply select the on-screen registration!

Hard copy schedules of classes also will become obsolete. Students will simply search out the courses of their choice on-line and register for them as previously indicated. They will have the option of registering for individual courses during a specific term, for their entire degree program, or for as much of that program as they feel comfortable with at one time. Institutions will want to encourage students to register for their entire degree program, indicating which courses they want to take in which semester. By scheduling classes to meet the collective needs of the student body (rather than trying to force students into classes they would otherwise choose not to attend), the institution will then be able to optimize the use of its resources, faculty, and classroom space.

On those occasions when there is insufficient enrollment to warrant a "live" class or when no faculty member is available to offer another section, a class can be made available electronically by broadcasting a course outside the classroom, by means of an interactive video link to another college or university offering the same course, or through computer-based instruction. Students will be less likely to be closed out of courses and may actually prefer to be able to choose the "distance education" or "virtual university" option described earlier.

Many adult students will be able to continue their education in their home or at their place of work, eliminating the need to travel to classes at what might be a distant location after a long day of work and then travel home late at night. Through the use of technology, recognized experts will be added to the teaching/learning experience without the costs and limitations that can make such efforts virtually impossible in a "live" classroom today.

Some of the pressures that registrars feel in the assignment of classroom facilities, as well as the continuing need for new and expanded instructional facilities, will be alleviated. Technology will soon make it not only possible, but indeed commonplace, to provide instruction at multiple sites through interactive video and computer-based instruction. In addition, it soon will be possible to substitute computer simulations of laboratory experiments for expensive and inherently limited laboratory facilities, thus increasing flexibility in that area.

These developments will alleviate many perceived headaches for registrars;

however, new problems involving the scheduling of highly sought-after high-tech classrooms and registering and providing services to students who do not need to come to the campus will soon take their place. In fact, these problems already exist to a degree but will become much more extensive in the future as more and more students find distance learning to their liking.

As a result of the rapid expansion in the capabilities and capacities of personal computers, mainframe computers will no longer be needed. Networks of personal computers linked to large file servers will make it possible to shift the control of computers and electronic data back to the users, in this case the registrars. User-friendly software packages and software development tools will make it possible for staff in the registrar's office to collect, maintain, manipulate, and report data without being dependent on the computer center staff. Local area and wide area networks will allow students, faculty, and staff throughout the campus, across the country, and around the world to access the data and procedures they need to register, drop and add courses, submit and obtain grades, request and send transcripts, and so on from wherever they are. The challenge to registrars will be to make sure their policies and procedures keep pace.

Information "kiosks" will be installed at strategic locations around the campus to provide students yet another form of access to information about the college or university, its faculty, and other students, as well as information from their own record.

Student records will continue to be maintained on-line. However, transcripts will be distributed electronically to other institutions and to employers, using electronic data interchange, upon receipt of electronic requests from either the student or another institution to which the student is seeking admission. At the receiving institution, if the data are going to a college or university, the data can be entered directly into the database so that admission, placement, articulation, and degree-audit processes can occur immediately. It soon will be possible for a student to apply for admission, have a transcript sent, have the application evaluated electronically, have any prior credit evaluated, be admitted and be given a degree audit report showing both the prior credit that has been accepted and recommending the classes that should be taken each term for the duration of the student's academic program—all in the same day, perhaps within the same brief session at a computer terminal.

Maintenance of inactive paper, microfilm, microfiche, and even imaged records will become obsolete. Inactive records will be transferred directly from on-line files to computer data warehouses where the data will remain accessible, in compressed form, for historical purposes, research, and analysis, all the while enabling the campus to reuse local mass storage devices for current data.

One of the most significant changes that will occur is the refinement of voice recognition software to the extent that keyboards will no longer be necessary as the primary means of entering data and instructions for manipulation of those data. This will permit another great reduction in the size of the computer, with the screen—as opposed to the keyboard—becoming the major determining factor. But even that may soon change!

In the very near future a person may be able to don headgear, with a microphone attached for communication and a faceplate where visual images will be displayed, and have the entire computer on his on her head. These are similar to the helmets used today for "virtual reality" games. They will use wireless communications and be tied to a power pack worn around the waist to make them entirely portable. Tiny video cameras mounted on computers or computer helmets will enable people we communicate with to see us and us to see them.

Viewers, much sharper and much more friendly on the eyes than today's computer screens, will be developed for use when one needs to view the data in a setting involving more than one person, such as a counseling session. The viewers can be large desktop or table-model devices or small, handheld devices that enable you to rapidly access the data you wish to view and page through them like a book or go directly to the item of interest.

In summary, technology can and will lead to dramatic changes in the way we do business. Paper will become largely obsolete as a means of collecting and sharing information and communicating with each other. All data collection, data maintenance, and communication will be electronic. Our archives will be maintained in an electronic warehouse, with data transferable from point to point on command. The mail system and postage, in the sense in which we are familiar with them, will become things of the past. There may be new fees for exchanging electronic data, but because of the vastly smaller number of people needed to handle distribution, costs should be much lower. At the same time, the delivery time will become almost instantaneous, and lost mail will be an infrequent occurrence.

Because technology enables us to access data and information from wherever we are, more and more people will spend more and more time working at home. In many cases, they will be able to work hours of their own choosing. This will improve efficiency and help reduce traffic congestion and pollution, but it will also present challenges. New ways will have to be found to supervise the work that is being done and to determine fair and equitable compensation.

The challenge to registrars and admissions personnel is to learn and implement the new technologies as rapidly as possible so as to obtain the many benefits they make possible.

Suggested Readings

Akerman, G. 1985. *Introduction to Electronic Data Interchange: A Primer*. Rockville, MD: GE Information Services.

Alexander, G. 1988. Should students permit the registrar to access their records? *CAUSE/EFFECT* (Winter): 47–50.

American Association of Collegiate Registrars and Admissions Officers (AACRAO). 1996. *Academic Record and Transcript Guide*. Washington, DC: AACRAO.

———. 1991. *AACRAO Member Guide 1992–93*. Washington, DC: AACRAO.

———. 1989a. *Certification of Students under Veterans' Laws*. Washington, DC: AACRAO, April.

———. 1989b. *Guide to NCAA Eligibility*. Washington, DC: AACRAO.

———. 1988. *Emerging Issues, Expectations, and Tasks for the 90s. Report of the Task Force of the 90s*. Washington, DC: AACRAO.

Bainbridge, L. 1994. "SPEEDE/ExPRESS Activity List." Washington, DC: American Association of Collegiate Registrars and Admissions Officers.

Bandura, A. 1982. Self-efficacy mechanism in human agency. *American Psychologist* 37(2): 122–147.

Barr, Margaret J., et al. 1988. *Student Services and the Law*. San Francisco: Jossey-Bass.

Bell, Melanie Moore. 1993. *Touch-tone Telephone/Voice Response Registration: A Guide to Successful Implementation*. Washington, DC: American Association of Collegiate Registrars and Admissions Officers.

Berman, J., and Goldman, J. 1989. *A Federal Right of Information Privacy: The Need for Reform* (4). Washington, DC: Benton Foundation.

Biderman, Beverly. 1993. Putting information technology to work for persons with a disability. *CAUSE/EFFECT* 16(2) (Summer): 21–27.

Bracker, J.S., and Pearson, J.N. 1986. Worker obsolescence: The H.R. dilemma of the 80's. *Personnel Administrator* 31: 109–116.

Brown v. Washington University, CA No. 88-1907-c-5 (settled May 11, 1990).

Buckley, Benjamin C., Director. Concurrent Admissions Program, Servicemembers Opportunity Colleges. Memo dated April 14, 1995.

Bursuck, W., Rose, E., Cowen, S., and Yahaya, M. 1989. Nationwide survey of postsecondary education services for students with learning disabilities. *Exceptional Children* 56: 236–245.

Byham, W.C. 1990. *Zapp! The Lightning of Empowerment.* New York: Harmony Books.

Cannon, E. 1993. *EDI Guide: A Step by Step Approach.* New York: Van Nostrand Reinhold.

Canon, Harry J. 1989. Guiding standards and principles. In *Student Services: A Handbook for the Profession,* by Ursula Delworth and Gary R. Hanson et al. San Francisco: Jossey-Bass.

Canon, Harry J., and Brown, Robert D. 1985. Applied ethics in student services. In *New Directions for Student Services.* San Francisco: Jossey-Bass.

Carey, J.H. *The Americans with Disabilities Act.* 1992. Baltimore: Venable, Baetjer, and Howard.

Carnegie Council on Policy Studies in Higher Education. 1979. *Fair Practices in Higher Education.* San Francisco: Carnegie Council on Policy Studies in Higher Education.

Carson, Eugene. 1987. Distributed access to administrative systems. *CAUSE/EFFECT* 10(5) (September): 6–12.

CAUSE and AACRAO. 1997. *Privacy and Handling of Student Information in the Electronic Networked Environments of Colleges and Universities.* Denver, CO: CAUSE and AACRAO.

Cavanaugh, P. 1994a. *Access to the Student Information Inquiry System.* University of Houston, Office of Registration and Academic Records, April 12.

———. 1994b. *RARSTU Training Session.* University of Houston, Office of Registration and Academic Records, April 12.

———. 1994c. *Request for Access to RARMNT (Record Maintenance).* University of Houston, Office of Registration and Academic Records, April 12.

CCSSO, AACRAO, and NCES. 1993. *SPEEDE/ExPRESS: An Electronic System for Exchanging Student Records.* Washington, DC: National Center for Education Statistics.

Civil Rights Restoration Act of 1987, P.L. 100-259, 29 U.S.C. Sec. 794 (a)(2)(A).

Clark, R.E., and Solomon, G. 1986. Media in teaching. In M.C. Wittrock, ed., *Handbook of Research on Teaching,* 3rd ed. New York: Macmillan.

Constantini, Jo Ann. 1994. Survival skills for information professionals in the decade of turbulence. *Records Management Quarterly* 28(1): 26–30.

Coovert, M.D., and Goldstein, M. 1980. Locus of control as a predictor of users' attitude toward computers. *Psychological Reports* 47: 1167–73.

Coovert, M.D., Salas, E., and Ramakrishna, K. 1992. The role of individual and system characteristics in computerized training systems. *Computers in Human Behavior* 8: 335–352.

Cornesky, R., McCool, S., Byrnes, L., and Weber, R. 1991. *Implementing Total Quality Management in Higher Education.* Madison, WI: Magna Publications.

Cornesky, R. et al. 1990. *Using Deming to Improve Quality in Colleges and Universities.* Madison, WI: Magna Publications.

Covey, S.R. 1992. *Principle-Centered Leadership.* New York: Simon and Schuster.

———. 1989. *The Seven Habits of Highly Effective People.* New York: Simon and Schuster.

Crook v. Baker, 57 *American Law Reports 4th*, Section 3, "View That a College or University Has Power to Revoke Degree," 1986.

Curran, R. 1989. Student privacy in the electronic era: Legal perspectives. *CAUSE/EFFECT* (Winter).

Dambrot, F., Watkins-Malek, M., Silling, S., Marshall, R., and Garver, J. 1985. Correlates of sex differences in attitudes toward and involvement with computers. *Journal of Vocational Behavior* 27: 71–86.

Data Interchange Standards Association. 1994. *1994 DISA Information Manual.* Alexandria, VA.

Davis, Glenn. 1992. *Disaster Recovery Plan for North Hall Computing Facility.* University of California, Santa Barbara. July.

Davis v. Southeastern Community College, 442 US 397 (1979).

DeLoughry, T.J. 1989. Computerization makes student records accessible, but raises issues of security and confidentiality. *The Chronicle of Higher Education* (May 10).

Dinsmore v. Pugh and the Regents of the University of California at Berkley (settled 1989).

Doe v. New York University, 666 F. 2d 761 (2d Cir. 1981).

Emmelhainz, M.A. 1990. *Electronic Data Interchange: A Total Management Guide.* New York: Van Nostrand Reinhold.

Evert, H. 1990. A day in the registrar's office circa 2003. *College and University* 65: 171–175.

Fagan, P. 1993. Organizational issues in IT security. *Computers and Security* 12: 710–715.

Fortson-Jones, Judith. 1983. How to develop a disaster plan for books and records repositories. *History News* (May): 30–31.

Fry, B. 1994. *Responsibility of McMurry Computer Users Regarding Confidentiality of Student Information.* Abilene, TX: Office of the Registrar, McMurry University.

Gist, M., and Mitchell, T. 1992. Self-efficacy: A theoretical analysis of its determinants and malleability. *Academy of Management Review* 17: 183–211.

Gist, M., Rosen, B., and Schwoerer, C. 1988. The influence of training method and trainee age on the acquisition of computer skills. *Personnel Psychology* 41: 255–265.

Goldstein, I. 1980. Training in work organizations. *Annual Review of Psychology* 31: 327–372.

Green, William B. 1993. *Introduction to Electronic Document Management Systems.* New York: Harcourt Brace Jovanovich.

Greenwood, Frank. 1990. A competitive suggestion. *Information Executive* 3(2): 63.

Grove City College v. Bell, 465 US 555, S. Ct. 1211 (1984).

Gunn, Mary. 1990. The date of birth and the student transcript. *College and University* 65(4).

Hansen, M. 1993. The ADA's wide reach. *ABA Journal* 79 (December): 14.

Harris, V. 1993. Educating the educators (who was Buckley anyway?) [summary]. *Proceedings Bulletin of the 72nd Annual Conference of the Texas Association of Collegiate Registrars and Admissions Officers*, November, 24–25.

Haugen, S.D., Korn, W.M., and LaBarre, J.L. 1996. Procedures for improving security of local area networks. *Mid-American Journal of Business* (March).

Hawk, S. 1989. Locus of control and computer attitude: The effect of user involvement. *Computers in Human Behavior* 5: 199–206.

Hawkins, B.L. 1989. *Organizing and Managing Information Resources on Campus.* Reading, MA: Addison-Wesley.

Henderson, C. 1992. *College Freshmen with Disabilities: A Statistical Profile.* Washington, DC: American Council on Education, HEATH Resource Center.

Henry, K.D. 1989. Civil rights and the disabled: A comparison of the Rehabilitation Act of 1973 and the Americans with Disabilities Act of 1990 in the employment setting. *Albany Law Review* 54: 123–140.

Highland, H.J. 1993. A view of information security tomorrow. *Computers and Security* 12: 634–639.

Hill, W.A., Jr. 1992. Americans with Disabilities Act of 1990: Significant overlap with Section 504 for colleges and universities. *Journal of College and University Law* 18: 389–417.

Holcombe, John. 1990. The Student Access System: Georgia Tech's do-it-yourself project. *AACRAO Conference Proceedings.* Washington, DC: American Association of Collegiate Registrars and Admissions Officers.

Hussain, D., and Hussain, K.M. 1985. *Information Processing Systems for Management.* Homewood, IL: Richard D. Irwin.

Hyman, Ursula H. 1982. The Family Educational Rights and Privacy Act of 1974 and college record systems of the future. *Computer/Law Journal* 3(4).

Jarrow, J. 1993. *Subpart E: The Impact of Section 504 on Postsecondary Education.* Columbus, OH: Association of Higher Education and Disabilities.

Jones, B. 1990. Imagine . . . for admissions officers and registrars. *College and University* 65: 235–241.

Katzenback, J.R., and Smith, D.K. 1993. *The Wisdom of Teams.* Boston: Harvard Business School Press.

Kerr, Clark. 1994. Knowledge ethics and the new academic culture. *Change, the Magazine of Higher Learning* (January/February).

Kincaid, J., and Simon, J. 1994. *Issues in Higher Education and Disability Law.* Columbus, OH: Association of Higher Education and Disabilities.

King, W., and Jarrow, J. 1992. *Testing Accommodations for Persons with Disabilities; A Guide for Licensure, Certification, and Credentialing.* Columbus, OH: Association of Higher Education and Disabilities.

Kitchener, Karen S. 1985. Ethical principles and ethical decisions in student affairs. In *Applied Ethics in Student Services,* ed. Harry J. Canon and Robert D. Brown. San Francisco: Jossey-Bass.

Kramer, Gary L., and Rasband, H. Garth. 1993. Providing students critical academic planning assistance using academic information management (AIM): A remote access program. *CUMREC Conference Proceedings.* San Antonio, TX, May.

Langemo, Mark. 1993. A rationale for and the fundamentals of electronic imaging systems. *Records Management Quarterly* 27(3) (July): 10.

Lawler, E.E., III. 1992. *The Ultimate Advantage: Creating the High Involvement Organization.* San Francisco: Jossey-Bass.

Lewis, Peter H. 1993. A glimpse into the future as seen by chairman Gates. *New York Times,* December 12.

Lonabocker, Louise. 1993. U-VIEW Plus for the MacIntosh: Registration using a graphical user interface. *AACRAO Conference Proceedings.* Washington, DC: American Association of Collegiate Registrars and Admissions Officers.

――――. 1990. Security in the age of distributed processing. *College and University* 65: 203–212.

――――. 1989. U-VIEW: A student public access recordkeeping system. *College and University* 64(4): 349–355.

Lugosi v. Universal Pictures, 25 Cal 3d 813, 1979, p. 425.

Mangrum, C., and Strichart, S. 1988. *College and the Learning Disabled Student*. Orlando, FL: Grune and Stratton.

Marchese, Ted. 1993. TQM: A time for ideas. *Change Magazine* 25(3) (May/June): 10–13.

May, William W. 1990. *Ethics and Higher Education*. New York: Macmillan.

Mazzeo, K., and Hartman, R. 1994. *Recruitment, Admissions and Students with Disabilities: A Guide for Compliance with Section 504 of the Rehabilitation Act of 1973 and Amendments of 1992 and the Americans with Disabilities Act of 1990*. Washington, DC: HEATH Resource Center, American Council on Education, and American Association of Collegiate Registrars and Admissions Officers.

McKinney, R.L., Schoot, J.S., Teeter, D.J., and Mannering, L.W. 1986. The role of institutional research in data administration and management. Paper presented at the Twenty-Sixth Annual AIR Forum, Orlando, FL, June.

Meier, S.T. 1985. Computer aversion. *Computers in Human Behavior* 1: 171–179.

Menkus, B. 1991. ''Control'' is fundamental to successful information security. *Computers and Security* 10: 293–297.

Moad, Jeff. 1990. Disaster proof your data. *Datamation* (November 1): 87–93.

National Association of College and University Business Officers (NACUBO). 1981. Management information systems. *College and University Business Administration* 6(3): 1–10.

――――. 1977. A personnel database. *College and University Business Administration* 2(9): 1–8.

Neary, M. 1993. *Introduction to EDI and the SPEEDE/ExPRESS Implementation Guide*. Washington, DC: Committee on the Standardization of Postsecondary Education Electronic Data Interchange (SPEEDE), American Association of Collegiate Registrars and Admission Officers, and the Task Force on the Exchange of Permanent Records Electronically for Students and Schools (ExPRESS), National Center for Educational Statistics and the Council of Chief State School Officers. October.

Noe, R.A., and Schmitt, N. 1986. The influence of trainee attitudes on training effectiveness: Test of a model. *Personnel Psychology* 39: 497–523.

Norwood, Bill R. 1993. Evolution of smart card technology: Impact on higher education information systems. *CUMREC Conference Proceedings*. San Antonio, TX, May.

Oakley, E., and Krug, D. 1991. *Enlightened Leadership*. New York: Simon and Schuster.

Olson, I.M., and Abrams, M.D. 1990. Computer access control policy choices. *Computers and Security* 9: 699–714.

Orsburn, J., Moran, L., Musselwhite, E., and Zenger, J. 1990. *Self-Directed Work Teams*. Homewood, IL: Business One Irwin.

Parfett, M. 1992. *What Is EDI? A Guide to Electronic Data, Interchange*. 2nd ed. Oxford, England: NCC Blackwell.

Penrod, J.I., and Dolence, M.G. 1991. Concepts for reengineering higher education. *CAUSE/EFFECT* 14(2) (Summer): 10–17.

Perkins, Helen L. 1996. *Electronic Imaging in Admissions, Records and Financial Aid Offices*. Washington, DC: American Association of Collegiate Registrars and Admissions Officers.

Pflieger, Fran, ed. 1992. *Emergency Preparedness*. Alexandria, VA: Association of Higher Education Facilities Officers.

Pomplun, J. 1996. Document imaging as an advertising tool. Presentation given at CUMREC Conference, Nashville, TN.

Pottas, D., and von Solms, S.H. 1991. A computerized management reporting aid for a mainframe security system. *Computers and Security* 10: 653–660.

Privacy Rights of Students in Educational Records. 1993. California State University, Fullerton. Dr. Charles W. Buck. Office of the Vice President for Student Affairs. Fullerton, CA 92634. October.

Pushkin v. Regents of the University of Colorado, 689 F. 2d 742 (7th Cir. 1982).

Quann, C. James. 1994. Changing the nom de plume: A name-change protocol. *College and University*.

Quann, C. James, et al. 1987. *Admissions, Academic Records, and Registrar Services*. San Francisco: Jossey-Bass.

Redden, M., Levering, C., and Guthrie, C. 1985. *Recruitment, Admissions and Handicapped Students: A Guide for Compliance with Section 504 of the Rehabilitation Act of 1973*. Washington, DC: HEATH Resource Center, American Council on Education, and American Association of Collegiate Registrars and Admissions Officers.

Regulations to Implement the Equal Employment Provisions of the Americans with Disabilities Act, 29 CFR Part 1630.

Rehabilitation Act of 1973, Section 504, P.L. 93-112, 29 U.S.C. Sec. 794 (1977).

Request to Prevent Disclosure of General Directory Information. 1990. California State University, Fullerton. Dr. Charles W. Buck. Office of the Vice President for Student Affairs. Fullerton, CA 92634. June.

Rich, John M. 1984. *Professional Ethics In Education*. Springfield, IL: Charles C. Thomas.

Ridenour, David. 1988. Allowing students read-access to their own computer records. *CAUSE/EFFECT* 11(2) (March): 12–16.

Rohde, Renate, and Haskett, Jim. 1990. Disaster recovery planning for academic computing centers. *Communications of the ACM* 33(6) (June): 652–657.

Rothstein, L. 1993. Legal issues. In S. Vogel and P. Adelman, eds., *Success for College Students with Learning Disabilities*. New York: Springer-Verlag, 21–35.

Sandhu, R., and Jajodia, S. 1991. Integrity principles and mechanisms in database management systems. *Computers and Security* 10: 413–427.

School Board of Nassau County v. Arline, 480 US 273 (1987).

Senge, P.M. 1990. *The Fifth Discipline*. New York: Doubleday.

SPEEDE/ExPRESS. 1994. *A Guide to the Implementation of the SPEEDE/ExPRESS Electronic Transcript*. Washington, DC: Committee on the Standardization of Postsecondary Education Electronic Data Interchange (SPEEDE), American Association of Collegiate Registrars and Admission Officers, and the Task Force on the Exchange of Permanent Records Electronically for Students and Schools (ExPRESS), National Center for Educational Statistics and the Council of Chief State School Officers. May.

Spillane, S., McGuire, J., and Norlander, K. 1992. Undergraduate admission policies, practices, and procedures for applicants with learning disabilities. *Journal of Learning Disabilities* 25: 665–670.

Stein, Harry. 1982. *Ethics and Other Liabilities*. New York: St. Martin's Press.

Stewart, J. 1992. The electronic exchange of student transcripts using the national ANSI ASC X12 Standard Format. South Campus, Miami-Dade Community College.

Swanson, R.A., and Gradous, D. 1986. *Performance at Work: A Systematic Program for Analyzing Work Behavior*. New York: John Wiley and Sons.

Taveras, Luis, Swann, Marie, Craig, Kenneth, Hawkins, J. Michael, and Ingoglia, Eugene. 1993. Hofstra University's student information kiosk. *CAUSE/EFFECT* 16(1) (Spring): 23–32.

Temple, L., and Lips, H.M. 1989. Gender differences and similarities in attitudes toward computers. *Computers in Human Behavior* 5: 215–226.

Thrasher, F. 1992. *The Impact of Titles II and III of the Americans with Disabilities Act of 1990 on Academic and Student Services at Colleges, Universities & Proprietary Schools*. Washington, DC: National Association of College and University Attorneys.

Trubow, G. 1989. *Watching the Watchers: The Coordination of Federal Privacy Policy* (5). Washington, DC: Benton Foundation.

U.S. Department of Education. 1991. *Veterans Education Outreach Program, Exemplary Projects*. Washington, DC: U.S. Government Printing Office (289-004/56061).

———. 1974. Fact sheet: Family Educational Rights and Privacy Act of 1974.

U.S. Department of Health, Education, and Welfare. 1993. Privacy act issuances; Rules and regulations. *Federal Register* 58(4).

———. 1991. Privacy act issuances; 1991 compilation. *Federal Register* 1.

———. 1988. Privacy act issuances; Final regulations. *Federal Register* 53(69).

U.S. Department of Veterans Affairs. 1993. Federal benefits for veterans and dependents. VA Pamphlet 80-93-1.

U.S. Equal Employment Opportunity Commission. Americans with Disabilities Act. 1992. *A Technical Assistance Manual on the Employment Provisions (Title I)*. Washington, DC: U.S. Equal Employment Opportunity Commission.

———. 1991. Publication 17. Washington, DC: U.S. Equal Employment Opportunity Commission.

———. 1990. P.L. 101-336, 42 U.S.C. Sec 12101. Washington, DC: U.S. Equal Employment Opportunity Commission.

Vaughn, R.B., Saiedian, H., and Unger, E.A. 1993. A survey of security issues in office computation and the application of secure computing models to office systems. *Computers and Security* 12: 79–97.

Waldman, D.A., and Avolio, B. 1986. A meta-analysis of age differences in job performance. *Journal of Applied Psychology* 71: 33–38.

Waliga v Board of Trustees, 57 *American Law Reports 4th*, Section 3, ''View That a College or University Has Power to Revoke Degree,'' 1986, 1246–47.

Webster, S. 1989. Ethics in the information age: After rules and locks, what do we do? *CAUSE/EFFECT* (Winter): 51.

Weeks, Kent M. 1994. *Managing Admissions, Records and the Law*. Nashville, TN: College Legal Information.

———. 1993. *Complying with Federal Law: A Manual for College Decision Makers*. Nashville, TN: College Legal Information.

Weiss, K.P. 1993. Data integrity and security: Who's in charge here anyway? *Information Management and Computer Security* 1(4): 4–9.

Wellins, R., Byham, W., and Wilson, J. *Empowered Teams*. San Francisco: Jossey-Bass.

Wermers, D.J., Patterson, L.M., and Scott, T.J. 1992. SPEEDE simplified: The user perspective. *CUMREC Conference Proceedings*, 276–289.

Westin, A.F., and Baker, M.A. 1972. *Databanks in a Free Society: Computers, Record-keeping and Privacy. Report of the Project on Computer Databanks of the Computer Science and Engineering Board. National Academy of Sciences*. New York: Quandrangle Books.

Wheeler, Elaine, Gunter, T. Luther, and Pietrzyk, Catherine. 1989. Disaster preparedness . . . and recovery. Are you ready? *AACRAO Conference Papers*, 77th Annual Meeting, April 1991. Washington, DC: American Association of Collegiate Registrars and Admissions Officers.

White, W., Alley, G., Deshler, D., Schumaker, J., Warner, M., and Clark, F. 1982. Are there learning disabilities after high school? *Exceptional Children* 49: 273–274.

Wilder, G., Mackie, D., and Cooper, J. 1985. Gender and computers: Two surveys of computer-related attitudes. *Sex Poles* 13(3/4): 215–228.

Wilson, D. 1992. New federal regulations on rights of the handicapped may force colleges to provide better access to technology. *The Chronicle of Higher Education* 38(1): 1, 21–22.

Wynne v. Tufts University School of Medicine, 932 F. 2d 19 (1st Cir. 1991).

Yarwood, W. 1988. Perceptions of college admissions decision makers concerning students with learning disabilities. Ed.D. diss., Temple University.

Index

About the Contributors

WAYNE E. BECRAFT has been Executive Director of AACRAO since 1989, following brief terms as Associate Executive Director and Interim Executive Director from 1987–1989. Prior to that he was Director of Admission and Registration Services at The University of Maryland University College, a position he held for fifteen years. During his term as Executive Director, he has worked closely with the AACRAO Board of Directors to implement a Strategic Plan for the Association and to expand the programs and services available to the membership.

DAVID M. BIRNBAUM is the University Counsel in the Office of the President at the University of California.

JOHN F. DEMITROFF served as Registrar at the University of Rhode Island until his retirement in 1995. He has been and is still active in the NCAA, having represented AACRAO on the Academic Requirements Committee of the NCAA.

JAMES S. FREY, President of Educational Credential Evaluators, Inc., a private, nonprofit foreign educational credential evaluation service, has been involved in international education since 1961. In addition to service at three universities, he has held a variety of positions in AACRAO and NAFSA: The Association of International Educators, and has been a consultant on international education in seven countries. He is the author, co-author, and/or editor of seven books and twenty-three articles concerned with international education.

BOBBYE G. FRY currently serves as the Registrar for McMurry University in Abilene, Texas. She has completed courses toward her educational doctorate with Texas Tech University.

ROMAN S. GAWKOSKI served Marquette University, Milwaukee, Wisconsin, for thirty-five years as Registrar. During that time he was also a tenured professor, teaching both undergraduate and graduate statistics. He is currently serving as Editor of the refereed journal *College and University*.

DAVID GUZMAN is the Associate Registrar and Director of Veterans Programs at Washington State University. He also serves on several state and national veterans committees and councils, including membership on the Air Force Association Veterans and Retiree Council, and Vice President of the National Association of Veteran Program Administrators (NAVPA).

VIRGINIA K. JOHNS is Associate Registrar at the University of California, Santa Barbara. She has worked there as the Manager of Student Systems and, since 1995, as the Associate Registrar for Enrollment and Academic Records. She is currently working on her MBA at California State University, Northridge.

LOUISE LONABOCKER is Associate Dean of Enrollment Management and University Registrar at Boston College. She is currently AACRAO Vice President for Regional Associations and Institutional Issues and an editor of and contributor to *Breakthrough Systems: Student Access and Registration*, published by AACRAO.

KAY MAGADANCE is the Senior Institutional Planner at the University of Wisconsin–Eau Claire. Prior to assuming the Senior Institutional Planner role, Kay served as Assistant Registrar for Student Records and Data Systems. In that role she was responsible for coordinating the development of student and curricular systems, along with authorizing and training users on these systems. In her current position she leads the analysis of institutional information used for enrollment management and university-wide planning.

SARA N. MCNABB, formerly the Assistant Vice President for Enrollment Services at Indiana University in Bloomington, now serves that institution as Special Assistant to the President.

JAMES F. MENZEL is Executive Director of the offices providing enrollment services to each of the six colleges within the Medical University of South Carolina. For over twenty-five years he has worked in admissions and records on campuses large and small, public and private, two-year and four-year, graduate and professional.

LAURA M. PATTERSON, formerly University Registrar at the University of Michigan, is now Director of the M-Pathways Project at the University of Michigan, Ann Arbor.

HELEN L. PERKINS serves as Registrar at the University of Montevallo, Montevallo, Alabama. She is the author of *Electronic Imaging in Admissions, Records and Financial Aid Offices*, published by AACRAO.

C. JAMES QUANN holds an indefinite appointment as Coordinator of Veterans' Research for Washington State University. He served as University Registrar and later Interim Vice Chancellor for Student Affairs at the University of California, Santa Cruz, from 1990 to 1995. Prior to that he served for many years as University Registrar at Washington State University. He holds a doctorate in higher education administration.

M. THERESE RUZICKA is Assistant Director of Enrollment Services at the University of Wisconsin–Milwaukee. Her professional background has been primarily within registration and records operations, but she recently accepted a challenge on a somewhat different track: directing a new Office of Adult and Returning Student Services at the University of Wisconsin–Milwaukee.

SALLY S. SCOTT is Co-Director of the Learning Disabilities Center at the University of Georgia in Athens.

ANTHONY D. TORTORELLA has more than thirty years of professional experience in directing registrations and maintaining academic records, and played a major role at Marquette University in the design and the enhancement of their student record database when it was developed in the late 1970s. In 1990 he served as the academic area project leader for the planning and implementation of the touchtone telephone registration system that was developed in-house by the University. He has been University Registrar at Marquette since 1993.

KENNETH P. WARREN, an evaluator for Educational Credential Evaluators, Inc. since 1992, specializes in education in the Baltic Republics, Finland, Germany, Hungary, Iran, Netherlands, Spain, Sweden, Switzerland, successor states to the USSR and former Yugoslavia, and in the professional fields of education and speech pathology. He is the author of *The ECE Presents the Educational System of Finland*, which will be published in late 1997.

BETH LEE WECKMUELLER serves as Director of Enrollment Services at the University of Wisconsin–Milwaukee. Her particular areas of professional interest are eclectic. At the moment they include implementation of Electronic Data Interchange and World Wide Web–based systems to support student enrollment services, competency based admission systems, and computer adaptive testing.

DONALD J. WERMERS serves as Registrar at the University of Wisconsin–Madison. He has served on the SPEEDE Committee since 1992.

ELAINE WHEELER is Director of the UCSC Academic Senate at the University of California, Santa Cruz.